A More Perfect Union

A MORE PERFECT UNION

Documents in U.S. History

FOURTH EDITION

Volume II: Since 1865

PAUL F. BOLLER, JR.

Professor Emeritus, Texas Christian University

RONALD STORY

University of Massachusetts, Amherst

Houghton Mifflin Company   Boston

Geneva, Illinois   Palo Alto   Princeton, New Jersey

To Martin and Eliza

Senior Sponsoring Editor: Sean W. Wakely
Senior Associate Editor: Jeffrey Greene
Senior Project Editor: Carol Newman
Senior Production/Design Coordinator: Carol Merrigan
Senior Manufacturing Coordinator: Marie Barnes
Marketing Manager: Pamela Shaffer

Cover designer: Harold Burch, Harold Burch Design, New York City.

Cover image: "Silver Inkstand, Independence Hall, Philadelphia, PA." Michael Bryant/Woodfin Comp.

Printed in the U.S.A.

ISBN: 0-395-74525-X

Library of Congress Catalog Card Number: 95-76925

1 2 3 4 5 6 7 8 9-QM-99 98 97 96 95

CONTENTS

✧

CHAPTER THREE

The Age of Industry

✧ CHAPTER FOUR ────────────

Empire and Uplift

CHAPTER FIVE

✦ ──────────────────────────

Crisis and Hope

CHAPTER EIGHT

✧ ——————————————

Modern Times

Preface

❖

Our two-volume reader, *A More Perfect Union: Documents in U.S. History*, presents students with the original words of speeches and testimony, political and legal writings, and literature that have reflected, precipitated, and implemented pivotal events of the past four centuries. The readings in Volume I cover the era from Columbus's voyage of discovery to Reconstruction. Volume II begins with the post-Civil War period, repeating some of the first volume's final readings, and concludes with contemporary selections. We are pleased with the reception that *A More Perfect Union* has received, and we have worked toward refining the contents of this new edition.

About a third of the material is new to this edition. New selections in Volume I include, for example, a letter from a Scotch-Irish farmer and a revolutionary speech by Patrick Henry, both from the eighteenth century, as well as Charles G. Finney's lecture on revivals of religion and General William T. Sherman's message to the citizens of Atlanta from the nineteenth century. Many new selections have been added to Volume II. Among them are Andrew Carnegie's "Wealth" and the Populist Party platform as well as an interview with Malcolm X and the Republican Party's "Contract with America."

The readings in these volumes represent a blend of social and political history, along with some cultural and economic trends, suitable for introductory courses in American history. We made our selections with three thoughts in mind. First, we looked for famous documents with a lustrous place in the American tradition—or the Gettysburg Address, for example, or Franklin D. Roosevelt's First Inaugural Address. These we chose for their great mythic quality, as expressions of fundamental sentiments with which students should be familiar. Second, we looked for writings that caused something to happen or had an impact when they appeared. Examples include the Virginia slave statutes, Thomas Paine's *The Crisis*, the Emancipation Proclamation, and Earl Warren's opinion in *Brown v. Board of Education of Topeka*—all of them influential pieces, some of them famous as well. Third, we looked for documents that seemed to reflect important attitudes or developments. Into this group fall Thomas Hart Benton's racial views as well as the writings of Upton Sinclair on industrial Chicago and of Martin Luther King, Jr. on Vietnam. In this category, where the need for careful selection from a wide field was most apparent, we looked especially for thoughtful pieces with a measure of fame and influence. Horace Mann's statement on schools reflected common attitudes; it also caused something to happen and is a well-known reform statement. We have also tried to mix a few unusual items into the stew, as with the "Report of the Joint Committee on Reconstruction" and a letter from a Catholic nun in early Colorado.

We have edited severely in places, mostly when the document is long or contains extraneous material or obscure references. We have also, in some cases, modernized spelling and punctuation.

Each document has a lengthy headnote that summarizes the relevant trends of the era, provides a specific setting for the document, and sketches the life of the author. There are also "Questions to Consider" to guide students through the prose and suggest ways of thinking about the selections.

We would like to thank the following people who reviewed the manuscript for one or both volumes:

John K. Alexander, University of Cincinnati; June G. Alexander, University of Cincinnati; Judith L. Demark, Northern Michigan University; Harvey Green, Northeastern University; Ben Rader, University of Nebraska at Lincoln; C. Elizabeth Raymond, University of Nevada–Reno; Thomas Templeton Taylor, Wittenberg University; and John Scott Wilson, University of South Carolina.

We also wish to express our appreciation to the editorial staff of Houghton Mifflin Company for their hard and conscientious work in producing these volumes.

P.F.B.
R.S.

A MORE PERFECT UNION

Columbia, South Carolina in the wake of Sherman's Army. (Chicago Historical Society)

CHAPTER ONE

Reconstructing the Union

1

✧

A HELPING HAND

The Thirteenth Amendment, which became part of the Constitution in 1865, freed about four million slaves in the South. But with freedom came uncertainty, insecurity, and perplexity. Unlike the peasants of France and Russia, who stayed on the land on which they had been working when they were freed from serfdom, the former American slaves were cast adrift at the end of the Civil War with no means of livelihood. They found themselves without property, legal rights, education, training, and any experience as independent farmers or laborers. Thousands began roaming the countryside looking for work and ways to survive. The first year of freedom brought hunger, disease, suffering, and death.

The freedmen did receive some assistance from the federal government after the war. In March 1865, Congress established the Bureau of Refugees, Freedmen, and Abandoned Lands (commonly called the Freedmen's Bureau) to provide them with food, clothing, shelter, and medical aid. Under the direction of General Oliver O. Howard (the "Christian General"), the Freedmen's Bureau also established schools and colleges for young blacks, founded savings banks, set up courts to protect their civil rights, and tried to get them jobs and fair contracts of employment. During its seven years of existence (1865–1872), the bureau spent more than $15 million for food and other aid and over $6 million on schools and educational work, and gave medical attention to nearly half a million patients. Bureau agents also registered black voters and encouraged political participation. The hostility of Southern whites and the growing indifference of whites in the North, however, negated much of the bureau's work.

The report excerpted below was written by Colonel Eliphalet Whittlesey, assistant bureau commissioner for North Carolina, in October 1865. Whittlesey later became a general and moved to Washington, where he served as a trustee of the national Freedman's Savings Bank. In North Carolina where blacks made up only a third of the population and therefore only a third of the potential voters, the Republican party and the national government soon began to lose political control. By

1871 the white Democratic party once again controlled the state, ending Reconstruction there.

Questions to Consider. Southern whites argued repeatedly that the fundamental objective of the Freedmen's Bureau was not to help the needy but to punish its foes by transforming Southern racial and economic relations. Does Whittlesey's report support this contention? Who received federal assistance in 1865? On what grounds was assistance given? Who made the decisions? Did Whittlesey sound like the commander of an occupying army? Of the bureau's four goals, which did he seem to feel were most urgent? Was he optimistic? Which of its goals was the bureau most likely to achieve in the short run?

————————✦————————

Report on the Freedmen's Bureau (1865)

On the 22d of June I arrived at Raleigh with instructions from you to take the control of all subjects relating to "refugees, freedmen, and the abandoned lands" within this State. I found these subjects in much confusion. Hundreds of white refugees and thousands of blacks were collected about this and other towns, occupying every hovel and shanty, living upon government rations, without employment and without comfort, many dying for want of proper food and medical supplies. A much larger number, both white and black, were crowding into the towns, and literally swarming about every depot of supplies to receive their rations. My first effort was to reduce this class of suffering and idle humanity to order, and to discover how large a proportion of these applicants were really deserving of help. The whites, excepting "loyal refugees," were referred to the military authorities. To investigate the condition of refugees and freedmen and minister to the wants of the destitute, I saw at once would require the services of a large number of efficient officers. As fast as suitable persons could be selected, application was made to the department and district commanders for their detail, in accordance with General Order No. 102, War Department, May 31, 1865. In many cases these applications were unsuccessful because the officers asked for could not be spared. The difficulties and delays experienced in obtaining the help needed for a proper organization of my work will be seen from the fact that upon thirty-four written requests, in due form, only eleven officers have been detailed by the department and district commanders. . . .

From *Report of the Joint Committee on Reconstruction, 1st Session, 39th Congress* (Government Printing Office, Washington, D.C., 1866), II: 186–192.

An early class at Hampton Institute. Uniformed African-American students in class at Virginia's Hampton Institute, founded in 1868 with white philanthropic help to "train selected Negro youth who should go out and teach and lead their people." (Gift of Leonard Kirstein, The Museum of Modern Art, NY)

With this brief history of my efforts to organize the bureau, I proceed to state

The Design and Work Proposed

In my circulars Nos. 1 and 2 (copies of which are herewith enclosed) the objects to be attained are fully stated. All officers of the bureau are instructed—

1. To aid the destitutes, yet in such a way as not to encourage dependence.
2. To protect freedmen from injustice.
3. To assist freedmen in obtaining employment and fair wages for their labor.
4. To encourage education, intellectual and moral.

Under these four divisions the operations of the bureau can best be presented.

Relief Afforded

It was evident at the outset that large numbers were drawing rations who might support themselves. The street in front of the post commissary's office was blocked up with vehicles of all the descriptions peculiar to North Carolina, and with people who had come from the country around, in some instances from a distance of sixty miles, for government rations. These were destitute whites, and were supplied by order of the department commander. Our own headquarters, and every office of the bureau, was besieged from morning till night by freedmen, some coming many miles on foot, others in wagons and carts. The rations issued would scarcely last till they reached home, and in many instances they were sold before leaving the town, in exchange for luxuries. To correct these evils, orders were issued that no able-bodied man or woman should receive supplies, except such as were known to be industrious, and to be entirely destitute. By constant inquiry and effort the throng of beggars was gradually removed. The homeless and helpless were gathered in camps, where shelter and food could be furnished, and the sick collected in hospitals, where they could receive proper care. . . .

Protection

Regarding this bureau as the appointed instrument for redeeming the solemn pledge of the nation, through its Chief Magistrate, to secure the rights of freedmen, I have made every effort to protect them from wrong. Suddenly set free, they were at first exhilarated by the air of liberty, and committed some excesses. To be sure of their freedom, many thought they must leave the old scenes of oppression and seek new homes. Others regarded the property accumulated by their labor as in part their own, and demanded a share of it. On the other hand, the former masters, suddenly stripped of their wealth, at first looked upon the freedmen with a mixture of hate and fear. In these circumstances some collisions were inevitable. The negroes were complained of as idle, insolent, and dishonest; while they complained that they were treated with more cruelty than when they were slaves. Some were tied up and whipped without trial; some were driven from their homes without pay for their labor, without clothing or means of support; others were forbidden to leave on pain of death, and a few were shot or otherwise murdered. All officers of the bureau were directed, in accordance with your circular No. 5, to investigate these difficulties between the two classes, to settle them by counsel and arbitration as far as possible, to punish light offences by fines or otherwise, and to report more serious cases of crime to the military authorities for trial. The exact number of cases heard and decided cannot be given; they have been so numerous that no complete record could be kept; one officer reported that he had heard and disposed of as many as 180 complaints in a single day. The method pursued may be best presented by citing a few cases and the action thereon. From the report of Captain James, for August, I quote the following:

"Reports had reached me of the way in which David Parker, of Gates county, treated his colored people, and I determined to ascertain for myself their truth. Accordingly, last Monday, August 20, accompanied by a guard of six men from this post, (Elizabeth City,) I proceeded to his residence, about forty miles distant. He is very wealthy. I ascertained, after due investigation, and after convincing his colored people that I was really their friend, that the worst reports in regard to him were true. He had twenty-three negroes on his farm, large and small. Of these, fourteen were fieldhands; they all bore unmistakable evidence of the way they had been worked; very much undersized, rarely exceeding, man or women, 4 feet 6 inches—men and women of thirty and forty years of age looking like boys and girls. It has been his habit for years to work them from sunrise to sunset, and often long after, only stopping one hour for dinner—food always cooked for them to save time. He had, and has had for many years, an old colored man, one-eyed and worn out in the service, for an overseer or 'over-looker,' as he called himself. In addition, he has two sons at home, one of whom has made it a point to be with them all summer long—not so much to superintend as to drive. The old colored overseer always went behind the gang with a cane or whip, and woe betide the unlucky wretch who did not continually do his part; he had been brought up to work, and had not the least pity for any one who could not work as well as he.

"Mr. Parker told me that he had hired his people for the season: that directly after the surrender of General Lee he called them up and told them they were free; that he was better used to them than to others, and would prefer hiring them; that he would give them board and two suits of clothing to stay with him till the 1st day of January, 1866, and one Sunday suit at the end of that time; that they consented willingly—in fact, preferred to remain with him, &c. But from his people I learned that though he did call them up, as stated, yet when one of them demurred at the offer his son James flew at him and cuffed and kicked him; that after that they were all 'perfectly willing to stay'; they were watched night and day; that Bob, one of the men, had been kept chained nights; that they were actually afraid to try to get away. There was no complaint of the food nor much of the clothing, but they were in constant terror of the whip. Only three days before my arrival, Bob had been stripped in the field and given fifty lashes for hitting Adam, the colored over-looker, while James Parker stood by with a gun, and told him to run if he wanted to, he had a gun there. About four weeks before, four of them who went to church and returned before sunset were treated to twenty-five lashes each. Some were beaten or whipped almost every day. Having ascertained these and other similar facts, I directed him to call them up and pay them for the first of May last up to the present time. I investigated each case, taking into consideration age, family, physical condition, &c., estimating their work from $8 down, and saw him pay them off then and there, allowing for clothing and medical bill. I then arrested him and his two sons, and brought them here, except Dr. Joseph Parker, whose sister is very sick, with all the colored people I thought necessary as witnesses, intending to send them to Newbern for trial. But on account of the want of immediate transportation I concluded to release them on their giving a bond in the sum of $2,000 to Colonel E. Whittlesey, assistant commissioner for the State of North Carolina, and to his successors in office, conditioned as follows:

"That whereas David Parker and James Parker have heretofore maltreated their colored people, and have enforced the compulsory system instead of the free labor system: Now, therefore, if they, each of them, shall hereafter well and kindly treat, and cause to be treated, the hired laborers under their or his charge, and shall adopt the free labor system in lieu of the compulsory system, then this bond to be void and of no effect; otherwise to remain in full force and effect, with good security."

Lieutenant Colonel Clapp, superintendent central district, reports three cases of cruel beating, which have been investigated, and the offenders turned over to the military authorities for trial; besides very many instances of defrauding freedmen of their wages. . . .

The following cases are taken from the report of Captain Barritt, assistant commissioner, at Charlotte:

"Morrison Miller charged with whipping a girl Hannah (colored.) Found guilty. Action: ordered to pay said Hannah fifty bushels of corn towards supporting herself and children, two of said children being the offspring of Miller.

"Wm. Wallace charged with whipping Martha (colored.) Plead guilty. Action: fined said Wallace $15, with assurance that if the above offence was repeated, the fine would be doubled.

"Council Best attempts to defraud six families of their summer labor, by offering to sell at auction the crop on his leased plantation. Action: sent military force and stopped the sale until contract with laborers was complied with."

A hundred pages of similar reports might be copied, showing, on the one side, that many freedmen need the presence of some authority to enforce upon them their new duties; and on the other, that so far from being true that "there is no county in which a freedman can be imposed upon," there is no county in which he is not oftener wronged; and these wrongs increase just in proportion to their distance from United States authorities. There has been great improvement, during the quarter, in this respect. The efforts of the bureau to protect the freedmen have done much to restrain violence and injustice. Such efforts must be continued until civil government is fully restored, just laws enacted, or great suffering and serious disturbance will be the result.

Industry

Contrary to the fears and predictions of many, the great mass of colored people have remained quietly at work upon the plantations of their former masters during the entire summer. The crowds seen about the towns in the early part of the season had followed in the wake of the Union army, to escape from slavery. After hostilities ceased these refugees returned to their homes, so that but few vagrants can now be found. In truth, a much larger amount of vagrancy exists among the whites than among the blacks. It is the almost uniform report of officers of the bureau that freedmen are industrious.

The report is confirmed by the fact that out of a colored population of nearly 350,000 in the State, only about 5,000 are now receiving support from the government. Probably some others are receiving aid from kind-hearted men who have enjoyed the benefit of their services from childhood. To the general quiet and industry of this people there can be no doubt that the efforts of the bureau have contributed greatly. I have visited some of the larger towns, as Wilmington, Newbern, Goldsborough, and both by public addresses and private instructions counselled the freedmen to secure employment and maintain themselves. Captain James has made an extensive tour through the eastern district for the same purpose, and has exerted a most happy influence. Lieutenant Colonel Clapp has spent much of his time in visiting the county seats of the central district, and everywhere been listened to by all classes with deep interest. Other officers have done much good in this way. They have visited plantations, explained the difference between slave and free labor, the nature and the solemn obligation of contracts. The chief difficulty met with has been a want of confidence between the two parties. The employer, accustomed only to the system of compulsory labor, is slow to believe that he can secure fruitful services by the stimulus of wages. The laborer is unwilling to trust the promises of those for whom he had toiled all his days without pay; hence but few contracts for long periods have been effected. The bargains for the present year are generally vague, and their settlement as the crops are gathered in requires much labor. In a great majority of cases the landowners seem disposed to do justly, and even generously; and when this year's work is done, and the proceeds divided, it is hoped that a large number of freedmen will enter into contracts for the coming year. They will, however, labor much more cheerfully for money, with prompt and frequent payments, than for a share of the crop, for which they must wait twelve months. A large farmer in Pitt county hires hands by the job, and states that he never saw negroes work so well. Another in Lenoir county pays monthly, and is satisfied so far with the experiment of free labor. Another obstacle to long contracts was found in the impression which had become prevalent to some degree, *i.e.,* that lands were to be given to freedmen by the government. To correct this false impression I published a circular, No. 3, and directed all officers of the bureau to make it as widely known as possible. From the statistical reports enclosed, it will be seen that during the quarter 257 written contracts for labor have been prepared and witnessed; that the average rate of wages, when paid in money, is from $8 to $10 per month; that 128 farms are under the control of the bureau and cultivated for the benefit of freedmen; that 8,540 acres are under cultivation, and 6,102 are employed. Many of the farms were rented by agents of the treasury as abandoned lands, previous to the establishing of this bureau, and were transferred to us with the leases upon them. Nearly all have been restored to their owners, under the President's proclamation of amnesty, and our tenure of the few that remain is so uncertain that I have not deemed it prudent to set apart any for use of refugees and freedmen, in accordance with the act of Congress approved March 3, 1865. But many freedmen are taking this matter into their own hands, and renting lands from the owners for one or more years. . . .

Education

The quarter has been one of vacation rather than active work in this department. Still some progress has been made, and much done to prepare for the coming autumn and winter. Rev. F. A. Fiske, a Massachusetts teacher, has been appointed superintendent of education, and has devoted himself with energy to his duties. From his report it will be seen that the whole number of schools, during the whole or any part of the quarter, is 63, the number of teachers 85, and the number of scholars 5,624. A few of the schools are self-supporting, and taught by colored teachers, but the majority are sustained by northern societies and northern teachers. The officers of the bureau have, as far as practicable, assigned buildings for their use, and assisted in making them suitable; but the time is nearly past when such facilities can be given. The societies will be obliged hereafter to pay rent for school-rooms and for teachers' homes. The teachers are engaged in a noble and self-denying work. They report a surprising thirst for knowledge among the colored people—children giving earnest attention and learning rapidly, and adults, after the day's work is done, devoting the evening to study. In this connexion it may be mentioned, as a result of moral instruction, that 512 marriages have been reported and registered, and 42 orphans provided with good homes.

2

✧

KLANSMEN OF THE CAROLINAS

Reconstruction developed in a series of moves and countermoves. In a white Southern backlash to Union victory and emancipation came the "black codes" for coercing black laborers and President Andrew Johnson's pardon of Confederate landowners. Then in a Northern backlash to these codes and pardons came the Civil Rights bills, the sweeping Reconstruction Acts of 1867, and the Fourteenth and Fifteenth Amendments, all designed to guarantee black political rights. White Southerners reacted to these impositions in turn with secret night-time terrorist or "night rider" organizations designed to shatter Republican political power. Congress tried to protect Republican voters and the freedmen with the Force Acts of 1870 allowing the use of the army to prevent physical assaults, but Northern willingness to commit troops and resources to the struggle was waning. By the mid-1870s only three states remained in Republican hands, and within three years racist Democrats controlled these, too. The night riders had turned the tide.

Although numerous secret societies for whites appeared in the Reconstruction South—including the Order of the White Camelia (Louisiana), the Pale Faces (Tennessee), the White Brotherhood (North Carolina), and the Invisible Circle (South Carolina)—the largest and most influential society, and the one that spawned these imitators, was the Ku Klux Klan, the so-called Invisible Empire. The Klan began in Tennessee in 1866 as a young men's social club with secret costumes and rituals similar to those of the Masons, the Odd-Fellows, and other popular societies. In 1867, however, following passage of the Reconstruction Acts, anti-Republican racists began to see the usefulness of such a spookily secret order, and the Klan was reorganized to provide for "dens," "provinces" (counties), and "realms" (states), all under the authority of a "Grand Wizard," who in 1867 was believed to have been Nathan B. Forrest, a former slave trader and Confederate general.

The Klan structure was probably never fully established because of the disorganized conditions of the postwar South. Other societies with different names emerged, and the Reconstruction-era "Ku-Klux" may have disbanded as a formal entity in the early 1870s. But it clearly survived in spirit and in loosely formed groups, continuing to terrorize

Republicans and their allies among the newly enfranchised freedmen into the 1870s and sowing fear among the black families who composed, after all, the labor force on which the white planters still depended. The excerpt reprinted below includes congressional testimony by David Schenck, a member of the North Carolina Klan seeking to portray it in the best possible light, followed by testimony from Elias Hill, a South Carolina black man victimized by a local "den" of the Klan. Schenck and Hill were testifying before a joint Senate-House committee concerned with antiblack terrorism.

Questions to Consider. The oath taken by David Schenck emphasizes the Klan's religious, constitutional, and benevolent qualities, whereas Elias Hill's story reveals its terrorist features. Are there elements in the Klan oath that seem to hint at or justify the use of violence? Why does the oath contain the phrases "original purity," "pecuniary embarrassments," and "traitor's doom"? What "secrets of this order" could deserve death? Klansmen later claimed that because they could terrorize the superstitious freedmen simply by using masks, odd voices, and ghostly sheets, no real violence was necessary. Opponents have claimed, on the other hand, that Klansmen were basically sadists acting out sexual phobias and deep paranoia. What light does Elias Hill's testimony shed on these conflicting claims? What position did Hill hold in the black community? Did the Klansmen seem to be assaulting him because of his condition or because of his position in the black community? Why did they ask Hill to pray for them? Would it be fair or accurate to call the Ku Klux Klan a terrorist organization that succeeded?

———————✧———————

Report of the Joint Committee on Reconstruction (1872)

A select committee of the Senate, upon the 10th of March, 1871, made a report of the result of their investigation into the security of person and property in the State of North Carolina. . . . A sub-committee of their number proceeded to the State of South Carolina, and examined witnesses in that State until July 29. . . .

David Schenck, esq., a member of the bar of Lincoln County, North Carolina . . . was initiated in October, 1868, as a member of the Invisible

From *Report of the Joint Select Committee to Inquire into the Condition of Affairs in the Late Insurrectionary States* (Government Printing Office, Washington, D.C., 1872), 25–27, 44–47.

Empire. . . . In his own words: "We were in favor of constitutional liberty as handed down to us by our forefathers. I think the idea incorporated was that we were opposed to the [fourteenth and fifteenth] amendments to the Constitution. I desire to explain in regard to that that it was not to be—at least, I did not intend by that that it should be—forcible resistance, but a political principle."

The oath itself is as follows:

> I, (name,) before the great immaculate Judge of heaven and earth, and upon the Holy Evangelist of Almighty God, do, of my own free will and accord, subscribe to the following sacred, binding obligation:
>
> I. I am on the side of justice and humanity and constitutional liberty, as bequeathed to us by our forefathers in its original purity.
>
> II. I reject and oppose the principles of the radical [Republican] party.
>
> III. I pledge aid to a brother of the Ku-Klux Klan in sickness, distress, or pecuniary embarrassments. Females, friends, widows, and their households shall be the special objects of my care and protection.
>
> IV. Should I ever divulge, or cause to be divulged, any of the secrets of this order, or any of the foregoing obligations, I must meet with the fearful punishment of death and traitor's doom, which is death, death, death, at the hands of the brethren. . . .

Elias Hill of York County, South Carolina, is a remarkable character. He is crippled in both legs and arms, which are shriveled by rheumatism; he cannot walk, cannot help himself . . .; was in early life a slave, whose freedom was purchased by his father. . . . He learned his letters and to read by calling the school children into the cabin as they passed, and also learned to write. He became a Baptist preacher, and after the war engaged in teaching colored children, and conducted the business correspondence of many of his colored neighbors. . . . We put the story of his wrongs in his own language:

"On the night of the 5th of May, after I had heard a great deal of what they had done in that neighborhood, they came . . . to my brother's door, which is in the same yard, and broke open the door and attacked his wife, and I heard her screaming and mourning. I could not understand what they said, for they were talking in an outlandish and unnatural tone, which I had heard they generally used at a negro's house. They said, 'Where's Elias?' She said, 'He doesn't stay here; yon is his house.' I had heard them strike her five or six licks. Someone then hit my door. . . .

"They carried me into the yard between the houses, my brother's and mine, and put me on the ground. . . . 'Who did that burning? Who burned our houses?' I told them it was not me. I could not burn houses. Then they hit me with their fists, and said I did it, I ordered it. They went on asking me didn't I tell the black men to ravish all the white women. No, I answered them. They struck me again. . . . 'Haven't you been preaching and praying about the Ku-Klux? Haven't you been preaching political sermons? Doesn't a [Republican Party newspaper] come to your house? Haven't you written letters?' Generally one asked me all the questions, but the rest were squatting over me—some six men I counted as I lay there. . . . I told them if they would take me back into the house, and lay me in the bed, which was close adjoining my books and papers, I would try and get it. They said I would never go back to that bed, for they were going to kill me. . . . They caught my leg and pulled me over the yard, and then left me there, knowing I could not walk nor crawl. . . .

"After they had stayed in the house for a considerable time, they came back to where I lay and asked if I wasn't afraid at all. They pointed pistols at me all around my head once or twice, as if they were going to shoot me. . . . One caught me by the leg and hurt me, for my leg for forty years has been drawn each year, more and more, and I made moan when it hurt so. One said, 'G–d d—n it, hush!' He had a horsewhip, [and] I reckon he struck me eight cuts right on the hip bone; it was almost the only place he could hit my body, my legs are so short. They all had disguises. . . . One of them then took a strap, and buckled it around my neck and said, 'Let's take him to the river and drown him.' . . .

"Then they said, 'Look here! Will you put a card in the paper to renounce all republicanism? Will you quit preaching?' I told them I did not know. I said that to save my life. . . . They said if I did not they would come back the next week and kill me. [After more licks with the strap] one of them went into the house where my brother and sister-and-law lived, and brought her to pick me up. As she stooped down to pick me up one of them struck her, and as she was carrying me into the house another struck her with a strap. . . . They said, 'Don't you pray against Ku-Klux, but pray that God may forgive Ku-Klux. Pray that God may bless and save us.' I was so chilled with cold lying out of doors so long and in such pain I could not speak to pray, but I tried to, and they said that would do very well, and all went out of the house. . . ."

Satisfied that he could no longer live in that community, Hill wrote to make inquiry about the means of going to Liberia. Hearing this, many of his neighbors desired to go also. . . . Others are still hoping for relief, through the means of this sub-committee.

3

✧

A KIND OF REUNION

Despite Congress's seizure of control over Reconstruction policy and Ulysses S. Grant's defeat of Andrew Johnson for the presidency in 1868, Radical Reconstruction—the garrisoning of the South, the disfranchisement of former rebels, and the control of Southern state governments by Republican votes—did not last long in most places. During President Grant's first term of office, the white-dominated Democratic Party gained control of North Carolina, Tennessee, and Virginia, the three ex-Confederate states with the lowest percentage of black population. During Grant's second term, Democrats seized control of Alabama, Arkansas, Georgia, Mississippi, and Texas. That left Republican governments (and federal troops) in Florida, Louisiana, and South Carolina, three states with large black populations.

Those states mattered greatly in national politics. During the election of 1876 both parties resorted to fraud. Two sets of electoral returns came in from the three states, and it was necessary for Congress to set up an electoral commission to decide whether Rutherford B. Hayes, the Republican candidate, or Samuel J. Tilden, the Democratic standard bearer, had won. By a strict party vote of 8 to 7, the commission awarded all 20 disputed electoral votes to the Republicans. Hayes became president, with 185 votes to Tilden's 184. In the end, Southern Democrats reached a compromise with Northern Republicans. The Democrats agreed to accept the commission's decision and the Republicans promised to withdraw the remaining federal troops from the South. In April 1877, the last federal soldiers left the South. Solid Democratic control—and stepped-up measures to disfranchise black voters—quickly followed.

Although political maneuvering was important in finally killing Republican Reconstruction, the underlying reason it died was simply that Northerners were losing the will to suppress an increasingly violent white South. The nation's approaching centennial celebration in 1876 triggered an especially strong outpouring of sentiment in favor of improving sectional feelings by withdrawing the troops, even if withdrawal meant the resurgence of the Democratic Party. That, in turn, would permit an overdue rebonding of the century-old republic. The following unsigned editorial ran in the August 1875 issue of *Scribner's Monthly,* an influential, generally Republican, New York magazine. It expressed, with unusual eloquence, this emotional yearning for peace.

Questions to Consider. What was the occasion of the *Scribner's* editorial? Was this a natural time to consider troop withdrawals? What, in the view of the editor, was the major accomplishment of the Civil War? What specific political theory had been tested and defeated? When addressing the "men of the South," was the editor speaking to all Southern men? What did the phrase "brotherly sympathy" mean? Was it naive or was it realistic for the writer to think that the upcoming centennial could "heal all the old wounds" and "reconcile all the old differences"? Would Abraham Lincoln have agreed with the spirit of this editorial?

———————◆———————

What the Centennial Ought to Accomplish (1875)

SCRIBNER'S MONTHLY

We are to have grand doings next year. There is to be an Exposition. There are to be speeches, and songs, and processions, and elaborate ceremonies and general rejoicings. Cannon are to be fired, flags are to be floated, and the eagle is expected to scream while he dips the tip of either pinion in the Atlantic and the Pacific, and sprinkles the land with a new baptism of freedom. The national oratory will exhaust the figures of speech in patriotic glorification, while the effete civilizations of the Old World, and the despots of the East, tottering upon their tumbling thrones, will rub their eyes and sleepily inquire, "What's the row?" The Centennial is expected to celebrate in a fitting way—somewhat dimly apprehended, it is true—the birth of a nation.

Well, the object is a good one. When the old colonies declared themselves free, they took a grand step in the march of progress; but now, before we begin our celebration of this event, would it not be well for us to inquire whether we have a nation? In a large number of the States of this country there exists not only a belief that the United States do not constitute a nation, but a theory of State rights which forbids that they ever shall become one. We hear about the perturbed condition of the Southern mind. We hear it said that multitudes there are just as disloyal as they were during the civil war. This, we believe, we are justified in denying. Before the war they

From *Scribner's Monthly* 10 (August 1875), 509–510.

Miss Liberty's torch. A display at the great 1876 Centennial Exposition, Philadelphia. (Samuel Castner Collection/Free Library of Philadelphia)

had a theory of State rights. They fought to establish that theory, and they
now speak of the result as "the lost cause." They are not actively in rebellion,
and they do not propose to be. They do not hope for the re-establishment
of slavery. They fought bravely and well to establish their theory, but the
majority was against them; and if the result of the war emphasized any
fact, it was that *en masse* the people of the United States constitute a

nation—indivisible in constituents, in interest, in destiny. The result of the war was without significance, if it did not mean that the United States constitute a nation which cannot be divided; which will not permit itself to be divided; which is integral, indissoluble, indestructible. We do not care what theories of State rights are entertained outside of this. State rights, in all the States, should be jealously guarded, and, by all legitimate means, defended. New York should be as jealous of her State prerogatives as South Carolina or Louisiana; but this theory which makes of the Union a rope of sand, and of the States a collection of petty nationalities that can at liberty drop the bands which hold them together, is forever exploded. It has been tested at the point of the bayonet. It went down in blood, and went down for all time. Its adherents may mourn over the fact, as we can never cease to mourn over the events which accompanied it, over the sad, incalculable cost to them and to those who opposed them. The great point with them is to recognize the fact that, for richer or poorer, in sickness and health, until death do us part, these United States constitute a nation; that we are to live, grow, prosper, and suffer together, united by bands that cannot be sundered.

Unless this fact is fully recognized throughout the Union, our Centennial will be but a hollow mockery. If we are to celebrate anything worth celebrating, it is the birth of a nation. If we are to celebrate anything worth celebrating, it should be by the whole heart and united voice of the nation. If we can make the Centennial an occasion for emphasizing the great lesson of the war, and universally assenting to the results of the war, it will, indeed, be worth all the money expended upon and the time devoted to it. If around the old Altars of Liberty we cannot rejoin our hands in brotherly affection and national loyalty, let us spike the cannon that will only proclaim our weakness, put our flags at half-mast, smother our eagles, eat our ashes, and wait for our American aloe to give us a better blossoming.

A few weeks ago, Mr. Jefferson Davis, the ex-President of the Confederacy, was reported to have exhorted an audience to which he was speaking to be as loyal to the old flag of the Union now as they were during the Mexican War. If the South could know what music there was in these words to Northern ears—how grateful we were to their old chief for them—it would appreciate the strength of our longing for a complete restoration of the national feeling that existed when Northern and Southern blood mingled in common sacrifice on Mexican soil. This national feeling, this national pride, this brotherly sympathy *must be restored*; and accursed be any Northern or Southern man, whether in power or out of power, whether politician, theorizer, carpet-bagger, president-maker or plunderer, who puts obstacles in the way of such a restoration. Men of the South, we want you. Men of the South, we long for the restoration of your peace and your prosperity. We would see your cities thriving, your homes happy, your plantations teeming with plenteous harvests, your schools overflowing, your wisest statesmen leading you, and all causes and all memories of discord wiped out forever. You do not believe this? Then you do not know the heart of the North. Have you cause of complaint against the politicians? Alas! so have we. Help us, as loving and loyal American citizens, to make our politicians better. Only remember and believe that there is nothing that the North wants so much to-day, as your recognition of the fact that the old relations between you and us are forever restored—that your hope, your pride, your policy, and your destiny are one with ours. Our children will grow up to despise our childishness, if we cannot do away with our personal hates so far, that in the cause of an established nationality we may join hands under the old flag.

To bring about this reunion of the two sections of the country in the old fellowship, should be the leading object of the approaching Centennial. A celebration of the national birth, begun, carried on, and finished by a section, would be a mockery and a shame. The nations of the world might well point at it the finger of scorn. The money expended upon it were better sunk in the sea, or devoted to repairing the waste places of the war. Men of the South, it is for you to say whether your magnanimity is equal to your valor—whether you are as reasonable as you are brave, and whether, like your old chief, you accept that definite and irreversible result of the war which makes you and yours forever members of the great American nation with us. Let us see to it, North and South, that the Centennial heals all the old wounds, reconciles all the old differences, and furnishes the occasion for such a reunion of the great American nationality, as shall make our celebration an expression of fraternal good-will among all sections and all States, and a corner-stone over which shall be reared a new temple to national freedom, concord, peace, and prosperity.

4

✧

AFTERMATH

Frederick Douglass regarded the Declaration of Independence as a "watchword of freedom." But he was tempted to turn it to the wall, he said, because its human rights principles were so shamelessly violated. A former slave himself, Douglass knew what he was talking about. Douglass thought that enslaving blacks fettered whites as well and that the United States would never be truly free until it ended chattel slavery. During the Civil War, he had several conversations with Lincoln, urging him to make emancipation his major aim. He also put unremitting pressure on the Union army to accept black volunteers, and after resistance to admitting blacks into the army gave way, he toured the country encouraging blacks to enlist and imploring the government to treat black and white soldiers equally in matters of pay and promotion.

Douglass had great hopes for his fellow blacks after the Civil War. He demanded they be given full rights—political, legal, educational, and economic—as citizens. He also wanted to see the wall of separation between the races crumble and see "the colored people of this country, enjoying the same freedom [as whites], voting at the same ballot-box, using the same cartridge-box, going to the same schools, attending the same churches, travelling in the same street cars, in the same railroad cars, on the same steam-boats, proud of the same country, fighting the same war, and enjoying the same peace and all its advantages." He regarded the Republican party as the "party of progress, justice and freedom" and at election time took to the stump and rallied black votes for the party. He was rewarded for these services by appointment as marshal of the District of Columbia in 1877, as recorder of deeds for the District in 1881, and as minister to Haiti in 1889. But he was also asked by Republican leaders to keep a low profile, was omitted from White House guest lists, and was excluded from presidential receptions even though one duty of the District marshal was to introduce the guests at White House state occasions.

Douglass was puzzled and then upset by the increasing indifference of Republican leaders to conditions among blacks after the Civil War. In 1883 he attended a convention of blacks in Louisville, Kentucky, which met to discuss their plight and reaffirm their demand for full civil rights. In his keynote address, which is reprinted here, Douglass vividly portrayed the discrimination and persecution his people encountered, but he continued to believe that "prejudice, with all its malign accomplishments, may yet be removed by peaceful means."

Born into slavery in Maryland in 1817, Frederick Augustus Washington Bailey learned to read and write despite efforts to keep him illiterate. In 1838 he managed to escape to freedom and adopted the name Frederick Douglass. Shortly afterward he became associated with William Lloyd Garrison and developed into such an articulate spokesman for the antislavery cause that people doubted he had ever been a slave. In 1845 he published his *Narrative of the Life of Frederick Douglass, an American Slave,* naming names, places, dates, and precise events to convince people he had been born in bondage. Douglass continued to be an articulate spokesman for the black cause throughout his life. Shortly before his death in 1895 a college student asked him what a young black could do to help the cause. "Agitate! Agitate! Agitate!" Douglass is supposed to have told him.

Questions to Consider. In the following address Douglass was speaking to a convention of blacks in Louisville, but his appeal was primarily to American whites. How did he try to convince them that blacks deserved the same rights and opportunities as all Americans? How powerful did he think the color line was? What outrages against his people did he report? What was his attitude toward the Republican party, which he had so faithfully served? Were the grievances he cited largely economic or were they social and political in nature?

Address to the Louisville Convention (1883)

FREDERICK DOUGLASS

Born on American soil in common with yourselves, deriving our bodies and our minds from its dust, centuries having passed away since our ancestors were torn from the shores of Africa, we, like yourselves, hold ourselves to be in every sense Americans, and that we may, therefore, venture to speak to you in a tone not lower than that which becomes earnest men and American citizens. Having watered your soil with our

From Philip Foner, ed., *The Life and Writings of Frederick Douglass* (4 v., International Publishers, New York, 1955), IV: 373–392. Reprinted by permission.

Frederick Douglass. Douglass's greatest work came before and during the Civil War. One of the most eloquent and magnetic of all the abolitionist leaders, he contributed enormously to the antislavery cause. During the Civil War he pressed hard for the enlistment of blacks to fight in the Union armies on an equal footing with whites. After the war he continued his efforts for civil rights, including black suffrage. For his services to the Republican party he received appointments as secretary to the Santo Domingo commission, marshal and recorder of deeds for the District of Columbia, and U.S. minister to Haiti. (National Portrait Gallery, Smithsonian Institution/Washington, DC)

tears, enriched it with our blood, performed its roughest labor in time of peace, defended it against enemies in time of war, and at all times been loyal and true to its best interests, we deem it no arrogance or presumption to manifest now a common concern with you for its welfare, prosperity, honor and glory. . . .

It is our lot to live among a people whose laws, traditions, and prejudices have been against us for centuries, and from these they are not yet free.

To assume that they are free from these evils simply because they have changed their laws is to assume what is utterly unreasonable and contrary to facts. Large bodies move slowly. Individuals may be converted on the instant and change their whole course of life. Nations never. Time and events are required for the conversion of nations. Not even the character of a great political organization can be changed by a new platform. It will be the same old snake though in a new skin. Though we have had war, reconstruction and abolition as a nation, we still linger in the shadow and blight of an extinct institution. Though the colored man is no longer subject to be bought and sold, he is still surrounded by an adverse sentiment which fetters all his movements. In his downward course he meets with no resistance, but his course upward is resented and resisted at every step of his progress. If he comes in ignorance, rags, and wretchedness, he conforms to the popular belief of his character, and in that character he is welcome. But if he shall come as a gentleman, a scholar, and a statesman, he is hailed as a contradiction to the national faith concerning his race, and his coming is resented as impudence. In the one case he may provoke contempt and derision, but in the other he is an affront to pride, and provokes malice. Let him do what he will, there is at present, therefore, no escape for him. The color line meets him everywhere, and in a measure shuts him out from all respectable and profitable trades and callings. In spite of all your religion and laws he is a rejected man.

He is rejected by trade unions, of every trade, and refused work while he lives, and burial when he dies, and yet he is asked to forget his color, and forget that which everybody else remembers. If he offers himself to a builder as a mechanic, to a client as a lawyer, to a patient as a physician, to a college as a professor, to a firm as a clerk, to a Government Department as an agent, or an officer, he is sternly met on the color line, and his claim to consideration in some way is disputed on the ground of color.

Not even our churches, whose members profess to follow the despised Nazarene, whose home, when on earth, was among the lowly and despised, have yet conquered this feeling of color madness, and what is true of our churches is also true of our courts of law. Neither is free from this all-pervading atmosphere of color hate. The one describes the Deity as impartial, no respecter of persons, and the other the Goddess of Justice as blindfolded, with sword by her side and scales in her hand held evenly between high and low, rich and low, white and black, but both are the images of American imagination, rather than American practices.

Taking advantage of the general disposition in this country to impute crime to color, white men *color* their faces to commit crime and wash off the hated color to escape punishment. In many places where the commission of crime is alleged against one of our color, the ordinary processes of law are set aside as too slow for the impetuous justice of the infuriated populace. They take the law into their own bloody hands and proceed to whip, stab, shoot, hang, or burn the alleged culprit, without the intervention of courts, counsel, judges, juries, or witnesses. In such cases it is not the business of the accusers to prove guilt, but it is for the accused to prove his innocence, a thing hard for him to do in these infernal Lynch courts. A man accused, surprised, frightened, and captured by a motley crowd, dragged with a rope about his neck in midnight-darkness to the nearest tree, and told in the coarsest terms of profanity to prepare for death, would be more than human if he did not, in his terror-stricken appearance, more confirm suspicion of guilt than the contrary. Worse still, in the presence of such hell-black outrages, the pulpit is usually dumb, and the press in the neighborhood is silent or openly takes side with the mob. There are occasional cases in which white men are lynched, but one sparrow does not make a summer. Every one knows that what is called Lynch law is peculiarly the law colored people and for nobody else. If there were no other grievance than this horrible and barbarous Lynch law custom, we should be justified in assembling, as we have now done, to expose and denounce it. But this is not all. Even now, after twenty years of so-called emancipation, we are subject to lawless raids of midnight riders, who, with blackened faces, invade our homes and perpetrate the foulest of crimes upon us and our families. This condition of things is too flagrant and notorious to require specifications or proof. Thus in all the relations of life and death we are met by the color line.

While we recognize the color line as a hurtful force, a mountain barrier to our progress, wounding our bleeding feet with its flinty rocks at every step, we do not despair. We are a hopeful people. This convention is a proof of our faith in you, in reason, in truth and justice—our belief that prejudice, with all its malign accomplishments, may yet be removed by peaceful means; that, assisted by time and events and the growing enlightenment of both races, the color line will ultimately become harmless. When this shall come it will then only be used, as it should be, to distinguish one variety of the human family from another. It will cease to have any civil, political, or moral significance, and colored conventions will then be dispensed with as anachronisms, wholly out of place, but not till then. Do not marvel that we are discouraged. The faith within us has a rational basis, and is confirmed by facts. When we consider how deep-seated this feeling against us is; the long centuries it has been forming; the forces of avarice which have been marshaled to sustain it; how the language and literature of the country have been pervaded with it; how the church, the press, the play-house, and other influences of the country have been arrayed in its support, the progress toward its extinction must be considered vast and wonderful. . . .

We do not believe, as we are often told, that the Negro is the ugly child of the national family, and the more he is kept out of sight the better it will be for him. You know that liberty given is never so precious as liberty sought for and fought for. The man outraged is the man to make the outcry. Depend upon it, men will not care much for a people who do not care for themselves. Our meeting here was opposed by some of our members, because it would disturb the peace of the Republican party. The suggestion came from coward lips and misapprehended the character of that party. If the Republican party cannot stand a demand for justice and fair play, it ought to go down. We were men before that party was born, and our manhood is more sacred than any party can be. Parties were made for men, not men for parties.

The colored people of the South are the laboring people of the South. The labor of a country is the source of its wealth; without the colored laborer to-day the South would be a howling wilderness, given up to bats, owls, wolves, and bears. He was the source of its wealth before the war, and has been the source of its prosperity since the war. He almost alone is visible in her fields, with implements of toil in his hands, and laboriously using them to-day.

Let us look candidly at the matter. While we see and hear that the South is more prosperous than it ever was before and rapidly recovering from the waste of war, while we read that it raises more cotton, sugar, rice, tobacco, corn, and other valuable products than it ever produced before, how happens it, we sternly ask, that the houses of its laborers are miserable huts, that their clothes are rags, and their food the coarsest and scantiest? How happens it that the land-owner is becoming richer and the laborer poorer?

The implication is irresistible—that where the landlord is prosperous the laborer ought to share his prosperity, and whenever and wherever we find this is not the case there is manifestly wrong somewhere. . . .

Flagrant as have been the outrages committed upon colored citizens in respect to their civil rights, more flagrant, shocking, and scandalous still have been the outrages committed upon our political rights by means of bull-dozing and Kukluxing, Mississippi plans, fraudulent courts, tissue ballots, and the like devices. Three States in which the colored people outnumber the white population are without colored representation and their political voice suppressed. The colored citizens in those States are virtually disfranchised, the Constitution held in utter contempt and its provisions nullified. This has been done in the face of the Republican party and successive Republican administrations. . . .

This is no question of party. It is a question of law and government. It is a question whether men shall be protected by law, or be left to the mercy of cyclones of anarchy and bloodshed. It is whether the Government or the mob shall rule this land; whether the promises solemnly made to us in the constitution be manfully kept or meanly and flagrantly broken. Upon this vital point we ask the whole people of the United States to take notice that whatever of political power we have shall be exerted for no man of any party who will not, in advance of election, promise to use every power given him by the Government, State or National, to make the black man's path to the ballot-box as straight, smooth and safe as that of any other American citizen. . . .

We hold it to be self-evident that no class or color should be the exclusive rulers of this country. If there is such a ruling class, there must of course be a subject class, and when this condition is once established this Government of the people, by the people, and for the people, will have perished from the earth.

Miss Liberty welcoming a family of Jewish immigrants. (YIVO Institute for Jewish Research)

CHAPTER TWO

⟡

Minorities

5

✧

A SISTER ON THE FRONTIER

Roman Catholics found a niche in predominantly Protestant North America when Charles I granted Lord Baltimore a charter to establish the colony of Maryland. But prejudice compelled even Lord Baltimore to enjoin Catholics to worship "as privately as may be" and to avoid public discussion of their beliefs. Elsewhere in the colonies, Catholics often faced hostility, and persevered by keeping their religious convictions to themselves. With the Revolution and the religious freedom it promised, Catholics expected their position to improve—after all, they had fought enthusiastically for the cause, and the Catholic Count Pulaski, the top cavalry commander in the southern campaign, had died a hero of the Revolution.

Things did get better. With greater numbers of European Catholic immigrants, churches and dioceses multiplied, missionaries went west, and schools were founded. As the Catholic population increased, however, so again did nativist suspicions. By the 1830s anti-Catholicism was so virulent that in Boston a mob burned the Ursuline convent school. The huge influx of Irish Catholics in the 1840s and 1850s further aroused American prejudices, which lessened only somewhat during the Civil War and its bitter aftermath.

Yet Catholics remained intent on spreading their faith. And in contrast to their reception in some urban areas, they were often welcome on the frontier. Of Catholic schools in the Ohio and Indiana wilderness one observer reported:

Everywhere in America, in the best society, the most accomplished and influential ladies have been educated in convents, and though they may never go over to Rome they love and respect their teachers. . . . Education is removing prejudices, and the chaotic condition of the Protestant community, divided into warring sects, increases the power of a Church whose characteristic is unity, and whose claim is infallibility.

Sister Blandina Segale was a Catholic missionary and teacher who found herself in the rough cowboy country of the Colorado Territory in the 1870s. Sent by the Sisters of Charity to the town of Trinidad, she labored in the Southwest (in what is today Colorado and New

Mexico) among the predominantly Mexican population for twenty-one years. Hers was hardly a monastic existence; Sister Blandina's experiences included an encounter with Billy the Kid, whom she charmed into inviting her to call on him should she ever need assistance, and the rescue of a man about to be lynched by a mob. Her indomitable spirit, shrewd insight, and quick-wittedness are illustrated in the document below, a fragment from a journal she kept in the form of letters to her sister, Sister Justina, in Cincinnati. Here she records how she was able to get a new school built, a tale that reflects both her resourcefulness as an individual and the self-sufficient fashion in which the Catholic church established itself on the frontier.

Following her days in the territory, Sister Blandina returned to Cincinnati, where she and her sister established the Santa Maria Institute, the oldest aid society for Italian immigrants. There she labored for thirty-five years, personally instructing nearly 80 percent of the Italian population in the Catholic faith.

Questions to Consider. What qualities made Sister Blandina particularly well suited to life in a frontier situation? What kind of relationship did she have with the people she served? To what extent did she respect local wisdom and customs? How would you describe the relationship between local people and women?

✧

Letter from Colorado (1876)

BLANDINA SEGALE

Dear Sister Justina:

To-day I asked Sister Eulalia if, in her opinion, we did not need a new school building, which would contain a hall and stage for all school purposes. She said: "Just what we need, Sister. Do you want to build it?" I answered, "Yes, I do." She added, "We have not enough cash to pay interest on our indebtedness. Have you a plan by which you can build without money? If so, I say build."

"Here is my plan, Sister. Borrow a crowbar, get on the roof of the schoolhouse and begin to detach the adobes. The first good Mexican who sees me will ask, "What are you doing, Sister?" I will answer, "Tumbling down this structure to rebuild it before the opening of the fall term of school."

You should have seen Sister Eulalia laugh! It did me good. After three days' pondering how to get rid of low ceilings, poor ventilation, acrobats

---

From Sister Blandina Segale, *At the End of the Santa Fe Trail* (Milwaukee, 1948), 62–65.

from log-rafters introducing themselves without notice, and now here is an opportunity to carry out a test on the good in human nature, so I took it. I borrowed a crowbar and went on the roof, detached some adobes and began throwing them down. The school building is only one story high.

The first person who came towards the schoolhouse was Doña Juanita Simpson, wife of the noted hero of Simpson's Rest. When she saw me at work, she exclaimed, *"Por amor de Dios, Hermana, qué está Vd. haciendo?"* (For the love of God, Sister, what are you doing?)

I answered, "We need a schoolhouse that will a little resemble those we have in the United States, so I am demolishing this one in order to rebuild."

"How many men do you need, Sister?"

"We need not only men, but also straw, moulds, hods, shovels—everything it takes to build a house with a shingle roof. Our assets are good-will and energy."

Earnestly Mrs. Simpson said: "I go to get what you need."

The crowbar was kept at its work. In less than an hour, Mrs. Simpson returned with six men. One carried a mould, another straw, etc. The mould carrier informed me at once that women only know how to *encalar* (whitewash), the men had the trades and they would continue what I began. In a few days the old building was thrown down, the adobes made and sunburnt. In two weeks all the rubbish was hauled away. The trouble began when we were ready for the foundation. Keep in mind it was only by condescension I was permitted to look on. At this juncture I remarked to the moulder:

"Of course, we will have a stone foundation."

"Oh, no!" he answered, "we use adobes laid in mud."

"Do you think if we laid a foundation with stone laid in mortar, the combination would resist the rainy season better than adobes laid in mud?"

"No, no, Sister we never use stone for any of our houses," he replied.

I was at the mercy of the good natives and my best move was to let them have their way. Moreover, I recalled the fact that in the Far East there are mud structures centuries old in a good state of preservation. No mistake would be made by not changing their mode of building in that one point. We got the necessary lumber, sashes and shingles from Chené's mill, sixty miles from Trinidad. Wagons hauled the material. As the Chené family has a daughter at our boarding school, there will be no difficulty in meeting our bill. Mr. Hermann's daughter is a resident student, and Mr. Hermann is a carpenter and will pay his bill by work.

When the schoolhouse was ready for roofing, a number of the town carpenters offered to help. The merchants gave nails, paints, brushes, lime, hair, etc.

But now came the big obstacle. There is but one man who calls himself a plasterer, and his method is to plaster with mud. It is impossible to get a smooth surface with mud. I remarked to the plasterer: "You will use lime, sand and hair to plaster the schoolrooms."

His look plainly said: "What do women know of men's work?" Yet he condescended to explain: "I am the plasterer of this part of the country; if I should use any material but mud, my reputation would be lost."

I said to him, "But if lime, sand and hair made a better job, your reputation would gain."

He made answer, "Sister, I'll make a bargain with you. I will do as you suggest, but I will tell my people I carried out your American idea of plastering."

We both agreed to this. Meanwhile, the other men had shouldered their implements and were on their way home. The plasterer had to mix the sand, lime and hair following my directions. All that was done satisfactorily to me, at least. But there was not a man to carry the mortar to the plasterer, so I got the bucket and supplied a man's place. The comedy follows:

Rev. Charles Pinto, S.J., pastor, took pleasure in telling his co-religionists that the study of human nature, combined with good will and tactfulness, were building a schoolhouse.

On this day of my hod-carrying, the Rt. Rev. Bishop Machebeuf of Denver, Colorado, arrived on his visitation. The first place to which he was taken was the schoolhouse being built without money. Bishop and Pastor had just turned the kitchen corner when the three of us came face to face. Both gentlemen stood amazed. I rested my hod-bucket. Father Pinto looked puzzled. The Bishop remarked:

"I see how you manage to build without money." I laughed and explained the situation.

They took the bucket, and the three of us went to where the plasterer was working. After the welcome to the Bishop, the plasterer said:

"Your Reverence, look at me, the only Mexican plasterer, and I am putting aside my knowledge to follow American ways of doing my trade; but I told Sister the failure will not be pointed at me." The Rt. Rev. Bishop analyzed the material at a glance, then said: "Juan, if this method of plastering is better than yours, come again to help Sister when she needs you. If it fails, report to me and between us we shall give her the biggest penance she ever received."

The schoolroom walls turned out smooth, the plaster adhesive, and the plasterer will now make a lucrative living at his American method of plastering.

6

✧

INDIAN AUTUMN

Conflict between whites and Native Americans began with the first colonial landings and continued undiminished into the late nineteenth century. At that time, the United States finally completed its conquest of the continent and extended its authority over all the lands formerly held by the indigenous peoples. After the Civil War, whites began moving in large numbers along the new rail lines west of the Mississippi River. As part of this movement, the U.S. Army fought continuous wars against the larger and more combative Native American nations— notably the Comanche, Apache, Kiowa, Cheyenne, and Sioux. The army also harassed most of the smaller nations. Native Americans won occasional victories, for example, the Sioux victory over former Civil War General George A. Custer at the Little Bighorn in 1876. Most of the time, however, the tribespeople fell victim to U.S. Army's superior organization, supplies, and firepower. Whites' slaughter of the vast buffalo herds on which the Native Americans had based their lives— thirteen million buffalo had been killed by 1883—virtually ensured that the tribes would be crushed. The last major military clash between the government and the Native Americans came with the slaughter of scores of Sioux families in 1890 at Wounded Knee, South Dakota.

The Plains peoples were confined almost entirely to reservations. These large tracts of land had been set aside by the U.S. government as places where, with the protection and economic aid of the Indian Office, the Plains peoples might continue their nomadic communal ways. But this policy was a failure. Tribal ranks, already severely de-pleted by the Plains wars, were further thinned by the growing scarcity of buffalo. Moreover, large tribes were often widely divided on scattered reservations, where resident U.S. government agents usually proved unwilling or unable to prevent looting by white settlers and theft of funds earmarked for tribal assistance.

"Chief Joseph's Story," excerpted below, is a commentary on events during the 1870s. It describes both the encounters—peaceful and other-wise—of the Nez Percés[1] of the Oregon and Idaho country with U.S.

---

1. "Nez Percé," like "Joseph," was a European-American name imposed by American explorers in place of the tribal name.

settlers and authorities and the betrayals that accompanied those en-counters. Born about 1840, "Young Joseph" was the son of a chief of a major Nez Percé band, who had also been christened Joseph by white missionaries. The father had refused to cede tribal lands to the U.S. government following the discovery of gold in the Oregon country, and he passively resisted white efforts to settle the area. When his father died in 1873, "Young Joseph"—named Hinmatonyalatkit, or Thunder Traveling Over The Mountains, in his native tongue—continued the policy of noncooperation. In early 1877 General O. O. Howard ordered the Nez Percés off the land, promising them a reservation elsewhere in the Oregon region. "Young Joseph," seeking to protect his people, agreed to leave, but other Nez Percés did not. A skirmish quickly escalated into a series of pitched battles that deci-mated the tribe. After armed resistance and a masterly retreat of 1,500 miles, "Young Joseph" surrendered in October 1877. He and his band were sent to Indian Territory, then in 1885 to Washington state. Chief "Young Joseph," by now a figure of legendary proportions to Native Americans and whites alike, died in 1904.

Questions to Consider. What were the key features in the history of relations between Native Americans and whites, as "Young Joseph" told it? In "Young Joseph's" eyes, was the U.S. Army merely an arm of westward expansion or was it an autonomous agent? Given the Nez Percé beliefs (as the chief summarized them), do you think the Americans' westward advance could have occurred without wrecking the tribal nations? In his policy proposals at the end of the passage, was "Young Joseph" advocating a policy of assimilation, separate but equal status, ethnic autonomy, or simple justice? Was his vision practi-cal at that time? Can you see any alternative that might have suited both sides?

Chief Joseph's Story (1879)

YOUNG JOSEPH

My friends, I have been asked to show you my heart. I am glad to have a chance to do so. I want the white people to understand my people. Some of you think an Indian is like a wild animal. This is a great mistake. I will tell you about our people, and then you can judge whether an Indian is a

From "Chief Joseph's Own Story," *North American Review* (April 1879), 415–433.

Young Joseph. A late-nineteenth-century Nez Percé chief. (Smithsonian Institution, Washington, D.C.)

man or not. I believe much trouble and blood would be saved if we opened our hearts more. I will tell you in my way how the Indian sees things. The white man has more words to tell you how they look to him, but it does not require many words to speak the truth. What I have to say will come from my heart, and I will speak with a straight tongue. Ah-cum-kin-i-ma-me-hut (the Great Spirit) is looking at me, and will hear me.

My name is In-mut-too-yah-lat-lat (Thunder-traveling-over-the-mountains). I am chief of the Wal-lam-wat-kin band of Chute-pa-lu, or Nez Percés (nose-pierced Indians). I was born in eastern Oregon, thirty-eight winters ago. My father was chief before me. When a young man he was called Joseph by Mr. Spalding, a missionary. He died a few years ago. There was no stain on his hands of the blood of a white man. He left a good name on the earth. He advised me well for my people.

Our fathers gave us many laws, which they had learned from their fathers. These laws were good. They told us to treat all men as they treated us; that we should never be the first to break a bargain; that it was a disgrace to tell a lie; that we should speak only the truth; that it was a shame for one man to take from another his wife, or his property, without paying for it. We were taught to believe that the Great Spirit sees and hears everything, and that He never forgets; that hereafter He will give every man a spirit-home according to his deserts; if he has been a good man, he will have a good home; if he has been a bad man, he will have a bad home. This I believe, and all my people believe the same.

The first white men of your people who came to our country were named Lewis and Clarke. They also brought many things that our people had never seen. They talked straight, and our people gave them a great feast, as a proof that their hearts were friendly. These men were very kind. They made presents to our chiefs and our people made presents to them. We had a great many horses of which we gave them what they needed, and they gave us guns and tobacco in return. All the Nez Percés made friends with Lewis and Clarke, and agreed to let them pass through their country, and never to make war on white men. This promise the Nez Percés have never broken. . . .

Next there came a white officer who invited all the Nez Percés to a treaty council. After the council was opened he made known his heart. He said there were a great many white people in the country, and many more would come; that he wanted the land marked out so that the Indians and white men could be separated. If they were to live in peace it was necessary, he said, that the Indians should have a country set apart for them, and in that country they must stay. My father, who represented his band, refused to have anything to do with the council, because he wished to be a free man. He claimed that no man owned any part of the earth, and a man could not sell what was not his own. . . .

For a short time we lived quietly. But this could not last. White men had found gold in the mountains around the land of the winding water. They stole a great many horses from us, and we could not get them back because we were Indians. . . . We could have avenged our wrongs many times, but we did not. Whenever the Government has asked us to help them against other Indians we have never refused. When the white men were few and we were strong we could have killed them off, but the Nez Percés wished to live at peace. . . .

Year after year we have been threatened, but no war was made upon my people until General Howard came to our country two years ago and told us that he was the white war-chief of all that country. He said: "I have a great many soldiers at my back. I am going to bring them up here, and then I will talk to you again. I will not let white men laugh at me the next time I come. The country belongs to the Government, and I intend to make you go upon the reservation."

I remonstrated with him against bringing more soldiers to the Nez Percé country. He had one house full of troops all the time at Fort Lapwei. . . .

When the party arrived there General Howard sent out runners and called all the Indians to a grand council. In the council General Howard informed us in a haughty spirit that he would give my people thirty days to go back home, collect all their stock, and move on to the reservation, saying, "If you are not here in that time, I shall consider that you want to fight, and will send my soldiers to drive you on." . . .

When I returned to Wallowa I found my people very much excited upon discovering that the soldiers were already in the Wallowa Valley. We held a council, and decided to move immediately to avoid bloodshed. . . .

We gathered all the stock we could find, and made an attempt to move. We left many of our horses and cattle in Wallowa, and we lost several hundred in crossing the river. All my people succeeded in getting across in safety. Many of the Nez Percés came together in Rocky Cañon to hold a grand council. . . .

Again I counseled peace, and I thought the danger was past. We had not complied with General Howard's order because we could not, but we intended to do so as soon as possible. I was leaving the council to kill beef for my family when news came that a young man whose father had been killed had gone out with several hot-blooded young braves and killed four white men. He rode up to the council and shouted: "Why do you sit here like women? The war has begun already." [Following many battles] I went to General [Colonel Nelson] Miles and gave up my gun, and said, "From where the sun now stands I will fight no more." . . .

Words do not pay for my dead people. They do not pay for my country, now overrun by white men. They do not protect my father's grave. They do not pay for my horses and cattle. Good words will not give me back my children. Good words will not make good the promise of your War Chief, General Miles, [of reservation land in Idaho]. Good words will not give my people good health and stop them from dying. Good words will not get my people a home where they can live in peace and take care of themselves. I am tired of talk that comes to nothing. . . .

I know that my race must change. We cannot hold our own with the white men as we are. We only ask an even chance to live as other men live. We ask to be recognized as men. We ask that the same law shall work alike on all men. If the Indian breaks the law, punish him by the law. If the white man breaks the law, punish him also.

Let me be a free man—free to travel, free to stop, free to work, free to trade where I choose, free to choose my own teachers, free to follow the religion of my fathers, free to think and talk and act for myself—and I will obey every law, or submit to the penalty.

Whenever the white man treats the Indian as they treat each other, then we shall have no more wars. We shall be all alike—brothers of one father and one mother, with one sky above us and one country around us, and one government for all. Then the Great Spirit Chief who rules above will smile upon this land, and send rain to wash out the bloody spots made by brothers' hands upon the face of the earth. For this time the Indian race are waiting and praying. I hope that no more groans of wounded men and women will ever go to the ear of the Great Spirit Chief above, and that all people may be one people..

In-mut-too-yah-lat-lat has spoken for his people.

Young Joseph

7

Newcomers

The sprawling city was as fundamental a fact of life as the great West or the bitter South in the late nineteenth century, and most Americans found it simultaneously exciting and unsettling. Cities were exciting because they symbolized prosperity and progress, cardinal virtues of the country for decades if not centuries. These urban centers were full of good and novel things to buy and do in a land lusting to do both. But cities were also unsettling—seething (so it seemed) with greedy landlords, corrupt politicians, and radical workers. Most unsettling of all, they were populated by foreigners, not "real" Americans— immigrants from a dozen lands, speaking as many languages and exhibiting as many objectionable habits. These newcomers spilled out from the waterfronts of New York, Baltimore, or Chicago into vast impoverished tenement districts that strained not only public morality but also public order and public health. They may have been lovers of liberty "yearning to be free," as it said on the Statue of Liberty, but they were also "huddled masses."

For most Americans, New York City—the country's largest city and chief port of European debarkation—was the epitome of the immigrant city. No U.S. city could claim more foreign-born inhabitants or more crowded housing conditions. Relatively little open space remained for new residential or business construction. But New York was more than an immigrant center; it was also the publishing and literary capital of the United States. By 1890, hundreds of reporters and writers lived in the city, working for dozens of newspapers and magazines, not counting the foreign-language press. When the United States developed an appetite for urban coverage, New York had a thriving industry to supply it.

Jacob Riis, a Danish immigrant, was a pioneer in the field of urban exposé journalism. Riis, who arrived in New York in 1870, wandered in semipoverty for several years before becoming a city police reporter, first for the *New York Tribune,* then for the *Evening Sun.* His beat was the lower East Side, a teeming immigrant district. For twenty-two years, until 1899, his office was directly across from police headquarters. Here, he wrote, "I was to find my lifework." But Riis was more than a reporter; he became a reformer, determined not only to describe slum life but to improve it. His goal was partly to establish better building codes, but chiefly to ensure that all immigrants learned English and were assimilated thoroughly into American life. This path, after all, was the one that Jacob Riis himself had followed. *How the Other Half Lives,* which first appeared as a series of newspaper essays (one of which is excerpted below), was a weapon in Riis's crusade.

Jacob Riis, born in Ribe, Denmark, in 1849, was educated by his father and became an apprentice carpenter before emigrating to the United States in 1870. By 1890 he had become one of the best-known, most colorful newspapermen in New York. *How the Other Half Lives,* which Riis illustrated with startling photographs of slum conditions, made him a byword in the nation as well. Among its readers was another budding reformer and member of the New York City police board—Theodore Roosevelt, who befriended Riis, accompanied him on forays into the slums, and supported his reform efforts. Riis carried on his crusade in later books, including several on immigrant children, and saw significant improvements in slum schools and recreational facilities. He died in Barre, Massachusetts, in 1914.

Questions to Consider. Modern readers will instantly notice Riis's constant use of stereotypes in discussing various immigrant groups. Why might an intelligent, sympathetic reporter of the 1890s resort to such stereotypes? How could such an author be seen (as Riis was) as a champion of liberal social reform? Riis was a reporter, not a social scientist. Are his descriptions and explanations of group social mobility persuasive? When he explains why immigrant groups tend to form separate enclaves, is he persuasive? Would a writer about homelessness in the 1990s approach the task as Riis did?

————————✧————————

How the Other Half Lives (1890)

JACOB RIIS

When once I asked the agent of a notorious Fourth Ward alley how many people might be living in it I was told: One hundred and forty families, one hundred Irish, thirty-eight Italian, and two that spoke the German tongue. Barring the agent herself there was not a native-born individual in the court. The answer was characteristic of the cosmopolitan character

From Jacob Riis, *How the Other Half Lives* (Scribner's, New York, 1907), 14–21.

Homeless men and women huddling at the Elizabeth Street police station in Lower Manhattan. Jacob Riis took this photograph in 1890, about the time he enlisted the aid of Theodore Roosevelt, then chairman of the New York Police Commission. (UPI/Bettmann)

of lower New York, very nearly so of the whole of it, wherever it runs to alleys and courts. One may find for the asking an Italian, a German, a French, African, Spanish, Bohemian, Russian, Scandinavian, Jewish, and Chinese colony. Even the Arab, who peddles "holy earth" from the Battery as a direct importation from Jerusalem, has his exclusive preserves at the lower end of Washington Street. The one thing you shall vainly ask for in the chief city of America is a distinctively American community. . . .

They are not here. In their place has come this queer conglomerate mass of heterogeneous elements, ever striving and working like whiskey and water in one glass, and with the like result: final union and a prevailing taint of whiskey. The once unwelcome Irishman has been followed in his turn by the Italian, the Russian Jew, and the Chinaman, and has himself taken a hand at opposition, quite as bitter and quite as ineffectual, against these later hordes. Wherever these have gone they have crowded him out, possessing the block, the street, the ward with their denser swarms. But the Irishman's revenge is complete. Victorious in defeat over his recent as over his more ancient foe, the one who opposed his coming no less than the one who drove him out, he dictates to both their politics, and, secure in possession of the offices, returns the native his greeting with interest, while collecting the rents of the Italian whose house he has bought with the profits of his saloon. . . .

In justice to the Irish landlord it must be said that like an apt pupil he was merely showing forth the result of the schooling he had received, reenacting, in his own way, the scheme of the tenements. It is only his frankness that shocks. The Irishman does not naturally take kindly to tenement life, though with characteristic versatility he adapts himself to its conditions at once. It does violence, nevertheless, to the best that is in him, and for that very reason of all who come within its sphere soonest corrupts him. The result is a sediment, the product of more than a generation in the city's slums, that, as distinguished from the larger body of his class, justly ranks at the foot of tenement dwellers, the so-called "low Irish." . . .

An impulse toward better things there certainly is. The German rag-picker of thirty years ago, quite as low in the scale as his Italian successor, is the thrifty tradesman or prosperous farmer of today.

The Italian scavenger of our time is fast graduating into exclusive control of the corner fruit-stands,while his black-eyed boy monopolizes the boot-blacking industry in which a few years ago he was an intruder. The Irish hod-carrier in the second generation has become a bricklayer, if not the Alderman of his ward, while the Chinese coolie is in almost exclusive possession of the laundry business. The reason is obvious. The poorest immigrant comes here with the purpose and ambition to better himself and, given half a chance, might be reasonably expected to make the most of it. To the false plea that he prefers the squalid homes in which his kind are housed there could be no better answer. . . .

As emigration from east to west follows the latitude, so does the foreign influx in New York distribute itself along certain well-defined lines that waver and break only under the stronger pressure of a more gregarious race or the encroachments of inexorable business. A feeling of dependence upon mutual effort, natural to strangers in a strange land, unacquainted with its language and customs, sufficiently accounts for this.

The Irishman is the true cosmopolitan immigrant. All-pervading, he shares his lodging with perfect impartiality with the Italian, the Greek, and the "Dutchman," yielding only to sheer force of numbers, and objects equally to them all. A map of the city, colored to designate nationalities, would show more stripes than on the skin of a zebra, and more colors than any rainbow. The city on such a map would fall into two great halves, green for the Irish prevailing in the West Side tenement districts, and blue for the Germans on the East side. But intermingled with these ground colors would be an odd variety of tints that would give the whole the appearance of an extraordinary crazy-quilt. From down in the Sixth Ward, upon the site of the old Collect Pond that in the days of the fathers drained the hills which are no more, the red of the Italian would be seen forcing its way northward along the line of Mulberry Street to the quarter of the French purple on Bleecker Street and South Fifth Avenue, to lose itself and reappear, after a lapse of miles, in the "Little Italy" of Harlem, east of Second Avenue. Dashes of red, sharply defined, would be seen strung through the Annexed District, northward to the city line. On the West Side the red would be seen overrunning the old Africa of Thompson Street, pushing the black of the negro rapidly uptown, against querulous but unavailing protests, occupying his home, his church, his trade, and all with merciless impartiality.

Hardly less aggressive than the Italian, the Russian and Polish Jew, having overrun the district between Rivington and Division Streets, east of the Bowery, to the point of suffocation, is filling the tenements of the old Seventh Ward to the river front, and disputing with the Italian every foot of available space in the back alleys of Mulberry Street. The two races, differing hopelessly in much, have this in common: they carry their slums with them wherever they go, if allowed to do it. Little Italy already rivals its parent, the "Bend," in foulness. Other nationalities that begin at the bottom make a fresh start when crowded up the ladder. Happily both are manageable, the one by rabbinical, the other by the civil law. Between the dull gray of the Jew, his favorite color, and the Italian red, would be seen squeezed in on the map a sharp streak of yellow, marking the narrow boundaries of Chinatown. Dovetailed in with the German population, the poor but thrifty Bohemian might be picked out by the sombre hue of his life as of his philosophy, struggling against heavy odds in the big human bee-hives of the East Side. Colonies of his people extend northward, with long lapses of space, from below the Cooper Institute more than three miles. The Bohemian is the only foreigner with any considerable representation in the city who counts no wealthy man of his race, none who has not to work hard for a living, or has got beyond the reach of the tenement.

Down near the Battery the West Side emerald would be soiled by a dirty stain, spreading rapidly like a splash of ink on a sheet of blotting paper, headquarters of the Arab tribe, that in a single year has swelled from the original dozen to twelve hundred, intent, every mother's son, on trade and barter. Dots and dashes of color here and there would show where the Finnish sailors worship their djumala (God), the Greek pedlars the ancient name of their race, and the Swiss the goddess of thrift. And so on to the end of the long register, all toiling together in the galling fetters of the tenement. Were the question raised who makes the most of life thus mortgaged, who resists most stubbornly its levelling tendency—knows how to drag even the barracks upward a part of the way at least toward the ideal plane of the home—the palm must be unhesitatingly awarded the Teuton. The Italian and the poor Jew rise only by compulsion. The Chinaman does not rise at all; here, as at home, he simply remains stationary. The Irishman's genius runs to public affairs rather than domestic life; wherever he is mustered in force the saloon is the gorgeous centre of political activity. The German struggles vainly to learn his trick; his Teutonic wit is too heavy, and the political ladder he raises from his saloon usually too short or too clumsy to reach the desired goal. The best part of his life is lived at home, and he makes himself a home independent of the surroundings, giving the lie to the saying, unhappily become a maxim of social truth, that pauperism and drunkenness naturally grow in the tenements. He makes the most of his tenement, and it should be added that whenever and as soon as he can save up money enough, he gets out and never crosses the threshold of one again.

8

✦

FROM ANOTHER SHORE

In 1882, Congress passed the Chinese Exclusion Act, prohibiting Chinese workers from entering this country for a period of ten years. As the date of expiration approached, however, pressure from powerful sources mounted for renewing the law. Leading the fight was the Immigration Committee of the House of Representatives, under the chairmanship of Representative Herman Stump of Maryland, who produced a stream of witnesses describing how the Chinese used drugs, committed crimes, and lusted after American women. Stump distilled the most important parts of this testimony in the report, reprinted below, that accompanied the committee's recommendation that the exclusion act be renewed.

The committee and its witnesses were persuasive. Not only did Congress extend the law for another ten years, but in 1893 President Grover Cleveland named Representative Stump superintendent of immigration. The exclusion act and Stump's appointment in turn set the stage for a treaty between the United States and China, signed in 1894, barring the immigration of Chinese laborers for ten years from the date of the exchange of ratifications. Those who had left the United States were permitted to return, provided they had wives, children, parents, or property worth $1,000 in this country. The treaty gave China the right to exclude American workers (of which there were none in China), but not American merchants and officials (who were numerous and important there). Chinese were thus all but barred from American soil, even as the Statue of Liberty (a gift of France) was unveiled in 1886 to welcome immigrants from Europe.

By 1900, Japanese workers, too, were entering the United States in sizable numbers; outcries against the "yellow peril" were again raised in the West. The so-called Gentleman's Agreement of 1907 between Washington and Tokyo instantly reduced the flow of unskilled Japanese laborers into the United States.

Questions to Consider. The congressional report of 1892 argued that the Chinese presence in the United States was a threat to American "institutions." What institutions did the Immigration Committee seem most concerned about? Why does the report mention the "vegetable" diets of the Chinese? One aim of the committee was evidently to reduce the "smuggling" of Chinese aliens into the country. Why might such smuggling have taken place,, and why did immigration officers seem unable to prevent it? The committee based much of its argument on the idea that the Chinese either could not or would not assimilate. Assuming that this lack of assimilation was a genuine problem, what alternatives might the committee have explored besides exclusion?

————————✧————————

Congressional Report on Immigration (1892)

There is urgent necessity for prompt legislation on the subject of Chinese immigration. The exclusion act approved May 6, 1882, and its supplement expires by limitation of time on May 6, 1892, and after that time there will be no law to prevent the Chinese hordes from invading our country in number so vast, as soon to outnumber the present population of our flourishing States on the Pacific slope. . . .

The popular demand for legislation excluding the Chinese from this country is urgent and imperative and almost universal. Their presence here is inimical to our institutions and is deemed injurious and a source of danger. They are a distinct race, saving from their earnings a few hundred dollars and returning to China. This they succeed in doing in from five to ten years by living in the most miserable manner, when in cities and towns in crowded tenement houses, surrounded by dirt, filth, corruption, pollution, and prostitution; and gambling houses and opium joints abound. When used as cooks, farm-hands, servants, and gardeners, they are more cleanly in habits and manners. They, as a rule, have no families here; all are men, save a few women, usually prostitutes. They have no attachment to our country, its laws or its institutions, nor are they interested in its prosperity. They never assimilate with our people, our manners, tastes, religion, or ideas. With us they have nothing in common.

Living on the cheapest diet (mostly vegetable), wearing the poorest clothing, with no family to support, they enter the field of labor in competition with the American workman. In San Francisco, and in fact throughout the whole Pacific slope, we learn from the testimony heretofore alluded to, that the Chinamen have invaded almost every branch of industry; manufacturers of cigars, cigar boxes, brooms, tailors, laundrymen, cooks, servants, farmhands, fishermen, miners and all departments of manual labor, for wages and prices at which white men and women could not support themselves and those dependent upon them. Recently this was a

Chinese-American merchant. A late-nineteenth-century Chinese-American dry goods store, San Francisco. (The Bancroft Library)

new country, and the Chinese may have been a necessity at one time, but now our own people are fast filling up and developing this rich and highly favored land, and American citizens will not and can not afford to stand idly by and see this undesirable race carry away the fruits of the labor which justly belongs to them. A war of races would soon be inaugurated; several times it has broken out, and bloodshed has followed. The town of Tacoma, in 1887, banished some 3,000 Chinamen on twenty-four hours' notice, and no Chinaman has ever been permitted to return.

Our people are willing, however, that those now here may remain, protected by the laws which they do not appreciate or obey, provided strong provision be made that no more shall be allowed to come, and that the smuggling of Chinese across the frontiers be scrupulously guarded against, so that gradually, by voluntary departures, death by sickness, accident, or old age, this race may be eliminated from this country, and the white race fill their places without inconvenience to our own people or to the Chinese, and thus a desirable change be happily and peacefully accomplished. It was thought that the exclusion act of 1882 would bring about this result; but it now appears that although at San Francisco the departures largely exceed the arrivals, yet the business of smuggling Chinese persons across the lines from the British Possessions and Mexico has so greatly increased that the number of arrivals now exceed the departures. This must be effectually stopped.

9

✦

New South, Old South

Following the Civil War, the South suffered two ordeals: racism and poverty. The problem of race touched all Southerners, from oppressed former slaves to anxious white farmers and city dwellers. Poverty, especially the bleak agricultural poverty characteristic of the South, intensified the already severe problem of race. These twin cauldrons finally boiled over in the 1890s, when more than one hundred and fifty blacks were lynched per year, and collapsing farm prices drove many thousands of families—black and white—into bankruptcy.

The Cotton States Exposition of Industry and the Arts, held in Atlanta in 1895, was designed to address the problem of poverty. Mainly the brainchild of Atlanta publishers and bankers, the exposition made much of the prospects for railroad expansion, iron and textile manufacturing, and lumber and tobacco processing. It was hoped their success would reduce the South's unhappy dependence on agriculture and tie the region to the rest of industrial America. But the explosive issue of race also loomed. To address it, the exposition organizers, almost as an afterthought, invited Booker T. Washington, head of the Tuskegee Institute, a black vocational school in Tuskegee, Alabama, to speak to the mostly white exposition gathering. The exposition produced only a slight effect on Southern industrialization—manufacturing did not become widespread there until the 1920s and industrial prosperity has barely arrived even today. Washington's speech, however, was of major importance. His moderate message, accommodating tone, and stress on business and hard work generally pleased his listeners, who marked him as a worthy spokesman for his race. His reputation soon spread to the white North and to blacks as well. Thus, almost overnight, Washington became a prominent figure whose message mattered to everyone, especially in the South.

Not everyone agreed with Washington's approach. Black intellectuals and reformers still found their inspiration in Frederick Douglass, the great abolitionist and stalwart of Radical Reconstruction and equal rights. In their eyes, Washington's acceptance of disfranchisement and segregation seemed a betrayal. They thought his refusal to condemn lynching was a surrender and viewed his influence as mostly negative.

One of the most forceful of these critics was Ida B. Wells, a Chicago woman born to Mississippi slaves. Well's *A Red Record,* excerpted below, told the gruesome story of antiblack violence in the South in persuasive, compelling terms. It thus formed an important counterpoint to Washington's conservative views.

Booker T. Washington was born a slave in Virginia in 1856, and he worked from the age of nine in West Virginia salt furnaces and coal mines. He later worked his way through Hampton Institute, a black school in Virginia, established by philanthropists following the Civil War. After graduating in 1875, he briefly attended a theological seminary in Washington, D.C. In 1881, he accepted the headship of Tuskegee Institute, which he built up from two small buildings and 40 pupils to one hundred buildings, 1,500 students, and a $1 million endowment a quarter-century later. Washington was successful at attracting funds from Northern tycoons and was at least tolerated by Southern politicians. His years of greatest fame came after the Atlanta speech and especially after President Theodore Roosevelt's invitation to dine at the White House in 1901. It was in these years that Washington developed what detractors called a "Tuskegee machine," based on the support of Tuskegee graduates and black businessmen and the willingness of Northern charities and politicians to seek his advice on donations and appointments. His well-known autobiography, *Up From Slavery,* appeared in 1901. He died, exhausted from overwork, in Tuskegee, Alabama, in 1915.

Ida B. Wells was born a slave in Holly Springs, Mississippi, in 1862. She was educated in a freedmen's school, became a teacher herself, and eventually moved to Memphis, Tennessee, where she taught school and attended Fisk University. She turned to journalism in 1891 after losing her teaching post for refusing to give up her seat in a "whites-only" railroad car. When she wrote against antiblack violence, whites retaliated by burning her newspaper office. She left the South in 1892, in time marrying Ferdinand Barnett, a prominent black Chicagoan. A tireless writer and speaker for both women's and black rights, Wells encouraged the Niagara Movement, a 1909 initiative of W.E.B. Du Bois and other militants opposed to the Tuskegee Machine. She refused to support its successor organization, the National Association for the Advancement of Colored People (NAACP), on the grounds that it was too moderate. She died in Chicago in 1931.

Questions to Consider. In reading Washington's Atlanta speech, consider especially the time in which it was delivered. Was Washington, as Wells and others accused, trading black rights for black work? Or was he attempting to use the leverage of black labor to achieve something even more precious—black safety—in the turbulent 1890s? Why might 1895 have seemed an especially good time to move whites in this way? When Washington said, "Cast down your bucket where you are," was he speaking mainly to whites or to blacks? Were there population movements in the 1890s that might have prompted him to address both groups?

Why did Ida B. Wells go to such enormous pains in *A Red Record* to establish the record, from white sources, of antiblack atrocities in the post–Civil War South? For whom does she appear to have been writing? Were there models elsewhere in American society for this kind of "exposé" journalism? In this excerpt, she also takes care to refute the arguments given by white Southerners to justify the violence. Do these passages constitute an attack on paternalism—male chauvinism—as well as on racism? If Wells wrote, as she said, "in no spirit of vindictiveness," why did whites burn her newspaper office for printing similar stories? Was vindictiveness inherent in the material, bound inevitably to provoke outrage and assault? What strategies did Wells devise to avoid this?

————————✧————————

Atlanta Exposition Address (1895)

BOOKER T. WASHINGTON

Mr. President and Gentlemen of the Board of Directors and Citizens: One-third of the population of the South is of the Negro race. No enterprise seeking the material, civil, or moral welfare of this section can disregard this element of our population and reach the highest success. I but convey to you, Mr. President and Directors, the sentiment of the masses of my race when I say that in no way have the value and manhood of the American Negro been more fittingly and generously recognized than by the managers of this magnificent Exposition at every stage of its progress. It is a recognition that will do more to cement the friendship of the two races than any occurrence since the dawn of our freedom.

Not only this, but the opportunity here afforded will awaken among us a new era of industrial progress. Ignorant and inexperienced, it is not strange that in the first years of our new life we began at the top instead of at the bottom; that a seat in Congress or the state legislature was more sought than real estate or industrial skill; that the political convention or stump speaking had more attractions than starting a dairy farm or truck garden.

From Booker T. Washington, *Up from Slavery: A Biography* (Doubleday, Page and Co., New York, 1901), 218–225.

A ship lost at sea for many days suddenly sighted a friendly vessel. From the mast of the unfortunate vessel was seen a signal, "Water, water; we die of thirst!" The answer from the friendly vessel at once came back, "Cast down your bucket where you are." A second time the signal, "Water, water; send us water!" ran up from the distressed vessel, and was answered, "Cast down your bucket where you are." And a third and fourth signal for water was answered, "Cast down your bucket where you are." The captain of the distressed vessel, at last heeding the injunction, cast down his bucket, and it came up full of fresh, sparkling water from the mouth of the Amazon River. To those of my race who depend on bettering their condition in a foreign land or who underestimate the importance of cultivating friendly relations with the Southern white man, who is their next-door neighbour, I would say: "Cast down your bucket where you are"—cast it down in making friends in every manly way of the people of all races by whom we are surrounded.

Cast it down in agriculture, mechanics, in commerce, in domestic service, and in the professions. And in this connection it is well to bear in mind that whatever other sins the South may be called to bear, when it comes to business, pure and simple, it is in the South that the Negro is given a man's chance in the commercial world, and in nothing is this Exposition more eloquent than in emphasizing this chance. Our greatest danger is that in the great leap from slavery to freedom we may overlook the fact that the masses of us are to live by the productions of our hands, and fail to keep in mind that we shall prosper in proportion as we learn to dignify and glorify common labour, and put brains and skill into the common occupations of life; shall prosper in proportion as we learn to draw the line between the superficial and the substantial, the ornamental gewgaws of life and the useful. No race can prosper till it learns that there is as much dignity in tilling a field as in writing a poem. It is at the bottom of life we must begin, and not at the top. Nor should we permit our grievances to overshadow our opportunities.

To those of the white race who look to the incoming of those of foreign birth and strange tongue and habits for the prosperity of the South, were I permitted I would repeat what I say to my own race, "Cast down your bucket where your are." Cast it down among the eight millions of Negroes whose habits you know, whose fidelity and love you have tested in days when to have proved treacherous meant the ruin of your firesides. Cast down your bucket among these people who have, without strikes and labour wars, tilled your fields, cleared your forests, builded your railroads and cities, and brought forth treasures from the bowels of the earth, and helped make possible this magnificent representation of the progress of the South. Casting down your bucket among my people, helping and encouraging them as you are doing on these grounds, and to education of head, hand, and heart, you will find that they will buy your surplus land, make blossom the waste places in your fields, and run your factories. While doing this, you can be sure in the future, as in the past, that you and your families will be surrounded by the most patient, faithful, law-abiding, and unresentful people that the world has seen. As we have proved our loyalty to you in the past, in nursing your children, watching by the sick-bed of your mothers and fathers, and often following them with tear-dimmed eyes to their graves, so in the future, in our humble way, we shall stand by you with a devotion that no foreigner can approach, ready to lay down our lives, if need be, in defense of yours, interlacing our industrial, commercial, civil, and religious life with yours in a way that shall make the interests of both races one. In all things that are purely social we can be as separate as the fingers, yet one as the hand in all things essential to mutual progress.

There is no defense or security for any of us except in the highest intelligence and development of all. If anywhere there are efforts tending to curtail the fullest growth of the Negro, let these efforts be turned into stimulating, encouraging, and making him the most useful and intelligent citizen. Effort or means so invested will pay a thousand per cent interest. These efforts will be twice blessed—"blessing him that gives and him that takes."

There is no escape through law of man or God from the inevitable:—

> "The laws of changeless justice bind
> Oppressor with oppressed;
> And close as sin and suffering joined
> We march to fate abreast."

Nearly sixteen millions of hands will aid you in pulling the load upward, or they will pull against you the load downward. We shall constitute one-third and more of the ignorance and crime of the South, or one-third its intelligence and progress; we shall contribute one-third to the business and industrial prosperity of the South, or we shall prove a veritable body of death, stagnating, depressing, retarding every effort to advance the body politic.

Gentlemen of the Exposition, as we present to you our humble effort at an exhibition of our progress, you must not expect overmuch. Starting thirty years ago with ownership here and there in a few quilts and pumpkins and chickens (gathered from miscellaneous sources), remember the path that has led from these to the inventions and production of agricultural implements, buggies, steam-engines, newspapers, books, statuary, carving, paintings, the management of drug stores and banks, has not been trodden without contact with thorns and thistles. While we take pride in what we exhibit as a result of our independent efforts, we do not for a moment forget that our part in this exhibition would fall far short of your expectations but for the constant help that has come to our educational life, not only from the Southern states, but especially from Northern philanthropists, who have made their gifts a constant stream of blessing and encouragement.

The wisest among my race understand that the agitation of questions of social equality is the extremest folly, and that progress in the enjoyment of all the privileges that will come to us must be the result of severe and constant struggle rather than of artificial forcing. No race that has anything to contribute to the markets of the world is long in any degree ostracized. It is important and right that all privileges of the law be ours, but it is vastly more important that we be prepared for the exercise of these privileges. The opportunity to earn a dollar in a factory just now is worth infinitely more than the opportunity to spend a dollar in an opera-house.

In conclusion, may I repeat that nothing in thirty years has given us more hope and encouragement, and drawn us so near to you of the white race, as this opportunity offered by the Exposition; and here bending, as it were, over the altar that represents the results of the struggles of your race and mine, both starting practically empty-handed three decades ago, I pledge that in your effort to work out the great and intricate problem which God has laid at the doors of the South, you shall have at all times the patient, sympathetic help of my race; only let this be constantly in mind, that, while from representations in these buildings of the product of field, of forest, of mine, of factory, letters, and art, much good will come, yet far above and beyond material benefits will be that higher good, that, let us pray God, will come, in a blotting out of sectional differences and racial animosities and suspicions, in a determination to administer absolute justice, in a willing obedience among all classes to the mandates of law. This, coupled with our material prosperity, will bring into our beloved South a new heaven and a new earth.

---------◇---------

A Red Record (1895)

IDA B. WELLS

Not all nor nearly all of the murders done by white men, during the past thirty years in the South, have come to light, but the statistics as gathered and preserved by white men, and which have not been questioned, show that during these years more than ten thousand Negroes have been killed in cold blood, without the formality of judicial trial and legal execution. And yet, as evidence of the absolute impunity with which the white man dares to kill a Negro, the same record shows that during all these years, and for all these murders only three white men have been tried, convicted, and executed. As no white man has been lynched for the murder of colored

Ida B. Wells, *A Red Record. Tabulated Statistics and Alleged Causes of Lynchings in the United States, 1892–1893–1894* (Chicago, n.d.), pp.9–15, 20, 43, 45–48.

people, these three executions are the only instances of the death penalty being visited upon white men for murdering Negroes.

Naturally enough the commission of these crimes began to tell upon the public conscience, and the Southern white man, as a tribute to the nineteenth century civilization, was in a manner compelled to give excuses for his barbarism.

The first excuse given to the civilized world for the murder of unoffending Negroes was the necessity of the white man to repress and stamp out alleged "race riots." For years immediately succeeding the war there was an appalling slaughter of colored people, and the wires usually conveyed to northern people and the world the intelligence, first, that an insurrection was being planned by Negroes, which, a few hours later, would prove to have been vigorously resisted by white men, and controlled with a resulting loss of several killed and wounded. It was always a remarkable feature in these insurrections and riots that only Negroes were killed during the rioting, and that all the white men escaped unharmed. . . .

Then came the second excuse, which had its birth during the turbulent times of reconstruction. By an amendment to the Constitution the Negro was given the right of franchise, and, theoretically at least, his ballot became his invaluable emblem of citizenship. In a government "of the people, for the people, and by the people," the Negro's vote became an important factor in all matters of state and national politics. But this did not last long. The southern white man would not consider that the Negro had any right which a white man was bound to respect, and the idea of a republican form of government in the southern states grew into general contempt.

The white man's victory soon became complete by fraud, violence, intimidation and murder. The franchise vouchsafed to the Negro grew to be a "barren ideality," and regardless of numbers, the colored people found themselves voiceless in the councils of those whose duty it was to rule. With no longer the fear of "Negro Domination" before their eyes, the white man's second excuse became valueless. With the Southern governments all subverted and the Negro actually eliminated from all participation in state and national elections, there could be no longer an excuse for killing Negroes to prevent "Negro Domination."

Brutality still continued; Negroes were whipped, scourged, exiled, shot and hung whenever and wherever it pleased the white man so to treat them, and as the civilized world with increasing persistency held the white people of the South to account for its outlawry, the murderers invented the third excuse—that Negroes had to be killed to avenge their assaults upon women. There could be framed no possible excuse more harmful to the Negro and more unanswerable if true in its sufficiency for the white man.

Humanity abhors the assailant of womanhood, and this charge upon the Negro at once placed him beyond the pale of human sympathy. With such unanimity, earnestness, and apparent candor was this charge made and reiterated that the world has accepted the story that the Negro is a monster which the Southern white man has painted him. . . .

A word as to the charge itself. In considering the third reason assigned by the Southern white people for the butchery of blacks, the question must be asked, what the white man means when he charges the black man with rape. Does he mean the crime which the statutes of the civilized states describe as such? Not by any means. With the Southern white man, any mésalliance existing between a white woman and a black man is a sufficient foundation for the charge of rape. The Southern white man says that it is impossible for a voluntary alliance to exist between a white woman and a colored man, and therefore, the fact of an alliance is a proof of force. In numerous instances where colored men have been lynched on the charge of rape, it was positively known at the time of lynching, and indisputably proven after the victim's death, that the relationship sustained between the man and woman was voluntary and clandestine, and that in no court of law could even the charge of assault have been successfully maintained.

It was for the assertion of this fact, in the defense of her own race, that the writer hereof became an exile; her property destroyed and her return to her home forbidden under penalty of death. . . .

But threats cannot suppress the truth, and while the Negro suffers the soul deformity, resultant from two and a half centuries of slavery, he is no more guilty of this vilest of all vile charges than the white man who would blacken his name.

During all the years of slavery, no such charge was ever made, not even during the dark days of the rebellion, when the white man, following the fortunes of war went to do battle for the maintenance of slavery. While the master was away fighting to forge the fetters upon the slave, he left his wife and children with no protectors save the Negroes themselves. And yet during those years of trust and peril, no Negro proved recreant to his trust and no white man returned to a home that had been dispoiled.

Likewise during the period of alleged "insurrection," and alarming "race riots," it never occurred to the white man, that his wife and children were in danger of assault. Nor in the Reconstruction era, when the hue and cry was against "Negro Domination," was there ever a thought that the domination would ever contaminate a fireside or strike to death the virtue of womanhood. . . .

In his remarkable apology for lynching, Bishop Haygood, of Georgia, says: "No race, not the most savage, tolerates the rape of woman, but it may be said without reflection upon any other people that the Southern people are now and always have been most sensitive concerning the honor of their women—their mothers, wives, sisters and daughters." It is not the purpose of this defense to say one word against the white women of the South. Such need not be said, but it is their misfortune that the chivalrous white men of that section, in order to escape the deserved execration of the civilized world, should shield themselves by their cowardly and infamously false excuse, and call into question that very honor about which their distinguished priestly apologist claims they are most sensitive. To justify their own barbarism they assume a chivalry which they do not possess. . . .

When emancipation came to the Negroes, there arose in the northern part of the United States an almost divine sentiment among the noblest, purest and best white women of the North, who felt called to a mission to educate and Christianize the millions of southern ex-slaves. From every nook and corner of the North, brave young white women answered that call and left their cultured homes, their happy associations and their lives of ease, and with heroic determination went to the South to carry light and truth to the benighted blacks. It was a heroism no less than that which calls for volunteers for India, Africa, and the Isles of the sea. To educate their unfortunate charges; to teach them the Christian virtues and to inspire in them the moral sentiments manifest in their own lives, these young women braved dangers whose record reads more like fiction than fact. They became social outlaws in the South. The peculiar sensitiveness of the southern white men for women, never shed its protecting influence about them. No friendly word from their own race cheered them in their work; no hospitable doors gave them the companionship like that from which they had come. No chivalrous white man doffed his hat in honor or respect. They were "Nigger teachers" —unpardonable offenders in the social ethics of the South, and were insulted, persecuted and ostracized, not by Negroes, but by the white manhood which boasts of its chivalry toward women.

And yet these northern women worked on, year after year, unselfishly, with a heroism which amounted almost to martyrdom. Threading their way through dense forests, working in schoolhouse, in the cabin and in the church, thrown at all times and in all places among the unfortunate and lowly Negroes, whom they had come to find and to serve, these northern women, thousands and thousands of them, have spent more than a quarter of a century in giving to the colored people their splendid lessons for home and heart and soul. Without protection, save that which innocence gives to every good woman, they went about their work, fearing no assault and suffering none. . . . Before the world adjudges the Negro a moral monster, a vicious assailant of womanhood and a menace to the sacred precints of home, the colored people ask the consideration of the silent record of gratitude, respect, protection, and devotion of the millions of the race in the South, to the thousands of northern white women who have served as teachers and missionaries since the war. . . .

These pages are written in no spirit of vindictiveness, for all who give the subject consideration must concede that far too serious is the condition of that civilized government in which the spirit of unrestrained outlawry constantly increases in violence, and casts its blight over a continually growing area of territory. We plead not for the colored people alone, but for all victims of the terrible injustice which puts men and women to death without form of law. During the year 1894, there were 132 persons executed in the United States by due form of law, while in the same year, 197 persons were put to death by mobs who gave the victims no opportunity to make a lawful defense. No comment need be made upon a condition of public sentiment responsible for such alarming results.

10

❖

THE SEGREGATED SOUTH

After the Dred Scott decision in 1857, the tide of federal decision making turned, becoming more favorable for blacks, at least through 1870 when the ratification of the Fifteenth Amendment to the Constitution guaranteed them the right to vote. But with President Rutherford B. Hayes's withdrawal of federal troops from the South in 1877, the current gradually shifted once more toward disfranchisement, exploitation, and increasingly, segregation. In the *Plessy* v. *Ferguson* case in 1896, the Supreme Court upheld a Louisiana law requiring separate railroad cars for blacks and whites.

Homer Plessy was one-eighth black; by sitting in the white section of a railway car en route from New Orleans to Covington, Louisiana, he violated a Louisiana "Jim Crow" (racial separation) law. He was arrested for refusing to move into a black section, and John H. Ferguson, the Louisiana judge who tried the case, found him guilty. Believing that the Jim Crow law violated the Fourteenth Amendment, Plessy appealed the decision. But the Supreme Court upheld the Louisiana law, stating that the Fourteenth Amendment, which forbids states to abridge the civil rights and liberties of citizens, requires only that separate facilities be equal.

This "separate but equal" doctrine allowed segregation not only of private commercial facilities like hotels, but also of public schools and even towns and cities. In practice it permitted the creation of facilities that were surely separate but hardly equal. The decision stood until 1954, when it was overturned by the Supreme Court in the landmark decision in *Brown* v. *The Board of Education of Topeka*.

Henry Billings Brown, the author of the Plessy decision, was born to wealthy parents in Massachusetts in 1836. He attended Yale College and set up a law practice in Detroit. Appointed to the Supreme Court by President Benjamin Harrison in 1890, Brown retired from the Court in 1906 and lived in New York until his death in 1913. His chief opinion besides Plessy was a concurrence in the decision in *Dawson* v. *Bidwell* (1901) that inhabitants of annexed territories, such as Puerto Rico, had no constitutional rights.

Questions to Consider. Several aspects of the Plessy opinion merit special attention. Note, for example, the dual themes of racism and growth. Did Henry Billings Brown believe his decision would segregate facilities in the South? Was it not, in fact, Southern industrial progress—new railroads, streetcars, hotels, and schools—and its effect on race relations that had brought the issue before the Court in the first place? Brown stated that although all citizens have a kind of "property" interest in their reputations because these can affect their future, segregation will not harm blacks' reputations unless they allow it to hurt their self-esteem. Whites in a minority position, said Brown, would not suffer diminished self-esteem; neither should blacks. What evidence is cited for this opinion? Note Brown's narrow view of the scope of the law. Law, he argued, can neither equalize nor unify society. In its Plessy decision, therefore, the Supreme Court declared actual racial experience—slavery, terrorism, and exploitation—to be irrelevant to the legal consideration of race relations. Do you agree with this reasoning?

Plessy v. Ferguson (1896)

HENRY BILLINGS BROWN

This case turns upon the constitutionality of an act of the general assembly of the state of Louisiana, passed in 1890, providing for separate railway carriages for the white and colored races. . . .

The constitutionality of this act is attacked upon the ground that it conflicts both with the 13th Amendment of the Constitution, abolishing slavery, and the 14th Amendment, which prohibits certain restrictive legislation on the part of the states.

That it does not conflict with the 13th Amendment, which abolished slavery and involuntary servitude, except as a punishment for crime, is too clear for argument. . . .

The object of the [14th] amendment was undoubtedly to enforce the absolute equality of the two races before the law, but in the nature of things it could not have been intended to abolish distinctions based upon color, or to enforce social, as distinguished from political, equality, or a commingling of the two races upon terms unsatisfactory to either. Laws permitting, and even requiring their separation in places where they are liable to be brought into contact do not necessarily imply the inferiority of either race to the other, and have been generally, if not universally, recognized as

Plessy v. Ferguson, 163 U.S. 537 (1896).

within the competency of the state legislatures in the exercise of their police power. The most common instance of this is connected with the establishment of separate schools for white and colored children, which have been held to be a valid exercise of the legislative power even by courts of states where the political rights of the colored race have been longest and most earnestly enforced. . . .

It is claimed by the plaintiff in error that, in any mixed community, the reputation of belonging to the dominant race, in this instance the white race, is property, in the same sense that a right of action, or of inheritance, is property. Conceding this to be so, for the purposes of this case, we are unable to see how this statute deprives him of, or in any way affects his right to, such property. If he be a white man and assigned to a colored coach, he may have his action for damages against the company for being deprived of his so-called property. Upon the other hand, if he be a colored man and be so assigned, he has been deprived of no property, since he is not lawfully entitled to the reputation of being a white man. . . .

So far, then, as a conflict with the 14th Amendment is concerned, the case reduces itself to the question whether the statute of Louisiana is a reasonable regulation, and with respect to this there must necessarily be a large discretion on the part of the legislature. In determining the question of reasonableness it is at liberty to act with reference to the established usages, customs, and traditions of the people, and with a view to the promotion of their comfort, and the preservation of the public peace and good order. Gauged by this standard, we cannot say that a law which authorizes or even requires the separation of the two races in public convey-ances is unreasonable or more obnoxious to the 14th Amendment than the acts of Congress requiring separate schools for colored children in the District of Columbia, the constitutionality of which does not seem to have been questioned, or the corresponding acts of state legislatures.

We consider the underlying fallacy of the plaintiff's argument to consist in the assumption that the enforced separation of the two races stamps the colored race with a badge of inferiority. If this be so, it is not by reason of anything found in the act, but solely because the colored race chooses to put that construction upon it. The argument necessarily assumes that if, as has been more than once the case, and is not unlikely to be so again, the colored race should become the dominant power in the state legislature, and should enact a law in precisely similar terms, it would thereby relegate the white race to an inferior position. We imagine that the white race, at least, would not acquiesce in this assumption. The argument also assumes that social prejudice may be overcome by legislation, and that equal rights cannot be secured to the Negro except by an enforced commingling of the two races. We cannot accept this proposition. If the two races are to meet on terms of social equality, it must be the result of natural affinities, a mutual appreciation of each other's merits and a voluntary consent of individuals. . . .

Legislation is powerless to eradicate racial instincts or to abolish distinctions based upon physical differences, and the attempt to do so can only result in accentuating the difficulties of the present situation. If the civil and political right of both races be equal, one cannot be inferior to the other civilly or politically. If one race be inferior to the other socially, the Constitution of the United States cannot put them upon the same plane.

11

✧

Bearing Gifts

Nativist bigotry was widespread in turn-of-the-century America, attaching itself with special force to immigrants from Eastern or Catholic Europe and perhaps most venomously to Jews. Anti-Semitism was a powerful current from czarist Russia to the democratic United States in the late nineteenth century, intensifying in the United States with the beginning of large-scale Jewish immigration in the 1880s. Thereafter, anti-Semitism emerged in all regions, classes, and parties. Resort hotels and exclusive men's clubs barred Jewish businessmen, and upper-class colleges established quota systems. Small-town Midwesterners and Southern farmers criticized not just Wall Street bankers but international Jewish bankers. Radical writers like Jack London cast a racist net that snared Jews as well as blacks. Even urban Catholic immigrants, who themselves experienced religious and nativist discrimination, harassed the "Christ-killers" and "Shylocks" who shared their ethnic slums.

Spokespersons for the various immigrant groups labored hard to counter nativist bigotry. They challenged stereotypes where they could, chiefly by publicizing their group's successes, including successful examples of Americanization. They also tried to portray the group's distinctive characteristics in positive terms, stressing how the country would benefit from Italian musical genius, for example, or Polish religious fervor. The Jewish community had no finer advocate than Mary Antin, a young writer and political activist whose speech before a New York convention of the General Federation of Women's Clubs is excerpted below.

Mary Antin was born in Russia in 1881 and emigrated with her parents to the United States in 1894. When she was still a teenager, Antin wrote her first book—in Yiddish—about the Jewish immigrant experience. After studying at Teachers College and Barnard College in New York City, she published *The Promised Land* (1912), perhaps our most beautiful version of the immigrant saga. An ardent socialist and union supporter, Antin continued to write and lecture on the subject of immigration; she was a notable opponent of congressional efforts to pass restrictive immigration laws. She died in Suffern, New York, on May 15, 1949.

Questions to Consider. Why didn't Mary Antin argue for the value of Jewish immigration by offering case studies, as immigrant defenders sometimes did, of successful individual Jews? What point was she trying to make by implicitly reinforcing a stereotype about Jews—that as a group they produced a disproportionate number of scholars, lawyers, and debaters? How did she attempt to connect the discussion about Jews and the law with her discussion later about the organization of the clothing industry? Was she right to argue that the passion for justice was fundamental to being a Jew, so that Jews were, in a sense, heirs to the "Spirit of '76" and therefore naturally American? What were the "false gods" Antin referred to in her final sentence?

———————✧———————

Russian Jews (1916)

MARY ANTIN

On the whole the Russian immigrant in this country is the Jewish immigrant, since we are the most numerous group out of Russia. But to speak for the Jews—the most misunderstood people in the whole of history—ten minutes, in which to clear away 2,000 years of misunderstanding! Your President has probably in this instance, as in other instances, been guided by some inspiration, the source of which none of us may know. I was called by name long before your President notified me that she would call me to this assembly. I was called by name to say what does the Jew bring to America—by a lady from Philadelphia. Miss Repplier, not long ago, in an article in her inimitable fashion, called things by their name, and sometimes miscalled them, spoke of "the Jew in America who has received from us so much and has given us so little." This comment was called down by something that I had said about certain things in American life that did not come up to the American standard. "The Jew who has given so little." Tonight I am the Jew—you are the Americans. Let us look over these things.

What do we bring you besides our poverty and our rags? Men, women, and children—the stuff that nations are built of. What sort of men and women? I shall not seek to tire you with a list of shining names of Jewish notables. If you want to know who's who among the Jews, I refer you to your biographical dictionary. You are as familiar as I am with the name of Jews who shine in the professions, who have done notable service to the state, in politics, in diplomacy, and where you will. . . .

You know as well as I what numbers of Jewish youth are always taking high ranks, high honors in the schools, colleges and universities. You know

From General Federation of Women's Clubs, *Thirteenth Biennial Convention* (New York, 1916).

as well as I do in what numbers our people crowd your lecture halls and your civic centers, in all those places where the spiritual wine of life may be added to our daily bread. These are things that you know. I don't want you to be thinking of any list of Jewish notables.

A very characteristic thing of Jewish life is the democracy of virtue that you find in every Jewish community. We Jews have never depended for our salvation on the supreme constellations of any chosen ones. . . . Our shining ones were to us always examples by means of which the whole community was to be disciplined to what was Jewish virtue.

Take a group of Jews anywhere, and you will have the essence of their Jewishness, though there be not present one single shining luminary. The average Jew presents the average of whatsoever there is of Jewish virtue, talent or capacity.

What is this peculiar Jewish genius? If I must sum it up in a word, I will say that the Jewish genius is a love for living out the things that they believe. What do we believe? We Jews believe that the world is a world of law. Law is another name for our God, and the quest after the law, the formulation of it, has always permeated our schools, and the incorporation of the laws of life, as our scholars noted it down, has been the chief business of the Jewish masses. No wonder that when we come to America, a nation founded as was our ancient nation, a nation founded on law and principle, on an ideal—no wonder that we so quickly find ourselves at home, that presently we fall into the regulation habit of speaking of America as our own country, until Miss Repplier reproves us, and then we do it no more. I used formerly when speaking of American sins, tribulations, etc., I used to speak of them as "ours"; no more—your sins. I have been corrected.

Why then, now that we have come here, to this nation builded on the same principle as was our nation, no wonder that we so quickly seize on the fundamentals. We make no virtue of the fact—it is the Jewishness in us—that has been our peculiar characteristics, our habit. We need no one from outside of our ranks to remind us of the goodly things we have found and taken from your hands. We have been as eloquent as any that has spoken in appreciation of what we have found here, of liberty, justice, and a square deal. We give thanks. We have rendered thanks, we Jews, some of you are witnesses. We know the value of the gifts that we have found here.

Who shall know the flavor of bread if not they that have gone hungry, and we, who have been for centuries without the bread of justice, we know the full flavor of American justice, liberty, and equality.

To formulate and again formulate, and criticise the law,—what do our Rabbis in the Ghetto besides the study of law? To them used to come our lawyers, to our Rabbis, not to find the way how to get around the law, but to be sure that we were walking straight in the path indicated by the law. So today in America we are busy in the same fashion.

The Jewish virtues, such as they are, are widespread throughout the

Jewish masses. Here in New York City is congregated the largest Jewish community in the whole world, and what is true of the Jews of New York, is true of the Jews of America, and the Jews of the world. If I speak of the characteristics of Jewish life on the East side, one of the great characteristics is its restlessness in physical form, due to the oppression of city life, and the greater restlessness, due to the unquenchable, turbulent quest for the truth, and more truth. You know that the East side of New York is a very spawning ground for debate, and debating clubs. There are more boys and girls in debating clubs than in boys' basket ball teams, or baseball teams. I believe in boys playing baseball, but I also believe in that peculiar enthusiasm of our Jewish people for studying the American law, just as they used to study their own law, to see whether any of the American principles find incorporation in American institutions and habits. We are the critics. We are never satisfied with things as they are. Go out and hear the boys and girls. They like to go to school and learn the names of liberty, and equality and justice, and after school they gather in their debating circles and discuss what might be the meaning of these names, and what is their application to life. That is the reason there is so much stirring, rebellion, and protest that comes out of the East side.

In the great labor movement, it is the effort of the people to arrive at a program of economic justice that shall parallel the political justice. Consider for a moment the present condition of the garment-making trade. That is a Jewish trade. Ages ago when the lords of the nations, among whom we lived, were preventing us from engaging in other occupations, they thrust into the hands of our people the needle, and the needle was our tool, why through the needle we have still thought to give expression to the Jewish genius in our life.

This immense clothing industry—a Jewish industry primarily—is today in a better condition as regards unionization, is further on the road to economic justice than any other great industry that you could name. Mind you, the sweatshop we found here when we came here. We took it just as it was, but the barring of the sweatshop and the organization of the clothing industry in such fashion that it is further in advance, more nearly on a basis that affords just treatment to all concerned—that has been the contribution of our tailor men and tailor women. We have done this thing. . . . The Protocol[1] is a piece of machinery for bringing about justice in this great industry. We have invented that thing, we Jews. We are putting it in operation, we are fighting for its perpetuation. Whatsoever good comes from it, we have done it. . . .

Consider us, if you will, in the most barbarous sense, but I point to this as our great contribution, we are always protesting, and if you want to

---

1. **The Protocol:** A labor-management agreement recognizing union rights and providing for improved working conditions in the garment industry.—*Eds.*

know the value of that contribution, I remind you that the formulae of the rights of men, which was a criticism of things as they used to be, and a formularizing of things as they ought to be, was at least as efficient as all the armies of the continent put together in the revolutionary war. The Spirit of '76 is the spirit of criticism. We Jews in America are busy at our ancient business of pulling down false gods.

12

✧

A MULTICULTURAL VISION

Fully half of white Americans with native grandparents have one or more pioneers among their ancestors. Whatever valuable race traits distinguish the American people from the parent European stocks are due to the efflorescence of this breed. . . . Now we confront the melancholy spectacle of this pioneer breed being swamped and submerged by an overwhelming tide of latecomers from the old-world hive. . . . The new blood now being injected into the veins of our people is "sub-common." Observe immigrants . . . in their Sunday best. You are struck by the fact that from ten to twenty per cent are . . . big-faced persons of low mentality. . . . Clearly they belong in skins, in wattled huts at the close of the Great Ice Age.

So Edward A. Ross argued in 1914 in *The Old World in the New,* an influential treatise based on the notion of Anglo-Saxon racial superiority. Like so many Americans during the era of World War I, Ross was convinced that the mingling of immigrant blood, that of southeastern Europeans in particular, with that of Anglo-Saxons would not only arrest the development of the United States, but would extinguish the Anglo-Saxon race. Thus he argued for restricted immigration in order to preserve America's quality of life. To fail to do so was to invite disaster.

More thoughtful persons were not threatened by the so-called new immigrants who came to American shores from Poland, Russia, Greece, Italy, and other nations. Many understood the immigration of diverse peoples as an opportunity to create not a "melting-pot" society, but one that was pluralistic and "cosmopolitan," according to Randolph A. Bourne. In contrast to Ross, he argued that Anglo-Saxon or "English-American conservatism" was America's "chief obstacle to social advance."

Writing two years after Ross wrote on restriction, Bourne made a case for what today we call "multiculturalism." Emphatically rejecting any notion that democratic tendencies reside in any particular race, he argued in *Trans-National America,* a part of which is reproduced below, that the capacity for excellence resides in all people. The United States, so attractive to immigrants, therefore had a unique opportunity to build a society that would reflect "a new ideal": a dynamic, tolerant community in which distinctive ethnic groups would make unique contributions to the whole. Although Ross and his supporters were to have their way—the Immigration Act of 1924 restricted European immigration and favored persons from northern and western European countries—it is Bourne's observations that ring true for most modern readers. It was he who reminded Americans that "we are all foreign-born or the descendants of foreign-born."

As a result of a fall in infancy, Bourne was hunchbacked and stunted and his head was deformed; persons he encountered were often unable to overlook his physical features. In writing of the "inferior" southeastern European, Ross had observed that "in every face there was something wrong. . . . There were so many sugarloaf heads, moon-faces, slit mouths, lantern-jaws, and goose-bill noses that one might imagine a malicious jinn had amused himself by casting human beings in a set of skew-molds discarded by the Creator." Cruel and unthinking statements like these doubtless went straight to Bourne's heart, and one might speculate that his sympathy for minorities may very well have derived from the reactions of others to his appearance.

Bourne was a native of New Jersey and attended Columbia University. As a writer for *The Masses* and *Seven Arts,* he attacked America's entry into World War I, but when the latter periodical was suspended in 1917, Bourne had trouble finding outlets for his writing and sank into dire poverty. Having made a name for himself as a brilliant social and literary critic with the publication of several books, Bourne died in 1918 at age thirty-two in the influenza pandemic that claimed the lives of millions.

Questions to Consider.   To what extent was Bourne skeptical of American institutions? How do Bourne's ideas compare with the popular notion of America as a "melting pot"? According to Bourne, of what value was cultural pluralism? Is his thinking persuasive?

Transnational America (1916)

RANDOLPH BOURNE

No reverberatory effect of the great war has caused American public opinion more solicitude than the failure of the "melting-pot." The discovery of diverse nationalistic feelings among our great alien population has come to most people as an intense shock. It has brought out the unpleasant

From *Atlantic Monthly,* July 1916.

European immigrants at Ellis Island. Women often wore head scarves aboard ship because of the damp cold and because they had worn them in public in Europe to avoid appearing immodest. (Library of Congress)

inconsistencies of our traditional beliefs. We have had to watch hard-hearted old Brahmins virtuously indignant at the spectacle of the immigrant refusing to be melted, while they jeer at patriots like Mary Antin who write about "our forefathers." We have had to listen to publicists who express themselves as stunned by the evidence of vigorous nationalistic and cultural movements in this country among Germans, Scandinavians, Bohemians, and Poles, while in the same breath they insist that the alien shall be forcibly assimilated to that Anglo-Saxon tradition which they unquestioningly label "American."

As the unpleasant truth has come upon us that assimilation in this country was proceeding on lines very different from those we had marked out for it, we found ourselves inclined to blame those who were thwarting our prophecies. The truth became culpable. We blamed the war, we blamed the Germans. And then we discovered with a moral shock that these movements had been making great headway before the war even began. We found that the tendency, reprehensible and paradoxical as it might be, has been for the national clusters of immigrants, as they became more and more firmly established and more and more prosperous, to cultivate more and more assiduously the literatures and cultural traditions of their home-lands. Assimilation, in other words, instead of washing out the memories of Europe, made them more and more intensely real. Just as these clusters became more and more objectively American, did they become more and more German or Scandinavian or Bohemian or Polish.

To face the fact that our aliens are already strong enough to take a share in the direction of their own destiny, and that the strong cultural movements represented by the foreign press, schools, and colonies are a challenge to our facile attempts, is not, however, to admit the failure of Americanization. It is not to fear the failure of democracy. It is rather to urge us to an investigation of what Americanism may rightly mean. It is to ask ourselves whether our ideal has been broad or narrow—whether perhaps the time has not come to assert a higher ideal than the "melting-pot." Surely we cannot be certain of our spiritual democracy when, claiming to melt the nations within us to a comprehension of our free and democratic institutions, we fly into panic at the first sign of their own will and tendency. We act as if we wanted Americanization to take place only on our own terms, and not by the consent of the governed. All our elaborate machinery of settlement and school and union, of social and political naturalization, however, will move with friction just in so far ås it neglects to take into account this strong and virile insistence that America shall be what the immigrant will have a hand in making it, and not what a ruling class, descendant of those British stocks which were the first permanent immigrants, decide that America shall be made. This is the condition which confronts us, and which demands a clear and general readjustment of our attitude and our ideal. . . .

Mary Antin is right when she looks upon our foreign-born as the people who missed the Mayflower and came over on the first boat they could find. But she forgets that when they did come it was not upon other Mayflowers, but upon a "Maiblume," a "Fleur de Mai," a "Fior di Maggio," a "Majblomst." These people were not mere arrivals from the same family, to be welcomed as understood and long-loved, but strangers to the neighborhood, with whom a long process of settling down had to take place. For they brought with them their national and racial characters, and each new national quota had to wear slowly away the contempt with which its mere alienness got itself greeted. Each had to make its way slowly from the lowest strata of unskilled labor up to a level where it satisfied the accredited norms of social success.

We are all foreign-born or the descendants of foreign-born, and if distinctions are to be made between us they should rightly be on some other ground than indigenousness. The early colonists came over with motives no less colonial than the later. They did not come to be assimilated in an American melting-pot. They did not come to adopt the culture of the American Indian. They had not the smallest intention of "giving themselves without reservation" to the new country. They came to get freedom to live as they wanted to. They came to escape from the stifling air and chaos of the old world; they came to make their fortune in a new land. They invented no new social framework. Rather they brought over bodily the old ways to which they had been accustomed. Tightly concentrated on a hostile frontier, they were conservative beyond belief. Their pioneer daring was reserved for the objective conquest of material resources. In their folkways, in their social and political institutions, they were, like every colonial people, slavishly imitative of the mother-country. So that, in spite of the "Revolution," our whole legal and political system remained more English than the English, petrified and unchanging, while in England law developed to meet the needs of the changing times.

It is just this English-American conservatism that has been our chief obstacle to social advance. We have needed the new peoples—the order of the German and Scandinavian, the turbulence of the Slav and Hun—to save us from our own stagnation. I do not mean that the illiterate Slav is now the equal of the New Englander of pure descent. He is raw material to be educated, not into a New Englander, but into a socialized American along such lines as those thirty nationalities are being educated in the amazing schools of Gary. I do not believe that this process is to be one of decades of evolution. The spectacle of Japan's sudden jump from mediaevalism to post-modernism should have destroyed that superstition. We are not dealing with individuals who are to "evolve." We are dealing with their children, who, with that education we are about to have, will start level with all of us. Let us cease to think of ideals like democracy as magical qualities inherent in certain peoples. Let us speak, not of inferior races, but of inferior civilizations. We are all to educate and to be educated. These peoples in America are in a common enterprise. It is not what we are now that concerns us, but what this plastic next generation may become in the light of a new cosmopolitan ideal. . . .

If freedom means the right to do pretty much as one pleases, so long as one does not interfere with others, the immigrant has found freedom, and the ruling element has been singularly liberal in its treatment of the invading hordes. But if freedom means a democratic cooperation in determining the ideals and purposes and industrial and social institutions of a country, then the immigrant has not been free, and the Anglo-Saxon element is guilty of just what every dominant race is guilty of in every European country: the imposition of its own culture upon the minority peoples. The fact that this imposition has been so mild and, indeed, semiconscious does not alter its quality. And the war has brought out just the degree to which that purpose of "Americanizing," that is, "Anglo-Saxonizing," the immigrant has failed. . . .

Let the Anglo-Saxon ask himself where he would have been if these races had not come? Let those who feel the inferiority of the non-Anglo-Saxon immigrant contemplate that region of the States which has remained the most distinctively "American," the South. Let him ask himself whether he would really like to see the foreign hordes Americanized into such an Americanization. Let him ask himself how superior this native civilization is to the great "alien" states of Wisconsin and Minnesota, where Scandinavians, Poles, and Germans have self-consciously labored to preserve their traditional culture, while being outwardly and satisfactorily American. Let him ask himself how much more wisdom, intelligence, industry and social leadership has come out of these alien states than out of all the truly American ones. The South, in fact, while this vast Northern development has gone on, still remains an English colony, stagnant and complacent, having progressed culturally scarcely beyond the early Victorian era. It is culturally sterile because it has had no advantage of cross-fertilization like the Northern states. What has happened in states such as Wisconsin and Minnesota is that strong foreign cultures have struck root in a new and fertile soil. America has meant liberation, and German and Scandinavian political ideas and social energies have expanded to a new potency.

A truer cultural sense would have told us that it is not the self-conscious cultural nuclei that sap at our American life, but these fringes. It is not the Jew who sticks proudly to the faith of his fathers and boasts of that venerable culture of his who is dangerous to America, but the Jew who has lost the Jewish fire and become a mere elementary, grasping animal. It is not the Bohemian who supports the Bohemian schools in Chicago whose influence is sinister, but the Bohemian who has made money and has got into ward politics. Just so surely as we tend to disintegrate these nuclei of nationalistic culture do we tend to create hordes of men and women without a spiritual country, cultural outlaws, without taste, without standards but those of the mob.

Already we have far too much of this insipidity—masses of people who are cultural half-breeds, neither assimilated Anglo-Saxons nor nationals of another culture. Each national colony in this country seems to retain in its foreign press, its vernacular literature, its schools, its intellectual and patriotic leaders, a central cultural nucleus. From this nucleus the colony extends out by imperceptible gradations to a fringe where national characteristics are all but lost. Our cities are filled with these half-breeds who retain their foreign names but have lost the foreign savor. This does not mean that they have actually been changed into New Englanders or Middle Westerners. It does not mean that they have been really Americanized. It means that, letting slip from them whatever native culture they had, they have substituted for it only the most rudimentary American—the American culture of the cheap newspaper, the "movies," the popular song, the ubiquitous automobile. The unthinking who survey this class call them assimilated, Americanized. The great American public school has done its work. With these people our institutions are safe. We may thrill with dread at the aggressive hyphenate, but this tame flabbiness is accepted as Americanization. The same moulders of opinion whose ideal is to melt the different races into Anglo-Saxon gold hail this poor product as the satisfying result of their alchemy. . . .

America is a unique sociological fabric, and it bespeaks poverty of imagination not to be thrilled at the incalculable potentialities of so novel a union of men. To seek no other goal than the weary old nationalism—belligerent, exclusive, inbreeding, the poison of which we are witnessing now in Europe—is to make patriotism a hollow sham, and to declare that, in spite of our boastings, America must ever be a follower and not a leader of nations. . . .

Only America, by reason of the unique liberty of opportunity and traditional isolation for which she seems to stand, can lead in this cosmopolitan enterprise. Only the American—and in this category I include the migratory alien who has lived with us and caught the pioneer spirit and a sense of new social vistas—has the chance to become that citizen of the world. America is coming to be, not a nationality but a trans-nationality, a weaving back and forth, with the other lands, of many threads of all sizes and colors. Any movement which attempts to thwart this weaving, or to dye the fabric any one color, or disentangle the threads of the strands, is false to this cosmopolitan vision. I do not mean that we shall necessarily glut ourselves with the raw product of humanity. It would be folly to absorb the nations faster than we could weave them. We have no duty either to admit or reject. It is purely a question of expediency. What concerns us is the fact that the strands are here. We must have a policy and an ideal for an actual situation. Our question is, What shall we do with our America? How are we likely to get the more creative America—by confining our imaginations to the ideal of the melting-pot, or broadening them to some such cosmopolitan conception as I have been vaguely sketching? . . .

The failure of the melting-pot, far from closing the great American democratic experiment, means that it has only just begun. Whatever American nationalism turns out to be, we see already that it will have a color richer and more exciting than our ideal has hitherto encompassed. In a world which has dreamed of internationalism, we find that we have all unawares been building up the first international nation. The voices which have cried for a tight and jealous nationalism of the European pattern are failing. From the ideal, however valiantly and disinterestedly it has been set for us, time and tendency have moved us further and further away. What we have achieved has been rather a cosmopolitan federation of national colonies, of foreign cultures, from whom the sting of devastating competition has been removed. America is already the world-federation in miniature, the continent where for the first time in history has been achieved that miracle of hope, the peaceful living side by side, with character substantially preserved, of the most heterogenous peoples under the sun. Nowhere else has such contiguity been anything but the breeder of misery. Here, notwithstanding our tragic failures of adjustment, the outlines are already too clear not to give us a new vision and a new orientation of the American mind in the world.

It is for the American of the younger generation to accept this cosmopolitanism, and carry it along with self-conscious and fruitful purpose. In his colleges, he is already getting, with the study of modern history and politics, the modern literatures, economic geography, the privilege of a cosmopolitan outlook such as the people of no other nation of today in Europe can possibly secure. If he is still a colonial, he is no longer the colonial of one partial culture, but of many. He is a colonial of the world. Colonialism has grown into cosmopolitanism, and his motherland is no one nation, but all who have anything life-enhancing to offer to the spirit. That vague sympathy which the France of ten years ago was feeling for the world—a sympathy which was drowned in the terrible reality of war—may be the modern American's, and that in a positive and aggressive sense. If the American is parochial, it is in sheer wantonness or cowardice. His provincialism is the measure of his fear of bogies or the defect of his imagination. . . .

All our idealisms must be those of future social goals in which all can participate, the good life of personality lived in the environment of the Beloved Community. No mere doubtful triumphs of the past, which redound to the glory of only one of our transnationalities, can satisfy us. It must be a future America, on which all can unite, which pulls us irresistibly toward it, as we understand each other more warmly.

To make real this striving amid dangers and apathies is work for a younger *intelligentsia* of America. Here is an enterprise of integration into which we can all pour ourselves, of a spiritual welding which should make us, if the final menace ever came, not weaker, but infinitely strong.

13

✧

CLOSING THE DOORS

For a half-century after the Civil War the United States maintained a relatively unrestrictive policy toward immigration from Europe. Yet the coming of so many millions of immigrants, particularly so many who were neither Protestant nor northern Europeans, caused growing alarm among "old-stock" Americans, who associated the newcomers with saloons, political corruption, and other "ills" of urban society. Labor leaders feared such floods of uncontrollable cheap labor; upper-class spokesmen were concerned about the possible "mongrelization" of the country.

The first broad effort to restrict immigration was the Literacy Test of 1917, which actually had little effect because most immigrants could in fact read and write. In 1921, Congress limited immigration from any country to 3 percent of that country's proportion of the American population as of 1910. By 1924 the public favored even more restrictive measures. The sweeping National Origins Act, excerpted below, brought the tradition of unrestricted entry by Europeans to a definitive close. Only people from the Western Hemisphere could come freely now. (A separate Oriental Exclusion Act later banned Asians altogether.) The national-origins standard, though modified, persisted until 1965, when the emphasis shifted from national origin to refugees, relatives, and occupational skills.

Questions to Consider. The Immigration Act of 1924 shows how American society rated the different nationalities at that time. According to the quotas listed in the act, for example, a Czech was worth thirty Chinese, a Swiss equaled twenty Syrians, and an Irishman ten Italians. Is this a fair interpretation of the act? Not even at this peak of feverish nationalism did the U.S. government discriminate arbitrarily between nationalities or allot immigration space on a random basis. With the notable exception of Asians, national quotas were figured on a percentage basis: limiting Armenians also meant limiting Austrians. Most of the Western Hemisphere, moreover, was exempt from the act. Nevertheless, by basing quotas on the 1890 rather than the 1910 census, the act did embody clear racial preferences. Why, then, was such care taken to employ percentages rather than absolute numbers?

————————✧————————

The Immigration Act of 1924

It will be remembered that the quota limit act of May 1921, provided that the number of aliens of any nationality admissible to the United States in any fiscal year should be limited to 3 per cent of the number of persons of such nationality who were resident in the United States according to the census of 1910, it being also provided that not more than 20 per cent of any annual quota could be admitted in any one month. Under the act of 1924 the number of each nationality who may be admitted annually is limited to 2 per cent of the population of such nationality resident in the United States according to the census of 1890, and not more than 10 per cent of any annual quota may be admitted in any month except in cases where such quota is less than 300 for the entire year.

Under the act of May, 1921, the quota area was limited to Europe, the Near East, Africa, and Australasia. The countries of North and South America, with adjacent islands, and countries immigration from which was otherwise regulated, such as China, Japan, and countries within the Asiatic barred zone, were not within the scope of the quota law. Under the new act, however, immigration from the entire world, with the exception of the Dominion of Canada, Newfoundland, the Republic of Mexico, the Republic of Cuba, the Republic of Haiti, the Dominican Republic, the Canal Zone, and independent countries of Central and South America, is subject to quota limitations. The various quotas established under the new law are shown in the . . . proclamation of the President, issued on the last day of the present fiscal year: . . .

Country or Area of Birth	Quota 1924–1925
Afghanistan	100
Albania	100
Andorra	100
Arabian peninsula	100
Armenia	124
Australia, including Papua, Tasmania, and all islands appertaining to Australia	121
Austria	785
Belgium	512
Bhutan	100
Bulgaria	100
Cameroon (proposed British mandate)	100
Cameroon (French mandate)	100
China	100

From the *Annual Report of the Commissioner-General of Immigration* (Government Printing Office, Washington, D.C., 1924).

Czechoslovakia	3,073
Danzig, Free City of	228
Denmark	2,789
Egypt	100
Estonia	124
Ethiopia (Abyssinia)	100
Finland	170
France	3,954
Germany	51,227
Great Britain and Northern Ireland	34,007
Greece	100
Hungary	473
Iceland	100
India	100
Iraq (Mesopotamia)	100
Irish Free State	28,567
Italy, including Rhodes, Dodekanesia, and Castellorizzo	3,845
Japan	100
Latvia	142
Liberia	100
Liechtenstein	100
Lithuania	344
Luxemburg	100
Monaco	100
Morocco (French and Spanish Zones and Tangier)	100
Muscat (Oman)	100
Nauru (Proposed British mandate)	100
Nepal	100
Netherlands	1,648
New Zealand (including appertaining islands)	100
Norway	6,453
New Guinea, and other Pacific Islands under proposed Australian mandate	100
Palestine (with Trans-Jordan, proposed British mandate)	100
Persia	100
Poland	5,982
Portugal	503
Ruanda and Urundi (Belgium mandate)	100
Rumania	603
Russia, European and Asiatic	2,248
Samoa, Western (proposed mandate of New Zealand)	100
San Marino	100
Siam	100
South Africa, Union of	100
South West Africa (proposed mandate of Union of South Africa)	100
Spain	131
Sweden	9,561
Switzerland	2,081
Syria and The Lebanon (French mandate)	100
Tanganyika (proposed British mandate)	100
Togoland (proposed British mandate)	100
Togoland (French mandate)	100

"The Only Way to Handle It." This 1921 cartoon from the *Providence Evening Bulletin* urged support for measures to restrict immigration according to the size of resident nationality groups. New England Yankees, such as the readers of the *Bulletin,* helped lead the restrictionist movement, with considerable assistance from Midwesterners and Californians. Restrictionists felt especially threatened by the renewal of mass European migration to America following the end of World War I. (Library of Congress)

A Bessemer steel plant. The Bessemer steel manufacturing process used at Andrew Carnegie's steelworks in Pittsburgh, Pennsylvania. (Granger Collection)

CHAPTER THREE

✧

The Age of Industry

14

✧

LABOR'S VISION

The decades following the Civil War brought an enormous expansion of activity in railroads, coal, steel, and other basic industries. This rapid rise in the development of America's natural resources was accompanied by a sharp rise in the country's per capita wealth and income and, in the long run, a higher standard of living for most people. But it resulted in other things as well: greater wealth and power for "capitalists," as the new leaders of industry were called; a deterioration in conditions for many workers; and a society repeatedly torn by class conflict.

The Noble Order of the Knights of Labor, formed as a secret workingmen's lodge in 1869, represented an early response to these trends. Secrecy seemed essential at first because of the hostility of employers toward labor unions. Not until 1881 did the Knights of Labor abandon secrecy and announce its objectives to the world. Its slogan was "An injury to one is the concern of all." The Knights took pride in their admission of all workers—regardless of race, sex, or level of skill—and in their moderate, public-spirited vision of a cooperative economic order. These factors, together with their support of successful railroad strikes, swelled the Knights of Labor membership rolls to nearly 800,000 by 1886. After that, however, a wave of antiradicalism, combined with internal problems and the loss of several bitter industrial struggles, sent membership plummeting. By 1900 the organization was gone. It was replaced by two other labor organizations: the American Federation of Labor (AFL), founded in 1886, which organized skilled labor and struck over wages and working conditions, and the Industrial Workers of the World (IWW), founded in 1905, which appealed to the unskilled and stood for industrial reorganization. The AFL, which opposed most of the Knights principles, endured; the IWW, which shared many of them, did not.

The American Federation of Labor was a combination of national craft unions with an initial membership of about 140,000. It was the result of craft disagreement with the Knights of Labor partly over tactics and partly over leadership. The unions that constituted the AFL were central players in a nationwide campaign in support of an eight-hour workday. Centered in Chicago but spreading rapidly to other cities, the campaign (whose major statement appears below) culminated in a series of mass strikes and demonstrations on May 1, 1886. The campaign failed in its efforts to impose a uniform eight-hour day throughout American industry. It succeeded, however, in making a shortened workday one of the cardinal ongoing demands of union organizers and negotiators. When major breakthroughs in union representation and influence came during the 1930s and 1940s, eight hours—"nine to five" with an hour for lunch—became in fact the standard workday everywhere.

Because the Knights of Labor was at first a secret organization, the preamble to its constitution, reprinted below, contained asterisks instead of the organization's name. The author of the preamble was Terence V. Powderly, Grand Master Workman of the Knights from 1879 to 1893. Powderly was born in Carbondale, Pennsylvania, in 1849 to Irish immigrant parents. After ten years as a railroad laborer and machinist, he became active in union affairs, joining the Knights in 1874 and rising rapidly in the organization. He was also a political activist during these years. He served as mayor of Scranton, Pennsylvania, supporting many prolabor candidates in the 1880s, though, like most American labor leaders, he refused to support a separate labor party. After the Knights' decline, Powderly studied law and then served in the Federal Bureau of Immigration. He died in Washington, D.C., in 1924.

The president of the AFL in 1886 and a key figure in the Eight-Hour Association, was Samuel Gompers. Gompers was a German-born cigarmaker who emigrated to New York City with his parents at age thirteen. At first a strong socialist, he became a leader of the Cigarmakers' Union in the 1870s, moving it away from social and political reform and toward "pure and simple unionism" based on demands for higher wages, benefits, and security. Gompers was president of the AFL every year but one from 1886 to 1924. During this time, he built an organization that was both powerful and conservative—one that was hostile to radicalism, party alignments, and the admission of the unskilled. He died in San Antonio, Texas, in 1924.

Questions to Consider. What general objectives did the Knights preamble set forth? What do the Knights' practical demands reveal about working conditions in America during the Gilded Age (the period from 1870 to 1890)? To what extent was the preamble idealistic? How radical was it? Does the preamble explain why the Knights barred doctors, lawyers, bankers, gamblers, and liquor dealers from membership, although it allowed farmers, merchants, and small capitalists to join? If you wanted to quote something from the preamble giving the gist of the Knights' philosophy, which passage would you select?

The statement of the Eight-Hour Association opened with a demand to reduce the workday from ten hours to eight. How long had the standard workday been ten hours? Was the ten-hour workday a national standard in 1886? How, according to the statement, would the U.S. economy be able to tolerate so drastic a shrinkage in the workweek? For whose eyes does this portion of the statement appear to have been written? How could a shorter workday benefit laborers? Who besides the individual workers would benefit from the new day?

———————◆———————

Preamble to the Constitution of the Knights of Labor (1878)

The recent alarming development and aggression of aggregated wealth, which, unless checked, will invariably lead to the pauperization and hopeless degradation of the toiling masses, render it imperative, if we desire to enjoy the blessings of life, that a check should be placed upon its power and upon unjust accumulation, and a system adopted which will secure to the laborer the fruits of his toil; and as this much-desired object can only be accomplished by the thorough unification of labor, and the united efforts of those who obey the divine injunction that "In the sweat of thy brow shalt thou eat bread," we have formed the ***** with a view of securing the organization and direction, by co-operative effort, of the power of the industrial classes; and we submit to the world the object sought to be accomplished by our organization, calling upon all who believe in securing "the greatest good to the greatest number" to aid and assist us:—

I. To bring within the folds of organization every department of productive industry, making knowledge a standpoint for action, and industrial and moral worth, not wealth, the true standard of individual and national greatness.

II. To secure to the toilers a proper share of the wealth that they create; more of the leisure that rightfully belongs to them; more societary advantages; more of the benefits, privileges, and emoluments of the world; in a word, all those rights and privileges necessary to make them capable of enjoying, appreciating, defending, and perpetuating the blessing of good government.

From Terence V. Powderly, *Thirty Years of Labor* (Excelsior Publishing House, Columbus, Ohio, 1890), 243–246.

Strikebreakers dragged from a train in Pittsburgh, 1877. The 1877 railroad strike was the first nationwide strike. Two weeks of fierce fighting left hundreds dead and damage in the millions of dollars. Industrial conflicts continued to convulse the industry in the 1880s, with workers sometimes winning concessions and sometimes losing them.

III. To arrive at the true condition of the producing masses in their educational, moral, and financial condition, by demanding from the various governments the establishment of bureaus of Labor Statistics.

IV. The establishment of co-operative institutions, productive and distributive.

V. The reserving of the public lands—the heritage of the people—for the actual settler;—not another acre for railroads or speculators.

VI. The abrogation of all laws that do not bear equally upon capital and labor, the removal of unjust technicalities, delays, and discriminations in the administration of justice, and the adopting of measures providing for the health and safety of those engaged in mining, manufacturing, or building pursuits.

VII. The enactment of laws to compel chartered corporations to pay their employees weekly, in full, for labor performed during the preceding week, in the lawful money of the country.

VIII. The enactment of laws giving mechanics and laborers a first lien on their work for their full wages.

IX. The abolishment of the contract system on national, state, and municipal work.

X. The substitution of arbitration for strikes, whenever and wherever employers and employees are willing to meet on equitable grounds.

XI. The prohibition of the employment of children in workshops, mines, and factories before attaining their fourteenth year.

XII. To abolish the system of letting out by contract the labor of convicts in our prisons and reformatory institutions.

XIII. To secure for both sexes equal pay for equal work.

XIV. The reduction of the hours of labor to eight per day, so that the laborers may have more time for social enjoyment and intellectual improvement, and be enabled to reap the advantages conferred by the labor-saving machinery which their brains have created.

XV. To prevail upon governments to establish a purely national circulating medium, based upon the faith and resources of the nation, and issued directly to the people, without the intervention of any system of banking corporations, which money shall be a legal tender in payment of all debts, public or private.

Statement of the Eight-Hour Association (1886)

The Eight-Hour Association asks for a reduction of all daily toil from ten hours to eight, for the reason that such reduction of time will give opportunity for two more men to work for every eight now employed. In other words, the work now performed by eight men will require ten men to achieve the same result. This will be twenty more men employed for every eighty, thus giving immediate, and for some years, constant labor to all who are willing and able to work.

That every one shall have steady employment at good wages, working eight hours daily, it is necessary that all agree and unite in this movement. In order for each workman to prosper it is essential that all other workmen prosper; because all people support each other by exchanging each others' production and services. Therefore everybody who has commodities or services for sale is interested in having everybody else have a sufficient

From *John Swinton's Paper* (May 2, 1886).

income from his own earnings to make a mutual exchange. United action in this effort means not only strength but prosperity for all.

The advocates of eight hours for a day's labor advise all workers to take for this number of hours an eight-hour price, allowing the law of supply and demand to regulate wages in the future. We fully believe that while merchants, manufacturers and all employers will be benefited, the wages for laborers will soon be higher than ever heretofore, for the following reasons: A reduction of one-fifth of laboring-time for all that work will make a reduction of one-fifth of all kinds of products in the near future, which will make proportionate scarcity. With scarcity will come advance in prices for every commodity, giving merchants and manufacturers a fair profit, and wage-workers an advance in wages. Ere long, all being employed, the production will be as great as now, but, all earning wages, the consumption and demand will be greater than now, so that prices and wages will still continue better than at present.

Eight hours, instead of ten, means a gain of two hours each day—more than one day each week—*seventy-eight days a year!*—a time sufficient to enable every unlettered person to learn to read and write; time in which every foreigner can learn to speak the English language and familiarize himself with his political duty as an American citizen. The extra time thus gained in the year will afford every workingman not only a sufficient recreation, but opportunity to attend the State and county fairs, the National Exposition, and make a visit to the childhood home, with time to spare for a journey to Europe.

This appeal is in the interest of capital as well as labor. The plain facts are that the strikes, lock-outs, business failures, general business depression throughout the world, overflowing prisons and poor-houses, are the result of the producing power of the country being far in excess of the practical ability to consume. We make, raise and produce more than we can readily eat, wear, or dispose of. This results, first, in a falling of prices; then a lowering of wages, succeeded by strikes and resistance of wage-workers, and a final discharge of workmen into idleness. Then, as men are unable to buy, there is a great under-consumption, goods piling up on one side, while great want and destitution exist on the other. To remedy this, productive power, temporarily, must be lessened. To do this by destroying machinery is barbarous. It is wiser far to accomplish this result, and benefit all mankind, by lessening the hours in which machines and men labor in the work of production. . . .

The advantage of eight hours to the laboring classes will be (1st) employment; (2d) steady employment; (3d) better wages; (4th) relief from anxiety that comes from idleness and poverty; (5th) an opportunity to lay aside the means for the purchase of a home; (6th) opportunity to see and get acquainted with the family by day-light; (7th) more time for intellectual improvement; (8th) a chance for outdoor recreation on the secular day, without being compelled to take Sunday for that purpose; (9th) the ability to obtain respectable dress and make a good appearance, whereby encouragement is given to attend church and social gatherings, resulting in intellectual, moral and spiritual improvement. . . .

To fully lay this matter before the people, through literature, discussion, lecture, sermon and study, *we recommend Saturday, April 24, 1886, as a general holiday for the laboring classes, preparatory to inaugurating the Eight-Hour Movement seven days afterwards, on the first day of May.*

In this effort we fervently invoke the aid of the press, the clergy, legislators, teachers, employers, and all persons in authority. Give us employment for the idle masses who are struggling for bread; give us a chance to send pauper and criminal back to shop, and field, and factory, where they may get an honest living; give us back again health and bloom for the sunken-eyed, starving sewing-woman; give us homes for working-people, and a chance to earn them; give us an honest opportunity for every human being to possess the reasonable comforts of life—GIVE US EIGHT HOURS!

15

✧

PRODUCTION AND WEALTH

During the late nineteenth century the United States experienced re-markable industrial development. In 1860 it was largely a nation of farms, villages, small businesses, and small-scale manufacturing estab-lishments; by 1900 it had become a nation of cities, machines, factories, offices, shops, and powerful business combinations. Between 1860 and 1900, railroad trackage increased, annual production of coal rose steadily, iron and steel production soared, oil refining flourished, and development of electric power proceeded apace. "There has never been in the history of civilization," observed economist Edward Atkin-son in 1891, "a period, or a place, or a section of the earth in which science and invention have worked such progress or have created such opportunity for material welfare as in these United States in the period which has elapsed since the end of the Civil War." By the end of the century, America's industrial production exceeded that of Great Britain and Germany combined, and the United States was exporting huge quantities of farm and factory goods to all parts of the world. The country had become one of the richest and most powerful nations in history.

More than any other single element, steel permitted and laid the foundation for industrialization. The process of steel production pow-ered industrial development, because it was from steel that railroad tracks and cars, bridges and girders, machines and farm equipment, elevators, ships, and automobiles were all manufactured. One key to rising steel production was the adaptation of the so-called Bessemer process to American conditions. The emergence of mass steel manufac-ture by this method involved a dynamic interplay between foreign and domestic production ideas, patent law, firm capitalization and competition, creative marketing, and, perhaps most important, constant technical adaptation on the factory floor.

At the other end of the production scale was Andrew Carnegie, the "King of Steel." Carnegie liked to boast of the accomplishments of efficient business organization in the American steel industry, as he did in the excerpt below from *Triumphant Democracy* (1886), a best seller. "Two pounds of ironstone mined upon Lake Superior and transported nine hundred miles to Pittsburgh; one pound and a half of coal mined and manufactured into coke, and transported to Pittsburgh; one-half pound of lime, mined and transported to Pittsburgh; a small amount of manganese ore mined in Virginia and brought to Pittsburgh—and these four pounds of materials manufactured into one pound of steel, for which the consumer pays one cent."

Carnegie preached what he called a "gospel of wealth." His gospel emphasized individual initiative, private property, competition, and the accumulation of wealth in the hands of those with superior ability and energy. But in the last quarter of the nineteenth century, less than 1 percent of the population controlled more than 50 percent of the nation's wealth, the highest concentration in U.S. history up to that time, and the benefits of spectacular industrial growth were hardly shared equitably. The nation had been built on the assumption that all men were created equal, and most Americans took for granted that in a republican society property and power would be widely distributed. Yet the disparity between the very rich and the very poor had grown extreme.

Thoughtful observers, troubled by the concentration of wealth and power in the hands of so few, raised their voices in protest. Andrew Carnegie was unusual in that, on the one hand, he defended the absolute right of the entrepreneur to accumulate wealth and also the Social Darwinist notion of "survival of the fittest." But at the same time, like some of the radicals of his era, Carnegie argued that the rich should dispense their wealth in ways that would benefit society. The "man who dies rich," he asserted, "dies disgraced." His thinking found its clearest expression in "Wealth," an essay first appearing in the *North American Review* and excerpted below.

Andrew Carnegie, the son of a handloom weaver, was born in Scotland in 1835. With his family, he moved to Allegheny, Pennsylvania, at the age of twelve and got a job in a textile mill at $1.20 a week. During this period he studied telegraphy, a skill that landed him a position as the personal secretary and telegrapher of a leading railroad executive. Carnegie was himself a railroad executive for a time, and then amassed a fortune selling bonds, dealing in oil, and building bridges. In 1873 he concentrated his efforts on steel and gradually built his Carnegie Steel Company into a massive industrial giant. In 1901 he sold the firm to J. P. Morgan, who made it the core of the world's first billion-dollar company, the United States Steel Corporation. Over the next two decades Carnegie gave away some $350 million for libraries and other public works. He died in Lenox, Massachusetts, in 1919.

Questions to Consider. The excerpt from *Triumphant Democracy* is typical of the many articles and books Andrew Carnegie wrote celebrating the American system. Why did Carnegie think life "has become vastly better worth living" than it had been a century before? What particular aspects of American life did he single out for special mention? In what ways did he think life in the United States was better than life in Europe? Was he writing mainly about the life of the average or of the well-to-do American? How did he relate America's economic achievements to democracy? In "Wealth," Carnegie argued that large fortunes should not be left to one's offspring. Is his reasoning valid? To what extent were his ideas about the administration of wealth fundamentally conservative? Do you agree with his argument that individuals should not be the recipients of great sums? Carnegie assumes that success will come to those who are competent and hard working. Given the conditions of his time, how sound was his thinking?

✧

Triumphant Democracy (1886)

ANDREW CARNEGIE

A community of toilers with an undeveloped continent before them, and destitute of the refinements and elegancies of life—such was the picture presented by the Republic sixty years ago. Contrasted with that of today, we might almost conclude that we were upon another planet and subject to different primary conditions. The development of an unequaled transportation system brings the products of one section to the doors of another, the tropical fruits of Florida and California to Maine, and the ice of New England to the Gulf States. Altogether life has become vastly better worth living than it was a century ago.

Among the rural communities, the change in the conditions is mainly seen in the presence of labor-saving devices, lessening the work in house and field. Mowing and reaping machines, horse rakes, steam plows and threshers, render man's part easy and increase his productive power. Railroads and highways connect him with the rest of the world, and he is no longer isolated or dependent upon his petty village. Markets for his produce are easy of access, and transportation swift and cheap. If the roads throughout the country are yet poor compared with those of Europe, the need of good roads has been rendered less imperative by the omnipresent railroad. It is the superiority of the iron highway in America which has diverted attention from the country roads. It is a matter of congratulation, however, that this subject is at last attracting attention. Nothing would contribute so much to the happiness of life in the country as such perfect roads as

From Andrew Carnegie, *Triumphant Democracy* (Scribners, New York, 1886), 164–183.

Andrew Carnegie. Carnegie was the country's biggest industrialist in the late 1800s, with a fortune estimated to be a half-billion dollars. He was also industry's most articulate spokesman, writing books and articles that were widely read. Carnegie exemplified two cherished American ideals: self-help in the accumulation of wealth and stewardship in the disposal of it. He endowed hundres of public libraries and donated to a wide range of charities. (The Bettmann Archive)

those of Scotland. It is a difficult problem, but its solution will well repay any amount of expenditure necessary. [British historian Thomas] Macaulay's test of the civilization of a people—the condition of their roads—must be interpreted, in this age of steam, to include railroads. Communication between great cities is now cheaper and more comfortable than in any other country. Upon the principal railway lines, the cars—luxurious drawing-rooms by day, and sleeping chambers by night—are ventilated by air, warmed and filtered in winter, and cooled in summer. Passenger steamers upon the lakes and rivers are of gigantic size, and models of elegance.

It is in the cities that the change from colonial conditions is greatest. Most of these—indeed all, excepting those upon the Atlantic coast—have been in great measure the result of design instead of being allowed, like Topsy, to "just grow." In these modern days cities are laid out under definite, far-seeing plans; consequently the modern city presents symmetry of form unknown in mediaeval ages. The difference is seen by contrasting the crooked cowpaths of old Boston with the symmetrical, broad streets of Washington or Denver. These are provided with parks at intervals for breathing spaces; amply supplied with pure water, in some cases at enormous expense; the most modern ideas are embodied in their sanitary arrangements; they are well lighted, well policed, and the fire departments are very efficient. In these modern cities an extensive fire is rare. The lessening danger of this risk is indicated by the steady fall in the rate of fire insurance.

The variety and quality of the food of the people of America excels that found elsewhere, and is a constant surprise to Europeans visiting the States. The Americans are the best-fed people on the globe. Their dress is now of the richest character—far beyond that of any other people, compared class for class. The comforts of the average American home compare favorably with those of other lands, while the residences of the wealthy classes are unequaled. The first-class American residence of today in all its appointments excites the envy of the foreigner. One touch of the electric button calls a messenger; two bring a telegraph boy; three summon a policeman; four give the alarm of fire. Telephones are used to an extent undreamt of in Europe, the stables and other out-buildings being connected with the mansion; and the houses of friends are joined by the talking wire almost as often as houses of business. Speaking tubes connect the drawing-room with the kitchen; and the dinner is brought up "piping hot" by a lift. Hot air and steam pipes are carried all over the house; and by the turning of a tap the temperature of any room is regulated to suit the convenience of the occupant. A passenger lift is common. The electric light is an additional home comfort. Indeed, there is no palace or great mansion in Europe with half the conveniences and scientific appliances which characterize the best American mansions. New York Central Park is no unworthy rival of Hyde Park and the Bois de Boulogne in its display of fine equipages; and in winter the hundreds of graceful sleighs dashing along the drives form a picture. The opera-houses, theatres, and public halls of the country excel in magnificence those of other lands, if we except the latter constructions in Paris and Vienna, with which the New York, Philadelphia, and Chicago opera-houses rank. The commercial exchanges, and the imposing structures of the life insurance companies, newspaper buildings, hotels, and many edifices built by wealthy firms, not only in New York but in the cities of the West, never fail to excite the Europeans' surprise. The postal system is equal in every respect to that of Europe. Mails are taken up by express trains, sorted on board, and dropped at all important points without stopping. Letters are delivered several times a day in every considerable town, and a ten-cent special delivery stamp insures delivery at once by special messenger in the large cities. The uniform rate of postage for all distances, often exceeding three thousand miles, is only two cents . . . per ounce.

In short, the conditions of life in American cities may be said to have approximated those of Europe during the sixty years of which we are speaking. Year by year, as the population advances, the general standard of comfort in the smaller Western cities rises to that of the East. Herbert Spencer [an English philosopher] was astonished beyond measure at what he saw in American cities. "Such books as I had looked into," said he, "had given me no adequate idea of the immense developments of material civilization which I have found everywhere. The extent, wealth, and magnificence of your cities, and especially the splendors of New York, have altogether astonished me. Though I have not visited the wonder of the West, Chicago, yet some of your minor modern places, such as Cleveland, have sufficiently amazed me by the marvelous results of one generation's activity. Occasionally, when I have been in places of some ten thousand inhabitants, where the telephone is in general use, I have felt somewhat ashamed of our own unenterprising towns, many of which, of fifty thousand inhabitants and more, make no use of it."

Such is the Democracy; such its conditions of life. In the presence of such a picture can it be maintained that the rule of the people is subversive of government and religion? Where have monarchical institutions developed a community so delightful in itself, so intelligent, so free from crime or pauperism—a community in which the greatest good of the greatest number is so fully attained, and one so well calculated to foster the growth of self-respecting men—which is the end civilization seeks?

> "For ere man made us citizens
> God made us men."

The republican is necessarily self-respecting, for the laws of his country begin by making him a man indeed, the equal of other men. The man who most respects himself will always be found the man who most respects the rights and feelings of others.

The rural democracy of America could be as soon induced to sanction the confiscation of the property of its richer neighbors, or to vote for any violent or discreditable measure, as it could be led to surrender the President for a king. Equal laws and privileges develop all the best and noblest characteristics, and these always lead in the direction of the Golden Rule.

These honest, pure, contented, industrious, patriotic people really do con-sider what they would have others do to them. They ask themselves what is fair and right. Nor is there elsewhere in the world so conservative a body of men; but then it is the equality of the citizen—just and equal laws—republicanism, they are resolved to conserve. To conserve these they are at all times ready to fight and, if need be, to die; for, to men who have once tasted the elixir of political equality, life under unequal conditions could possess no charm.

To every man is committed in some degree, as a sacred trust, the man-hood of man. This he may not himself infringe or permit to be infringed by others. Hereditary dignities, political inequalities, do infringe the right of man, and hence are not to be tolerated. The true democrat must live the peer of his fellows, or die struggling to become so.

The American citizen has no further need to struggle, being in possession of equality under the laws in every particular. He has not travelled far in the path of genuine Democracy who would not scorn to enjoy a privilege which was not the common birthright of all his fellows.

Wealth (1889)

ANDREW CARNEGIE

The Socialist or Anarchist who seeks to overturn present conditions is to be regarded as attacking the foundation upon which civilization itself rests, for civilization took its start from the day that the capable, industrious workman said to his incompetent and lazy fellow, "If thou dost not sow, thou shalt not reap," and thus ended primitive Communism by separating the drones from the bees. One who studies this subject will soon be brought face to face with the conclusion that upon the sacredness of property civilization itself depends—the right of the laborer to his hundred dollars in the savings bank, and equally the legal right of the millionaire to his millions. To those who propose to substitute Communism for this intense Individualism the answer, therefore, is: The race has tried that. All progress from that barbarous day to the present time has resulted from its displace-ment. Not evil, but good, has come to the race from the accumulation of wealth by those who have the ability and energy that produce it. . . .

We might as well urge the destruction of the highest existing type of man because he failed to reach our ideal as to favor the destruction of Individualism, Private Property, the Law of Accumulation of Wealth, and the Law of Competition; for these are the highest results of human experi-

From *North American Review* (June 1889).

ence, the soil in which society so far has produced the best fruit. Unequally or unjustly, perhaps, as these laws sometimes operate, and imperfect as they appear to the Idealist, they are, nevertheless, like the highest type of man, the best and most valuable of all that humanity has yet accomplished.

We start, then, with a condition of affairs under which the best interests of the race are promoted, but which inevitably gives wealth to the few. Thus far, accepting conditions as they exist, the situation can be surveyed and pronounced good. The question then arises,—and, if the foregoing be correct, it is the only question with which we have to deal,—What is the proper mode of administering wealth after the laws upon which civilization is founded have thrown it into the hands of the few? And it is of this great question that I believe I offer the true solution. It will be understood that *fortunes* are here spoken of, not moderate sums saved by many years of effort, the returns from which are required for the comfortable maintenance and education of families. This is not *wealth*, but only *competence*, which it should be the aim of all to acquire.

There are but three modes in which surplus wealth can be disposed of. It can be left to the families of the decedents; or it can be bequeathed for public purposes; or, finally, it can be administered during their lives by its possessors. Under the first and second modes most of the wealth of the world that has reached the few has hitherto been applied. Let us in turn consider each of these modes. The first is the most injudicious. In monarchical countries, the estates and the greatest portion of the wealth are left to the first son, that the vanity of the parent may be gratified by the thought that his name and title are to descend to succeeding generations unimpaired. The condition of this class in Europe to-day teaches the futility of such hopes or ambitions. The successors have become impoverished through their follies or from the fall in the value of land. Even in Great Britain the strict law of entail has been found inadequate to maintain the status of an hereditary class. Its soil is rapidly passing into the hands of the stranger. Under republican institutions the division of property among the children is much fairer, but the question which forces itself upon thoughtful men in all lands is: Why should men leave great fortunes to their children? If this is done from affection, is it not misguided affection? Observation teaches that, generally speaking, it is not well for the children that they should be so burdened. Neither is it well for the state. . . . .

It is not suggested that men who have failed to educate their sons to earn a livelihood shall cast them adrift in poverty. If any man has seen fit to rear his sons with a view to their living idle lives, or, what is highly commendable, has instilled in them the sentiment that they are in a position to labor for public ends without reference to pecuniary considerations, then, of course, the duty of the parent is to see that such are provided for *in moderation*. There are instances of millionaires' sons unspoiled by wealth, who, being rich, still perform great services in the community. Such are the very salt of the earth, as valuable as, unfortunately, they are rare; still it is not the exception, but the rule, that men must regard, and, looking at the usual result of enormous sums conferred upon legatees, the thoughtful man must shortly say, "I would as soon leave to my son a curse as the almighty dollar," and admit to himself that it is not the welfare of the children, but family pride, which inspires these enormous legacies.

As to the second mode, that of leaving wealth at death for public uses, it may be said that this is only a means for the disposal of wealth, provided a man is content to wait until he is dead before it becomes of much good in the world. Knowledge of the results of legacies bequeathed is not calculated to inspire the brightest hopes of much posthumous good being accomplished. The cases are not few in which the real object sought by the testator is not attained, nor are they few in which his real wishes are thwarted. In many cases the bequests are so used as to become only monuments of his folly. It is well to remember that it requires the exercise of not less ability than that which acquired the wealth to use it so as to be really beneficial to the community. Besides this, it may fairly be said that no man is to be extolled for doing what he cannot help doing, nor is he to be thanked by the community to which he only leaves wealth at death. Men who leave vast sums in this way may fairly be thought men who would not have left it at all, had they been able to take it with them. The memories of such cannot be held in grateful remembrance, for there is no grace in their gifts. It is not to be wondered at that such bequests seem so generally to lack the blessing.

The growing disposition to tax more and more heavily large estates left at death is a cheering indication of the growth of a salutary change in public opinion. The State of Pennsylvania now takes—subject to some exceptions—one-tenth of the property left by its citizens. The budget presented in the British Parliament the other day proposes to increase the death-duties; and, most significant of all, the new tax is to be a graduated one. Of all forms of taxation, this seems the wisest. Men who continue hoarding great sums all their lives, the proper use of which for public ends would work good to the community, should be made to feel that the community, in the form of the state, cannot thus be deprived of its proper share. By taxing estates heavily at death the state marks its condemnation of the selfish millionaire's unworthy life. . . .

There remains, then, only one mode of using great fortunes; but in this we have the true antidote for the temporary unequal distribution of wealth, the reconciliation of the rich and the poor—a reign of harmony—another ideal, differing, indeed, from that of the Communist in requiring only the further evolution of existing conditions, not the total overthrow of our civilization. It is founded upon the present most intense individualism, and the race is prepared to put it in practice by degrees whenever it pleases. Under its sway we shall have an ideal state, in which the surplus wealth of the few will become, in the best sense, the property of the many, because administered for the common good, and this wealth, passing through the hands of the few, can be made a much more potent force for the elevation of our race than if it had been distributed in small sums to the people themselves. Even the poorest can be made to see this, and to agree that great sums gathered by some of their fellow-citizens and spent for public purposes, from which the masses reap the principal benefit, are more valuable to them than if scattered among them through the course of many years in trifling amounts. . . .

Poor and restricted are our opportunities in this life; narrow our horizon; our best work most imperfect; but rich men should be thankful for one inestimable boon. They have it in their power during their lives to busy themselves in organizing benefactions from which the masses of their fellows will derive lasting advantage, and thus dignify their own lives.

16

✧

RURAL REVOLT

Rapid agricultural expansion was a crucial part of the nation's amazing economic growth in the late nineteenth century. Nevertheless, average farm income went down during this era, and the farmer gradually lost preeminent status in American society. Farmers in the Midwest suffered from bad weather, and farmers in the South from weevils and other pests. Everywhere growers received lower prices because of overproduction but paid higher borrowing and shipping costs because of what they saw as greedy and unresponsive banks and railroads. This network of transportation and finance quickly became a target of rural frustration, and farmers joined organizations such as the Grange and the Farmers' Alliance to promote their own interests. In 1890 state alliances in the Midwest formed political parties to challenge the Republicans and Democrats; in the South, alliance members, facing the problem of race relations, sought to take over the Democratic party. Encouraged by local victories, the alliances created a national People's, or Populist, party in 1892.

From the Populist point of view, "a vast conspiracy" of the wealthy few was rapidly dividing American society into two great classes, "tramps and millionaires"; the labor of the farmer and the workingman was being "stolen." When they met in convention on the the Fourth of July in Omaha, the Populists created a platform (excerpted below) that, in tone, is reminiscent of the Declaration of Independence, and punctuated it with words and phrases from the Constitution. Although the Populists considered themselves conservative—after all, theirs was an effort to "restore the government of the Republic to the hands of the 'plain people' with which class it originated"—most Americans found their demands extremely radical.

The People's party did remarkably well for a new party. James B. Weaver of Iowa, the Populist candidate for president, carried four states (with twenty-two electoral votes) in 1892 and received over a million popular votes. The Populists also succeeded in electing a number of congressmen and some state officials.

Questions to Consider. Does the Populists' platform suggest that they were nostalgic reactionaries who sought to reverse the direction of an increasingly industrial society, or do you think they heralded the great reform movements of the early twentieth century? Ultimately, some of the Populists' demands were enacted into law. Why was their platform considered so radical at the time? To what extent was their view of society legitimate? Do you think they had faith in democracy?

The Populist Party Platform (1892)

Assembled upon the 116th anniversary of the Declaration of Independence, the People's Party of America, in their first national convention, invoking upon their action the blessing of Almighty God, put forth in the name and on behalf of the people of this country, the following preamble and declaration of principles:

Preamble

The conditions which surround us best justify our co-operation; we meet in the midst of a nation brought to the verge of moral, political, and material ruin. Corruption dominates the ballot-box, the Legislatures, the Congress, and touches even the ermine of the bench. The people are demoralized; most of the States have been compelled to isolate the voters at the polling places to prevent universal intimidation and bribery. The newspapers are largely subsidized or muzzled, public opinion silenced, business prostrated, homes covered with mortgages, labor impoverished, and the land concentrating in the hands of capitalists. The urban workmen are denied the right to organize for self-protection, imported pauperized labor beats down their wages, a hireling standing army, unrecognized by our laws, is established to shoot them down, and they are rapidly degenerating into European conditions. The fruits of the toil of millions are boldly stolen to build up colossal fortunes for a few, unprecedented in the history of mankind; and the possessors of these, in turn, despise the Republic and endanger liberty. From the same prolific womb of governmental injustice we breed the two great classes—tramps and millionaires.

The national power to create money is appropriated to enrich bondholders; a vast public debt payable in legal-tender currency has been funded into gold-bearing bonds, thereby adding millions to the burdens of the people.

Silver, which has been accepted as coin since the dawn of history, has been demonetized to add to the purchasing power of gold by decreasing

E. McPherson, *A Handbook of Politics for 1892* (New York, 1893).

the value of all forms of property as well as human labor, and the supply of currency is purposely abridged to fatten usurers, bankrupt enterprise, and enslave industry. A vast conspiracy against mankind has been organized on two continents, and it is rapidly taking possession of the world. If not met and overthrown at once it forebodes terrible social convulsions, the destruction of civilization, or the establishment of an absolute despotism.

We have witnessed for more than a quarter of a century the struggles of the two great political parties for power and plunder, while grievous wrongs have been inflicted upon the suffering people. We charge that the controlling influences dominating both these parties have permitted the existing dreadful conditions to develop without serious effort to prevent or restrain them. Neither do they now promise us any substantial reform. They have agreed together to ignore, in the coming campaign, every issue but one. They propose to drown the outcries of a plundered people with the uproar of a sham battle over the tariff, so that capitalists, corporations, national banks, rings, trusts, watered stock, the demonetization of silver and the oppressions of the usurers may all be lost sight of. They propose to sacrifice our homes, lives, and children on the altar of mammon; to destroy the multitude in order to secure corruption funds from the millionaires.

Assembled on the anniversary of the birthday of the nation, and filled with the spirit of the grand general and chief who established our independence, we seek to restore the government of the Republic to the hands of the "plain people," with which class it originated. We assert our purposes to be identical with the purposes of the National Constitution: to form a more perfect union and establish justice, insure domestic tranquility, provide for the common defence, promote the general welfare, and secure the blessings of liberty for ourselves and our posterity. . . .

Platform

We declare, therefore—

First.—That the union of the labor forces of the United States this day consummated shall be permanent and perpetual; may its spirit enter into all hearts for the salvation of the Republic and the uplifting of mankind.

Second.—Wealth belongs to him who creates it, and every dollar taken from industry without an equivalent is robbery. "If any will not work, neither shall he eat." The interests of rural and civil labor are the same; their enemies are identical.

Third.—We believe that the time has come when the railroad corporations will either own the people or the people must own the railroads; and should the government enter upon the work of owning and managing all railroads, we should favor an amendment to the constitution by which all persons engaged in the government service shall be placed under a civil-service regulation of the most rigid character, so as to prevent the increase of the power of the national administration by the use of such additional government employes.

FINANCE.—We demand a national currency, safe, sound, and flexible issued by the general government only, a full legal tender for all debts, public and private, and that without the use of banking corporations; a just, equitable, and efficient means of distribution direct to the people, at a tax not to exceed 2 per cent, per annum, to be provided as set forth in the sub-treasury plan of the Farmers' Alliance, or a better system; also by payments in discharge of its obligations for public improvements.

1. We demand free and unlimited coinage of silver and gold at the present legal ratio of 16 to 1.
2. We demand that the amount of circulating medium be speedily increased to not less than $50 per capita.
3. We demand a graduated income tax.
4. We believe that the money of the country should be kept as much as possible in the hands of the people, and hence we demand that all State and national revenues shall be limited to the necessary expenses of the government, economically and honestly administered.
5. We demand that postal savings banks be established by the government for the safe deposit of the earnings of the people and to facilitate exchange.

TRANSPORTATION.—Transportation being a means of exchange and a public necessity, the government should own and operate the railroads in the interest of the people. The telegraph and telephone, like the post-office system, being a necessity for the transmission of news, should be owned and operated by the government in the interest of the people.

LAND.—The land, including all the natural sources of wealth, is the heritage of the people, and should not be monopolized for speculative purposes, and alien ownership of land should be prohibited. All land now held by railroads and other corporations in excess of their actual needs, and all lands now owned by aliens should be reclaimed by the government and held for actual settlers only.

17

✧

SIDE EFFECTS

Industrialization brought, among other things, the factory system: big machines in large buildings where thousands of workers did specialized tasks under strict supervision. The factory system vastly increased America's output of such products as glass, machinery, newspapers, soap, cigarettes, beef, and beer. Factories thus provided innumerable new goods and millions of new jobs for Americans. But factories also reduced workers' control over their place of work, made the conditions of labor more dangerous, and played no small part in destroying the dignity of that labor. The first part of the following excerpt from Upton Sinclair's novel *The Jungle* offers a glimpse into the factory system as it operated in a Chicago meat-packing plant around 1905.

Industrialization produced not only big factories but also big cities, particularly in the Northeast and Midwest. Sinclair therefore took pains to show the role of industry and new production techniques in creating urban transportation and other services. The second part of the excerpt suggests a few of the links between industrial growth and Chicago's leaders—the so-called gray wolves who controlled the city's government and businesses. Here again, Sinclair indicates the high toll in human life exacted by unrestrained development.

The Jungle caused a sensation when it was first published. The pages describing conditions in Chicago's meat-packing plants aroused horror, disgust, and fury, and sales of meat dropped precipitously. "I aimed at the public's heart," said Sinclair ruefully, "and hit it in the stomach." President Theodore Roosevelt ordered a congressional investigation of meat-packing plants in the nation, and Congress subsequently passed the Meat Inspection Act. But Sinclair, a socialist, did not seek to inspire reform legislation. He was concerned mainly with dramatizing the misery of workers under the capitalist mode of production and with winning recruits to socialism.

Upton Sinclair was born in Baltimore, Maryland, in 1878. After attending college in New York City, he began to write essays and fiction, experiencing his first real success with the publication of *The Jungle* in 1906. Dozens of novels on similar subjects—the coal and oil industries, newspapers, the liquor business, the persecution of radicals, the threat of dictatorship—poured from his pen in the following years, though none had the immediate impact of *The Jungle*. Sinclair's style, with its emphasis on the details of everyday life, resembles the realism of other writers of the time. But he also wrote as a "muckraker" (as Theodore Roosevelt called journalists who wrote exposés), trying to alert readers to the deceit and corruption then prevalent in American life. Unlike most muckrakers, however, Sinclair was politically active, running in California in the 1920s as a socialist candidate for the U.S. Congress. In 1934 he won the Democratic nomination for governor with the slogan "End Poverty in California"(EPIC), but he lost the election. During World War II he was a warm supporter of President Franklin D. Roosevelt and wrote novels about the war, one of which won a Pulitzer Prize. Not long before Sinclair's death in 1968 in Bound Brook, New Jersey, President Lyndon Johnson invited him to the White House to be present at the signing of the Wholesome Meat Act.

Questions to Consider. The Jungle has been regarded as propaganda, not literature, and has been placed second only to Harriet Beecher Stowe's *Uncle Tom's Cabin* in its effectiveness as a propagandistic novel. Why do you think the novel caused demands for reform rather than converts to socialism? What seems more shocking in the passages from the novel reprinted below, the life of immigrant workers in Chicago in the early twentieth century or the filthy conditions under which meat was prepared for America's dining tables? What did Sinclair reveal about the organization of the work force in Chicago's meat-packing plants? Sinclair centered his story on a Lithuanian worker named Jurgis Rudkus and his wife, Ona. In what ways did he make Jurgis's plight seem typical of urban workers of his time? Why did Jurgis deny that he had ever worked in Chicago before? What did Sinclair reveal about the attitude of employers toward labor unions at that time?

✧

The Jungle (1906)

UPTON SINCLAIR

There was another interesting set of statistics that a person might have gathered in Packingtown—those of the various afflictions of the workers. When Jurgis had first inspected the packing plants with Szedvilas, he had

From Upton Sinclair, *The Jungle* (Doubleday, Page and Co., New York, 1906), 116–117, 265–269. Published in the British Commonwealth by Penguin Books, Ltd. Reprinted by permission of the Estate of Upton Sinclair.

A meat packing house. Trimmers wielding razor-sharp knives in a Chicago packing house in 1892, more than a decade before the publication of *The Jungle*. (From *Views in the Chicago Stock Yards and Packing Industry*, published by A. Wittemann, NY, 1892; photo from Chicago Historical Society)

marveled while he listened to the tale of all the things that were made out of the carcasses of animals and of all the lesser industries that were maintained there; now he found that each one of these lesser industries was a separate little inferno, in its way as horrible as the killing-beds, the source and fountain of them all. The workers in each of them had their own peculiar diseases. And the wandering visitor might be skeptical about all the swindles, but he could not be skeptical about these, for the worker bore the evidence of them about on his own person—generally he had only to hold out his hand.

There were the men in the pickle rooms, for instance, where old Antanas had gotten his death; scarce a one of these had not some spot of horror on his person. Let a man so much as scrape his finger pushing a truck in the pickle rooms, and he might have a sore that would put him out of the world; all the joints in his fingers might be eaten by the acid, one by one. Of the butchers and floormen, the beef boners and trimmers, and all those who used knives, you could scarcely find a person who had the use of his thumb; time and time again the base of it had been slashed, till it was a mere lump of flesh against which the man pressed the knife to hold it. The hands of these men would be criss-crossed with cuts, until you could no longer pretend to count them or to trace them. They would have no nails—they had worn them off pulling hides; their knuckles were swollen so that their fingers spread out like a fan. There were men who worked in the cooking rooms, in the midst of steam and sickening odors, by artificial light; in these rooms the germs of tuberculosis might live for two years, but the supply was renewed every hour. There were the beef luggers, who carried two-hundred-pound quarters into the refrigerator cars, a fearful kind of work, that began at four o'clock in the morning, and that wore out the most powerful man in a few years. There were those who worked in the chilling rooms, and whose special disease was rheumatism; the time limit that a man could work in the chilling rooms was said to be five years. There were the wool pluckers, whose hands went to pieces even sooner than the hands of the pickle men; for the pelts of the sheep had to be painted with acid to loosen the wool, and then the pluckers had to pull out this wool with their bare hands, till the acid had eaten their fingers off. There were those who made the tins for the canned meat, and their hands, too, were a maze of cuts, and each cut represented a chance for blood poisoning. Some worked at the stamping machines, and it was very seldom that one could work long there at the pace that was set, and not give out and forget himself, and have a part of his hand chopped off. There were the "hoisters," as they were called, whose task it was to press the lever which lifted the dead cattle off the floor. They ran along upon a rafter, peering down through the damp and the steam, and as old Durham's architects had not built the killing room for the convenience of the hoisters, at every few feet they would have to stoop under a beam, say four feet above the one they ran on, which got them into the habit of stooping, so that in a few years they would be walking like chimpanzees. Worst of any, however, were the fertilizer men, and those who served in the cooking rooms. These people could not be shown to the visitor—for the odor of a fertilizer man would scare any ordinary visitor at a hundred yards, and as for the other men, who worked in tank rooms full of steam and in some of which there were open vats near the level of the floor, their peculiar trouble was that they fell into the vats; and when they were fished out, there was never enough of them left to be worth exhibiting—sometimes they would be overlooked for days, till all but the bones of them had gone out to the world as Durham's Pure Leaf Lard!

*　*　*　*　*

Early in the fall Jurgis set out for Chicago again. All the joy went out of tramping as soon as a man could not keep warm in the hay; and, like many thousands of others, he deluded himself with the hope that by coming early he could avoid the rush. He brought fifteen dollars with him, hidden away in one of his shoes, a sum which had been saved from the saloon-keepers, not so much by his conscience, as by the fear which filled him at the thought of being out of work in the city in the wintertime.

He traveled upon the railroad with several other men, hiding in freight cars at night, and liable to be thrown off at any time, regardless of the speed of the train. When he reached the city he left the rest, for he had money and they did not, and he meant to save himself in this fight. He would bring to it all the skill that practice had brought him, and he would stand, whoever fell. On fair nights he would sleep in the park or on a truck or an empty barrel or box, and when it was rainy or cold he would stow himself upon a shelf in a ten-cent lodging-house, or pay three cents for the privileges of a "squatter" in a tenement hallway. He would eat at free lunches, five cents a meal, and never a cent more—so he might keep alive for two months and more, and in that time he would surely find a job. He would have to bid farewell to his summer cleanliness, of course, for he would come out of the first night's lodging with his clothes alive with vermin. There was no place in the city where he could wash even his face, unless he went down to the lake front—and there it would soon be all ice.

First he went to the steel mill and the harvester works, and found that his places there had been filled long ago. He was careful to keep away from the stockyards—he was a single man now, he told himself, and he meant to stay one, to have his wages for his own when he got a job. He began the long, weary round of factories and warehouses, tramping all day, from one end of the city to the other, finding everywhere from ten to a hundred men ahead of him. He watched the newspapers, too—but no longer was he to be taken in by the smooth-spoken agents. He had been told of all those tricks while "on the road."

In the end it was through a newspaper that he got a job, after nearly a month of seeking. It was a call for a hundred laborers, and though he thought it was a "fake," he went because the place was near by. He found a line of men a block long, but as a wagon chanced to come out of an alley and break the line, he saw his chance and sprang to seize a place. Men threatened him and tried to throw him out, but he cursed and made a disturbance to attract a policeman, upon which they subsided, knowing that if the latter interfered it would be to "fire" them all.

An hour or two later he entered a room and confronted a big Irishman behind a desk.

"Ever worked in Chicago before?" the man inquired; and whether it was a good angel that put it into Jurgis's mind, or an intuition of his sharpened wits, he was moved to answer, "no, sir."

"Where do you come from?"

"Kansas City, sir."

"Any references?"

"No sir. I'm just an unskilled man, I've got good arms."

"I want men for hard work—it's all underground, digging tunnels for telephones. Maybe it won't suit you."

"I'm willing, sir—anything for me. What's the pay?"

"Fifteen cents an hour."

"I'm willing, sir."

"All right; go back there and give your name."

So within half an hour he was at work, far underneath the streets of the city. The tunnel was a peculiar one for telephone wires; it was about eight feet high, and with a level floor nearly as wide. It had innumerable branches—a perfect spider-web beneath the city; Jurgis walked over half a mile with his gang to the place where they were to work. Stranger yet, the tunnel was lighted by electricity, and upon it was laid a double-tracked, narrow gauge railroad!

But Jurgis was not there to ask questions, and he did not give the matter a thought. It was nearly a year afterward that he finally learned the meaning of this whole affair. The City Council had passed a quiet and innocent little bill allowing a company to construct telephone conduits under the city streets; and upon the strength of this, a great corporation had proceeded to tunnel all Chicago with a system of railway freight subways. In the city there was a combination of employers, representing hundreds of millions of capital, and formed for the purpose of crushing the labor unions. The chief union which troubled it was the teamsters'; and when these freight tunnels were completed, connecting all the big factories and stores with the railroad depots, they would have the teamsters' union by the throat. Now and then there were rumors and murmurs in the Board of Aldermen, and once there was a committee to investigate—but each time another small fortune was paid over, and the rumors died away; until at last the city woke up with a start to find the work completed. There was a tremendous scandal, of course; it was found that the city records had been falsified and other crimes committed, and some of Chicago's big capitalists got into jail—figuratively speaking. The aldermen declared that they had had no idea of it all, in spite of the fact that the main entrance to the work had been in the rear of the saloon of one of them. . . .

In a work thus carried out, not much thought was given to the welfare of the laborers. On an average, the tunneling cost a life a day and several manglings; it was seldom, however, that more than a dozen or two men heard of any one accident. The work was all done by the new boring-machinery, with as little blasting as possible; but there would be falling rocks and crushed supports and premature explosions—and in addition all the dangers of railroading. So it was that one night, as Jurgis was on his way out with his gang, an engine and a loaded car dashed round one of the innumerable right-angle branches and struck him upon the shoulder, hurling him against the concrete wall and knocking him senseless.

When he opened his eyes again it was to the clanging of the bell of an ambulance. He was lying in it, covered by a blanket, and it was heading its way slowly through the holiday-shopping crowds. They took him to the county hospital, where a young surgeon set his arm, then he was washed and laid upon a bed in a ward with a score or two more of maimed and mangled men.

18

✧

THE MANAGERIAL SPIRIT

Mass production involved two steps: the substitution of machines for the human hand in manufacturing; and the substitution of steam, electric, or other nonanimal power for human energy to drive the machines. The place where these two things occurred was the factory. Factories first appeared in the New England textile industry of the early nineteenth century. By 1900 they were the chief feature of the urban landscape, dominating every industry from meatpacking, steel, and clothing to paper, cigarettes, and automobiles. Factories had reached huge proportions, with thousands of workers—"hands"—in many places.

In spite of the best efforts of industrialists to simplify and mechanize the processes of production, human labor remained a central element in manufacturing. This was especially true where workers possessed skills that could not easily be mechanized or where unions were strong enough to resist management authority. It was true as well in the case of the unskilled laborer unwilling or unable to perform rote tasks efficiently. The human element was also a central concern in large nonmanufacturing businesses, such as department stores, mail-order houses, insurance firms, and telegraph companies, which employed clerical and white-collar workers away from the shop floor.

A great interest therefore arose in management technique and theory, an interest that led to the establishment of schools of business administration, the appearance of management journals, and the emergence of management consultants. By far the most important management theory of the period took the form of the "scientific management" principles of Frederick W. Taylor. Taylor was an industrial engineer who believed it was possible to establish more realistic times for doing most industrial tasks, thus reducing labor-management friction and boosting productivity. Taylor's system involved time-and-motion studies, analysis of work flows, divided foremanship, and other techniques. The following passage from Taylor's writing conveys his perspective on the workplace, including his inclination to break down work into more and more detailed and minute tasks.

Born in 1856 in Germantown, Pennsylvania, Frederick Taylor apprenticed at several factories, eventually becoming chief engineer in a steel mill. In the mill, he began to take notes on worker tasks and output. Concluding that bosses usually expected too much from workers, he devised better machinery and also systematized the time allotted for every task in the making of steel. Productivity at the mill rose sharply, and Taylor's ideas quickly spread throughout industrial America, including Bethlehem Steel Company and other corporate giants. Notorious in some labor circles for saying that a "first-class man is the same as a first-class horse" and for making other remarks considered demeaning, Taylor resigned his management post to devote himself to popularizing his ideas on industrial engineering and administration. The titles of his books suggest the tenor and focus of his thinking: *Note on Belting* (1893), *The Adjustment of Wages to Efficiency* (1896), *Shop Management* (1903), *On the Art of Cutting Metals* (1906), and *The Principles of Scientific Management* (1911). Taylor died in Philadelphia in 1915.

Questions to Consider. Even though "Taylorism" was widely identified with efficiency devices such as time-and-motion study and premium-and-bonus systems, he took great pains to say that scientific management was more than this. What larger principle was he trying to assert? Why do you think managers generally liked Taylor's ideas more than workers did, even though he argued that his methods would benefit everyone?

———————— ✧ ————————

Scientific Management (1911)

FREDERICK TAYLOR

Modern engineering can almost be called an exact science; each year removes it further from guess work and from rule-of-thumb methods and establishes it more firmly upon the foundation of fixed principles.

The writer feels that management is also destined to become more of an art, and that many of the elements which are now believed to be outside the field of exact knowledge will soon be standardized, tabulated, accepted, and used, as are now many of the elements of engineering. Management will be studied as an art and will rest upon well recognized, clearly defined, and fixed principles instead of depending upon more or less hazy ideas received from a limited observation of the few organizations with which the individual may have come in contact. There will, of course, be various

From Frederick Winslow Taylor, *Scientific Management* (Harper & Bros., New York and London, 1911), 63–72.

successful types, and the application of the underlying principles must be modified to suit each particular case. The writer has already indicated that he thinks the first object in management is to unite high wages with a low labor cost. He believes that this object can be most easily attained by the application of the following principles:

(*a*) A LARGE DAILY TASK.—Each man in the establishment, high or low, should daily have a clearly defined task laid out before him. This task should not in the least degree be vague or indefinite, but should be circumscribed carefully and completely, and should not be easy to accomplish.

(*b*) STANDARD CONDITIONS.—Each man's task should call for a full day's work, and at the same time the workman should be given such standardized conditions and appliances as will enable him to accomplish his task with certainty.

(*c*) HIGH PAY FOR SUCCESS.—He should be sure of large pay when he accomplishes his task.

(*d*) LOSS IN CASE OF FAILURE.—When he fails he should be sure that sooner or later he will be the loser by it.

When an establishment has reached an advanced state of organization, in many cases a fifth element should be added, namely: the task should be made so difficult that it can only be accomplished by a first-class man.

There is nothing new nor startling about any of these principles and yet it will be difficult to find a shop in which they are not daily violated over and over again. They call, however, for a greater departure from the ordinary types of organization than would at first appear. In the case, for instance, of a machine shop doing miscellaneous work, in order to assign daily to each man a carefully measured task, a special planning department is required to lay out all of the work at least one day ahead. All orders must be given to the men in detail in writing; and in order to lay out the next day's work and plan the entire progress of work through the shop, daily returns must be made by the men to the planning department in writing, showing just what has been done. Before each casting or forging arrives in the shop the exact route which it is to take from machine to machine should be laid out. An instruction card for each operation must be written out stating in detail just how each operation on every piece of work is to be done and the time required to do it, the drawing number, any special tools, jigs, or appliances required, etc. Before the four principles above referred to can be successfully applied it is also necessary in most shops to make important physical changes. All of the small details in the shop, which are usually regarded as of little importance and are left to be regulated according to the individual taste of the workman, or, at best, of the foreman, must be thoroughly and carefully standardized; such details, for instance, as the care and tightening of the belts; the exact shape and quality of each cutting tool; the establishment of a complete tool room from which properly ground tools, as well as jigs, templets, drawings, etc., are issued under a good check system, etc.; and as a matter of importance (in fact, as the foundation of scientific management) an accurate study of unit times must be made by one or more men connected with the planning department, and each machine tool must be standardized and a table or slide rule constructed for it showing how to run it to the best advantage.

At first view the running of a planning department, together with the other innovations, would appear to involve a large amount of additional work and expense, and the most natural question would be whether the increased efficiency of the shop more than offsets this outlay? It must be borne in mind, however, that, with the exception of the study of unit times, there is hardly a single item of work done in the planning department which is not already being done in the shop. Establishing a planning department merely concentrates the planning and much other brainwork in a few men especially fitted for their task and trained in their especial lines, instead of having it done, as heretofore, in most cases by high priced mechanics, well fitted to work at their trades, but poorly trained for work more or less clerical in its nature. . . .

The writer, while still a young man, had all lingering doubt as to the value of a drafting room dispelled by seeing the chief engineer, the foreman of the machine shop, the foreman of the foundry, and one or two workmen, in one of our large and successful engineering establishments of the old school, stand over the cylinder of an engine which was being built, with chalk and dividers, and discuss for more than an hour the proper size and location of the studs for fastening on the cylinder head. This was simplicity, but not economy. About the same time he became thoroughly convinced of the necessity and economy of a planning department with time study, and with written instruction cards and returns. He saw over and over again a workman shut down his machine and hunt up the foreman to inquire, perhaps, what work to put into his machine next, and then chase around the shop to find it or to have a special tool or templet looked up or made. He saw workmen carefully nursing their jobs by the hour and doing next to nothing to avoid making a record, and he was even more forcibly convinced of the necessity for a change while he was still working as a machinist by being ordered by the other men to slow down to half speed under penalty of being thrown over the fence.

No one now doubts the economy of the drafting room, and the writer predicts that in a very few years from now no one will doubt the economy and necessity of the study of unit times and of the planning department. . . .

There is no question that the average individual accomplishes the most when he either gives himself, or some one else assigns him, a definite task, namely, a given amount of work which he must do within a given time; and the more elementary the mind and character of the individual the more necessary does it become that each task shall extend over a short period of time only. No school teacher would think of telling children in a general way to study a certain book or subject. It is practically universal to assign each day a definite lesson beginning on one specified page and line and ending on another; and the best progress is made when the conditions are such that a definite study hour or period can be assigned in which the lesson must be learned. Most of us remain, through a great part of our lives, in this respect, grown-up children, and do our best only under pressure of a task of comparatively short duration.

Another and perhaps equally great advantage of assigning a daily task as against ordinary piece work lies in the fact that the success of a good workman or the failure of a poor one is thereby daily and prominently called to the attention of the management. Many a poor workman might be willing to go along in a slipshod way under ordinary piece work, careless as to whether he fell off a little in his output or not. Very few of them, however, would be willing to record a daily failure to accomplish their task even if they were allowed to do so by their foreman; and also since on ordinary piece work the price alone is specified without limiting the time which the job is to take, a quite large falling off in output can in many cases occur without coming to the attention of the management at all. It is for these reasons that the writer has above indicated "a large daily task" for each man as the first of four principles which should be included in the best type of management. . . .

The four principles above referred to can be successfully applied either under day work, piece work, task work with a bonus, or differential rate piece work, and each of these systems has its own especial conditions under which it is to be preferred to either of the other three. In no case, however, should an attempt be made to apply these principles unless accurate and thorough time study has previously been made of every item entering into the day's task.

They should be applied under day work only when a number of miscellaneous jobs have to be done day after day, none of which can occupy the entire time of a man throughout the whole of a day and when the time required to do each of these small jobs is likely to vary somewhat each day. In this case a number of these jobs can be grouped into a daily task which should be assigned, if practicable, to one man, possibly even to two or three, but rarely to a gang of men of any size. To illustrate: In a small boiler house in which there is no storage room for coal, the work of wheeling the coal to the fireman, wheeling out the ashes, helping clean fires and keeping the boiler room and the outside of the boilers clean can be made into the daily task for a man, and if these items do not sum up into a full day's work, on the average, other duties can be added until a proper task is assured. Or, the various details of sweeping, cleaning, and keeping a certain section of a shop floor windows, machines, etc., in order can be united to form a task. Or, in a small factory which turns out a uniform product and in uniform quantities day after day, supplying raw materials to certain parts of the factory and removing finished product from others may be coupled with other definite duties to form a task. The task should call for a large day's work, and the man should be paid more than the usual day's pay so that the position will be sought for by first-class, ambitious men. Clerical work can very properly be done by the task in this way, although when there is enough of it, piece work at so much per entry is to be preferred.

In all cases a clear cut, definite inspection of the task is desirable at least once a day and sometimes twice. When a shop is not running at night, a good time for this inspection is at seven o'clock in the morning, for instance. The inspector should daily sign a printed card, stating that he has inspected the work done by——, and enumerating the various items of the task. The card should state that the workman has satisfactorily performed his task, "except the following items," which should be enumerated in detail.

Doughboys home from the Great War. (UPI/Bettmann Newsphotos)

CHAPTER FOUR

Empire and Uplift

19

✧

THE LURE OF THE EAST

The United States went to war with Spain over Cuba in 1898. But the U.S. victory in the brief war brought acquisitions in the Pacific (the Philippines and Guam) as well as in the Caribbean (Puerto Rico): at this time the United States also got control of the Hawaiian Islands and Wake Island. In part these acquisitions represented the resumption of a long tradition of westward territorial expansion that had been abandoned since the purchase of Alaska in 1867. In part they represented America's desire for "great power" status at a time when the European nations were winning colonies in Asia and Africa. But powerful economic forces were at work, too, as they had been in the formulation of the recent Open Door policy or, for that matter, in President James Monroe's assertion of his famous Doctrine in 1823.

At the beginning of the war, President William McKinley was unsure himself whether or not the United States should take over the Philippines, and if it did, whether its forces would take only Manila, or the whole island of Luzon, or the entire archipelago. Not until December 1898 did the president finally announce that the United States would pursue a policy of "benevolent assimilation" toward the whole territory. This decision gave rise to a small but vocal anti-imperialist movement at home and, more important, a strong Filipino resistance struggle against the American occupation.

At this point, however, forceful advocates of imperialism rose to defend the president in the most vigorous terms. Of these none was more forceful or more important than Senator Albert J. Beveridge. His Senate speech of January 1900 in support of a (successful) resolution urging colonial status for the Philippines, excerpted below, provided the broadest possible grounds for the president's policy. With the fight thus in hand at home, McKinley turned to winning the fight abroad. Having made his decision, moreover, he stuck doggedly with it. In fact, the Americans overcame the insurgents only after another year's hard fighting and the death of more than a hundred thousand Filipinos.

President McKinley's ally and fellow Ohioan, Albert Beveridge, was only thirty-seven at the time of his imperialist speech of 1900, but he was already known as a proponent of military strength and Anglo-Saxon supremacy. This speech further enhanced his standing in Republican circles. Beveridge left the Senate in 1912 to devote himself to writing. In 1919, eight years before his death in Indiana, his *Life of John Marshall* was awarded the Pulitzer Prize for historical biography.

Questions to Consider. Beveridge's speech makes enormous claims for the strategic importance of the Philippines. On what grounds did Beveridge make these claims? Has history borne out Beveridge's predictions about the Pacific Ocean and world commerce? Did Beveridge think acquiring the Philippines would increase or reduce the chances of war? How did he seem to view the Declaration of Independence and the Constitution? Was Beveridge's main concern economics or race?

❖

America's Destiny (1900)

ALBERT BEVERIDGE

Mr. President, the times call for candor. The Philippines are ours forever, "territory belonging to the United States," as the Constitution calls them. And just beyond the Philippines are China's illimitable markets. We will not retreat from either. We will not repudiate our duty in the archipelago. We will not abandon our opportunity in the Orient. We will not renounce our part in the mission of our race, trustee, under God, of the civilization of the world. And we will move forward to our work, not howling out regrets like slaves whipped to their burdens, but with gratitude for a task worthy of our strength, and thanksgiving to Almighty God that He has marked us as His chosen people, henceforth to lead in the regeneration of the world.

This island empire is the last land left in all the oceans. If it should prove a mistake to abandon it, the blunder once made would be irretrievable. If it proves a mistake to hold it, the error can be corrected when we will. Every other progressive nation stands ready to relieve us.

But to hold it will be no mistake. Our largest trade henceforth must be with Asia. The Pacific is our ocean. More and more Europe will manufacture the most it needs, secure from its colonies the most it consumes. Where shall we turn for consumers of our surplus? Geography answers the question. China is our natural customer. She is nearer to us than to England, Germany, or Russia, the commercial powers of the present and the future.

From the *Congressional Record,* 56th Congress, 1st session, 704–712.

They have moved nearer to China by securing permanent bases on her borders. The Philippines give us a base at the door of all the East.

Lines of navigation from our ports to the Orient and Australia; from the Isthmian Canal to Asia; from all Oriental ports to Australia, converge at and separate from the Philippines. They are a self-supporting, dividend-paying fleet, permanently anchored at a spot selected by the strategy of Providence, commanding the Pacific. And the Pacific is the ocean of the commerce of the future. Most future wars will be conflicts for commerce. The power that rules the Pacific, therefore, is the power that rules the world. And, with the Philippines, that power is and will forever be the American Republic. . . .

Nothing is so natural as trade with one's neighbors. The Philippines make us the nearest neighbors of all the East. Nothing is more natural than to trade with those you know. This is the philosophy of all advertising. The Philippines bring us permanently face to face with the most sought-for customers of the world. National prestige, national propinquity, these and commercial activity are the elements of commercial success. The Philippines give the first; the character of the American people supply the last. It is a providential conjunction of all the elements of trade, of duty, and of power. If we are willing to go to war rather than let England have a few feet of frozen Alaska, which affords no market and commands none, what should we not do rather than let England, Germany, Russia, or Japan have all the Philippines? And no man on the spot can fail to see that this would be their fate if we retired. . . .

Here, then, Senators, is the situation. Two years ago there was no land in all the world which we could occupy for any purpose. Our commerce was daily turning toward the Orient, and geography and trade developments made necessary our commercial empire over the Pacific. And in that ocean we had no commercial, naval, or military base. Today we have one of the three great ocean possessions of the globe, located at the most commanding commercial, naval, and military points in the eastern seas, within hail of India, shoulder to shoulder with China, richer in its own resources than any equal body of land on the entire globe, and peopled by a race which civilization demands shall be improved. Shall we abandon it? That man little knows the common people of the Republic, little understands the instincts of our race, who thinks we will not hold it fast and hold it forever, administering just government by simplest methods. We may trick up devices to shift our burden and lessen our opportunity; they will avail us nothing but delay. We may tangle conditions by applying academic arrangements of self-government to a crude situation; their failure will drive us to our duty in the end. . . .

But, Senators, it would be better to abandon this combined garden and Gibraltar of the Pacific, and count our blood and treasure already spent a profitable loss, than to apply any academic arrangement of self-government to these children. They are not capable of self-government. How could they be? They are not of a self-governing race. They are Orientals, Malays, instructed by Spaniards in the latter's worst estate.

They know nothing of practical government except as they have witnessed the weak, corrupt, cruel, and capricious rule of Spain. What magic will anyone employ to dissolve in their minds and characters those impressions of governors and governed which three centuries of misrule have created? What alchemy will change the oriental quality of their blood and set the self-governing currents of the American pouring through their Malay veins? How shall they, in the twinkling of an eye, be exalted to the heights of self-governing peoples which required a thousand years for us to reach, Anglo-Saxon though we are . . . ?

The Declaration of Independence does not forbid us to do our part in the regeneration of the world. If it did, the Declaration would be wrong, just as the Articles of Confederation, drafted by the very same men who signed the Declaration, was found to be wrong. The Declaration has no application to the present situation. It was written by self-governing men for self-governing men. . . .

Senators in opposition are stopped from denying our constitutional power to govern the Philippines as circumstances may demand, for such power is admitted in the case of Florida, Louisiana, Alaska. How, then, is it denied in the Philippines? Is there a geographical interpretation to the Constitution? Do degrees of longitude fix constitutional limitations? Does a thousand miles of ocean diminish constitutional power more than a thousand miles of land . . . ?

No; the oceans are not limitations of the power which the Constitution expressly gives Congress to govern all territory the nation may acquire. The Constitution declares that "Congress shall have power to dispose of and make all needful rules and regulations respecting the territory belonging to the United States." . . .

Mr. President, this question is deeper than any question of party politics; deeper than any question of the isolated policy of our country even; deeper even than any question of constitutional power. It is elemental. It is racial. God has not been preparing the English-speaking and Teutonic peoples for a thousand years for nothing but vain and idle self-contemplation and self-admiration. No! He has made us the master organizers of the world to establish system where chaos reigns. He has given us the spirit of progress to overwhelm the forces of reaction throughout the earth. He has made us adepts in government that we may administer government among savage and senile peoples. Were it not for such a force as this the world would relapse into barbarism and night. And of all our race He has marked the American people as His chosen nation to finally lead in the regeneration of the world. This is the divine mission of America, and it holds for us all the profit, all the glory, all the happiness possible to man. We are trustees of the world's progress, guardians of its righteous peace. The judgment of the Master is upon us: "Ye have been faithful over a few things; I will make you ruler over many things."

What shall history say of us? Shall it say that we renounced that holy trust, left the savage to his base condition, the wilderness to the reign of waste, deserted duty, abandoned glory, forgot our sordid profit even, because we feared our strength and read the charter of our powers with the doubter's eye and the quibbler's mind? Shall it say that, called by events to captain and command the proudest, ablest, purest race of history in history's noblest work, we declined that great commission? Our fathers would not have had it so. No! They founded no paralytic government, incapable of the simplest acts of administration. They planted no sluggard people, passive while the world's work calls them. They established no reactionary nation. They unfurled no retreating flag. . . .

Mr. President and Senators, adopt the resolution offered, that peace may quickly come and that we may begin our saving, regenerating, and uplifting work. . . . Reject it, and the world, history, and the American people will know where to forever fix the awful responsibility for the consequences that will surely follow such failure to do our manifest duty. . . .

20

✧

GUNBOAT DIPLOMACY

Although the Monroe Doctrine of 1823 had proclaimed a special interest in Latin American affairs, it was neither militaristic nor especially interventionist in spirit. But the Spanish-American War signaled a new military and economic aggressiveness in Washington and a new determination to assert the country's diplomatic ambitions. It was perhaps inevitable, therefore, that President Theodore Roosevelt should modify the Monroe Doctrine to provide a rationale for direct intervention by armed force on behalf of "progress" and "responsible government."

A hero of the U.S. Army's recent Cuban campaign against Spain and an admirer of Admiral George Dewey, victor in the Battle of Manila, Roosevelt urged a policy of expanding the country's military might. Advising the United States to "speak softly and carry a big stick," Roosevelt believed the United States should act as the policeman of Central America and the Caribbean. This role was especially necessary, he explained in the following 1905 message to Congress on the Dominican Republic, in cases where European powers might intervene to protect investments. Roosevelt seems to have won his argument. During the first twenty-five years of the twentieth century, the United States sent troops into Latin American countries on sixteen different occasions (including twice to the Dominican Republic).

Theodore Roosevelt, who inaugurated this era of "gunboat diplomacy," was born to well-to-do parents in New York City in 1858. After college he juggled politics, writing, ranching, and hunting, until McKinley appointed him assistant secretary of the navy in 1897. He resigned in 1898 to lead a cavalry unit called the Rough Riders in Cuba, but he returned to win the governorship of New York in 1899 and 1900. He moved on to the vice-presidency in 1901 and, in that same year, to the presidency when McKinley was assassinated. Over the next ten years Roosevelt promised a "square deal" and a "new nationalism," both embodying his notions of social and military progress. In 1912 he bolted the Republican party to head a Progressive ticket that lost to Woodrow Wilson, a Democrat whose internationalism Roosevelt relentlessly castigated until his death in 1919.

Questions to Consider. In what ways did Roosevelt's justification of U.S. intervention in the Caribbean differ from Senator Albert Beveridge's argument for seizing the Philippines? What role did Europe play in shaping U.S. policy in the area? What impression of Central America and the Caribbean did Roosevelt convey in this message? Did he establish any limits on the right of the United States to intervene in Latin American affairs? Who would decide when intervention was warranted or would cease? Given the likely increase in U.S. investment in the area in future years, was U.S. intervention also likely to increase?

Message on the Caribbean (1905)

THEODORE ROOSEVELT

The conditions in the Republic of Santo Domingo [Dominican Republic] have been growing steadily worse for many years. There have been many disturbances and revolutions, and debts have been contracted beyond the power of the Republic to pay. Some of these debts were properly contracted and are held by those who have a legitimate right to their money. Others are without question improper or exorbitant, constituting claims which should never be paid in full and perhaps only to the extent of a very small portion of their nominal value.

Certain foreign countries have long felt themselves aggrieved because of the nonpayment of debts due their citizens. The only way by which foreign creditors could ever obtain from the Republic itself any guaranty of payment would be either by the acquisition of territory outright or temporarily, or else by taking possession of the custom-houses, which would of course in itself, in effect, be taking possession of a certain amount of territory.

It has for some time been obvious that those who profit by the Monroe Doctrine must accept certain responsibilities along with the rights which it confers; and that the same statement applies to those who uphold the doctrine. It can not be too often and too emphatically asserted that the United States has not the slightest desire for territorial aggrandizement at the expense of any of its southern neighbors, and will not treat the Monroe Doctrine as an excuse for such aggrandizement on its part. We do not propose to take any part of Santo Domingo, or exercise any other control over the island save what is necessary to its financial rehabilitation in connection with the collection of revenue, part of which will be turned over to the Government to meet the necessary expense of running it, and

From Theodore Roosevelt, *Presidential Addresses and State Papers* (New York, 1910), III: 241–260.

Theodore Roosevelt. Roosevelt inspects the construction of the Panama Canal, a critical feature of TR's vision of the United States as a Great Power and a dominant commercial and military force in the Caribbean, Central America, and the Pacific. (Brown Brothers)

part of which will be distributed pro rata among the creditors of the Republic upon a basis of absolute equity. The justification for the United States taking this burden and incurring this responsibility is to be found in the fact that it is incompatible with international equity for the United States to refuse to allow other powers to take the only means at their disposal of satisfying the claims of their creditors and yet to refuse, itself, to take any such steps.

An aggrieved nation can without interfering with the Monroe Doctrine take what action it sees fit in the adjustment of its disputes with American

States, provided that action does not take the shape of interference with their form of government or of the despoilment of their territory under any disguise. But, short of this, when the question is one of a money claim, the only way which remains, finally, to collect it is a blockade, or bombardment, or the seizure of the custom-houses, and this means, as has been said above, what is in effect a possession, even though only a temporary possession, of territory. The United States then becomes a party in interest, because under the Monroe Doctrine it can not see any European power seize and permanently occupy the territory of one of these Republics; and yet such seizure of territory, disguised or undisguised, may eventually offer the only way in which the power in question can collect any debts, unless there is interference on the part of the United States.

One of the difficult and increasingly complicated problems, which often arise in Santo Domingo, grows out of the violations of contracts and concessions, sometimes improvidently granted, with valuable privileges and exemptions stipulated for upon grossly inadequate considerations which were burdensome to the State, and which are not infrequently disregarded and violated by the governing authorities. . . . There are Governments which do sometimes take energetic action for the protection of their subjects in the enforcement of merely contractual claims, and thereupon American concessionaires, supported by powerful influences, make loud appeal to the United States Government in similar cases for similar action. They complain that in the actual posture of affairs their valuable properties are practically confiscated, that American enterprise is paralyzed, and that unless they are fully protected even by the enforcement of their merely contractual rights, it means the abandonment to the subjects of other Governments of the interests of American trade and commerce through the sacrifice of their investments. . . .

The conditions in the Dominican Republic not only constitute a menace to our relations with other foreign nations, but they also concern the prosperity of the people of the island, as well as the security of American interests, and they are intimately associated with the interests of the South Atlantic and Gulf States, the normal expansion of whose commerce lies in that direction. At one time, and that only a year ago, three revolutions were in progress in the island at the same time. . . .

If the United States Government declines to take action and other foreign Governments resort to action to secure payment of their claims, the latter would be entitled . . . to the preferential payment of their claims; and this would absorb all the Dominican revenues and would be a virtual sacrifice of American claims and interests in the island. If moreover, any such action should be taken by them, the only method to enable them to secure the payment of their claims would be to take possession of the custom-houses, and considering the state of the Dominican finances this would mean a definite and very possibly permanent occupation of Dominican territory. . . .

The United States Government could not interfere to prevent such seizure and occupation of Dominican territory without either itself proposing some feasible alternative in the way of action, or else virtually saying to European Governments that they would not be allowed to collect their claims. This would be an unfortunate attitude for the Government of the United States to be forced to maintain at present. It can not with propriety say that it will protect its own citizens and interests, on the one hand, and yet on the other hand refuse to allow other Governments to protect their citizens and interests. . . .

The ordinary resources of diplomacy and international arbitration are absolutely impotent to deal wisely and effectively with the situation in the Dominican Republic. . . . Either we must abandon our duty under our traditional policy toward the Dominican people, who aspire to a republican form of government while they are actually drifting into a condition of permanent anarchy, in which case we must permit some other Government to adopt its own measures in order to safeguard its own interests, or else we must ourselves take reasonable and appropriate action. . . .

I call attention to the urgent need of prompt action on this matter. We now have a great opportunity to secure peace and stability in the island, without friction or bloodshed, by acting in accordance with the cordial invitation of the governmental authorities themselves. It will be unfortunate from every standpoint if we fail to grasp this opportunity; for such failure will probably mean increasing revolutionary violence in Santo Domingo, and very possibly embarrassing foreign complications in addition. This protocol affords a practical test of the efficiency of the United States Government in maintaining the Monroe Doctrine.

21

◈

CITY LIGHTS

Progressivism was a powerful force in turn-of-the century America. Progressives believed in efficiency, so they fought to reform the civil service and to make government as effective and accountable as private business. They believed that capital, labor, and government should work together, so they urged the mediation of labor conflicts and the regulation of giant corporations. Believing in citizen participation, Progressives pioneered women's suffrage, the secret ballot, and the removal from office of corrupt officials by popular vote. Concerned with the suffering poor, Progressives promoted charity work, better public schools, university extension service, and better housing. They thought saloons and liquor caused trouble, so they struggled for prohibition. Most Progressives were educated, middle-class, native-born Protestants who felt uneasy around corporate greed and slum violence; they could be both self-righteous and narrow-minded. But they cared about the country. They were confident they could change things, and tried energetically to do just that. As President Theodore Roosevelt once cried on their behalf, "We stand at Armageddon and do battle for the Lord."

Settlement houses were quintessential Progressive institutions. Established throughout urban America between 1880 and 1920, settlement houses—largely the handiwork of women reformers—arose to serve the vast swarm of newcomers to the country's great cities. These new "settlers" were European immigrants for the most part, but they also included recent arrivals, black and white, from the rural South. The settlement houses provided meeting halls. The staffs sponsored lectures, encouraged political participation and sometimes union activity, taught English classes, agitated for tighter health codes, and held citizenship and naturalization classes. These early social workers paid special attention to the problems of poor women and inevitably, therefore, to the problems of immigrant families.

Urban youth were a particular concern of the settlements. Settlement workers labored ceaselessly for child labor laws, more playgrounds, better schools. They worked to heal the generation gap between immigrant parents clinging to older ways and children rejecting everything old and old-fashioned, including the parents. The social workers tried to explain the new land to these children and to give them a smattering of self-improvement and urban survival skills. The following excerpt was written by Jane Addams, founder of Chicago's Hull House and in 1909 probably the country's most illustrious woman—almost certainly its most famous reformer. She did settlement work to benefit local Chicagoans. She then used local Chicagoans as case studies to demonstrate how badly the industrial system was damaging urban youth and how the system might be counteracted. This approach understandably brought great credit to the settlement houses and also great prestige to the reformers. Eventually their influence spread from neighborhood to city to state to, at last, nation.

Jane Addams was born in 1860 into a small-town middle-class Illinois family. After her graduation from college in 1881, Addams visited Europe, where she became inspired by a pioneer English settlement house that worked with the London poor. By 1889 she had founded a similar house in a ramshackle Chicago mansion. Addams attracted numerous bright, dedicated young women to work with her, including Florence Kelley, later an Illinois factory inspector, and Mary Kenny, a labor organizer. Together the three made Hull House famous. Addams's writings and speeches helped spread its reputation. *The Spirit of Youth and the City Streets* alone sold twenty thousand copies, and Addams's autobiography far more. She received the Nobel Peace Prize in 1931, four years before her death.

Questions to Consider. Why did Addams see the theater as a serious urban problem, and how did she propose to combat it? Does her distinction between baseball and theater seem valid? How did she account for the popularity of saloons among youth? What would she offer as a substitute? What role did factory labor play in the lives of the urban youth described by Addams? How did factory labor affect their behavior? Did she propose fundamental changes? Do her alternatives seem realistic? Would the problems of the theater, the saloon, and the factory have affected small-town youth, too?

————————✧————————

The Spirit of Youth (1909)

JANE ADDAMS

This spring a group of young girls accustomed to the life of a five-cent theater, reluctantly refused an invitation to go to the country for a day's

From Jane Addams, *The Spirit of Youth and the City Streets* (The Macmillan Company, New York, 1909).

Jane Addams. Addams never used the words "adolescent" or "teenager." She thought the first too dry and academic; the second, slang. But it was this age group that most concerned her, as indeed it worried other adults of that period, who often wanted to pound delinquency out of the young by finger-wagging, confinement, and force. "Saint Jane" hoped to bury the bad tendencies of young people by giving their good ones a fighting chance. (Brown Brothers)

outing because the return on a late train would compel them to miss one evening's performance. They found it impossible to tear themselves away not only from the excitements of the theater itself but from the gaiety of the crowd of young men and girls invariably gathered outside discussing the sensational posters.

A steady English shopkeeper lately complained that unless he provided his four daughters with the money for the five-cent theaters every evening they would steal it from his till, and he feared that they might be driven to procure it in even more illicit ways. Because his entire family life had been thus disrupted he gloomily asserted that "this cheap show had ruined his 'ome and was the curse of America." This father was able to formulate the anxiety of many immigrant parents who are absolutely bewildered by the keen absorption of their children in the cheap theater. This anxiety is not, indeed, without foundation. An eminent alienist[1] of Chicago states that he has had a number of patients among neurotic children whose emotional natures have been so over-wrought by the crude appeal to which they had been so constantly subjected in the theaters, that they have become victims of hallucination and mental disorder. . . .

This testimony of a physician that the conditions are actually pathological, may at last induce us to bestir ourselves in regard to procuring a more wholesome form of public recreation. Many efforts in social amelioration have been undertaken only after such exposures; in the meantime, while the occasional child is driven distraught, a hundred children permanently injure their eyes watching the moving films, and hundreds more seriously model their conduct upon the standards set before them on this mimic stage.

Three boys, aged nine, eleven, and thirteen years, who had recently seen depicted the adventures of frontier life including the holding up of a stage coach and the lassoing of the driver, spent weeks planning to lasso, murder, and rob a neighborhood milkman, who started on his route at four o'clock in the morning. They made their headquarters in a barn and saved enough money to buy a revolver, adopting as their watchword the phrase "Dead Men Tell no Tales." . . . Fortunately for him, as the lariat was thrown the horse shied, and, although the shot was appropriately fired, the milkman's life was saved. Such a direct influence of the theater is by no means rare, even among older boys. Thirteen young lads were brought into the Municipal Court in Chicago during the first week that "Raffles, the Amateur Cracksman" was upon the stage, each one with an outfit of burglar's tools in his possession, and each one shamefacedly admitting that the gentlemanly burglar in the play had suggested to him a career of similar adventure.

In so far as the illusions of the theater succeed in giving youth the rest and recreation which comes from following a more primitive code of morality, it has a close relation to the function performed by public games. It is, of course, less valuable because the sense of participation is largely confined to the emotions and the imagination, and does not involve the entire nature. . . .

---

1. **Alienist:** psychiatrist.—*ed.*

Well considered public games easily carried out in a park or athletic field, might both fill the mind with the imaginative material constantly supplied by the theater, and also afford the activity which the cramped muscles of the town dweller so sorely need. Even the unquestioned ability which the theater possesses to bring men together into a common mood and to afford them a mutual topic of conversation, is better accomplished with the one national game which we already possess, and might be infinitely extended through the organization of other public games.

The theater even now by no means competes with the baseball league games which are attended by thousands of men and boys who, during the entire summer, discuss the respective standing of each nine and the relative merits of every player. During the noon hour all the employees of a city factory gather in the nearest vacant lot to cheer their own home team in its practice for the next game with the nine of a neighboring manufacturing establishment and on a Saturday afternoon the entire male population of the city betakes itself to the baseball field; the ordinary means of transportation are supplemented by gay stage-coaches and huge automobiles, noisy with blowing horns and decked with gay pennants. The enormous crowd of cheering men and boys are talkative, good-natured, full of the holiday spirit, and absolutely released from the grind of life. They are lifted out of their individual affairs and so fused together that a man cannot tell whether it is his own shout or another's that fills his ears; whether it is his own coat or another's that he is wildly waving to celebrate a victory. He does not call the stranger who sits next to him his "brother" but he unconsciously embraces him in an overwhelming outburst of kindly feeling when the favorite player makes a home run. Does not this contain a suggestion of the undoubted power of public recreation to bring together all classes of a community in the modern city unhappily so full of devices for keeping men apart? . . .

We are only beginning to understand what might be done through the festival, the street procession, the band of marching musicians, orchestral music in public squares or parks, with the magic power they all possess to formulate the sense of companionship and solidarity. . . .

As it is possible to establish a connection between the lack of public reaction and the vicious excitements and trivial amusements which become their substitutes, so it may be illuminating to trace the connection between the monotony and dullness of factory work and the petty immoralities which are often the youth's protest against them.

There are many city neighborhoods in which practically every young person who has attained the age of fourteen years enters a factory. When the work itself offers nothing of interest, and when no public provision is made for recreation, the situation becomes almost insupportable to the youth whose ancestors have been rough-working and hard-playing peasants.

In such neighborhoods the joy of youth is well nigh extinguished; and in that long procession of factory workers, each morning and evening, the young walk almost as wearily and listlessly as the old. Young people working in modern factories situated in cities still dominated by the ideals of Puritanism face a combination which tends almost irresistibly to overwhelm the spirit of youth. When the Puritan repression of pleasure was in the ascendant in America the people it dealt with lived on farms and villages where, although youthful pleasures might be frowned upon and crushed out, the young people still had a chance to find self-expression in their work. Plowing the field and spinning the flax could be carried on with a certain joyousness and vigor which the organization of modern industry too often precludes. Present industry based upon the inventions of the nineteenth century has little connection with the old patterns in which men have worked for generations. The modern factory calls for an expenditure of nervous energy almost more than it demands muscular effort, or at least machinery so far performs the work of the massive muscles, that greater stress is laid upon fine and exact movements necessarily involving nervous strain. But these movements are exactly of the type to which the muscles of a growing boy least readily respond, quite as the admonition to be accurate and faithful is that which appeals the least to his big primitive emotions. . . .

In vast regions of the city which are completely dominated by the factory, it is as if the development of industry had outrun all the educational and social arrangements.

The revolt of youth against uniformity and the necessity of following careful directions laid down by some one else, many times results in such nervous irritability that the youth, in spite of all sorts of prudential reasons, "throws up his job," if only to get outside the factory walls into the freer street, just as the narrowness of the school inclosure induces many a boy to jump the fence.

When the boy is on the street, however, and is "standing around on the corner" with the gang to which he mysteriously attaches himself, he finds the difficulties of direct untrammeled action almost as great there as they were in the factory, but for an entirely different set of reasons. The necessity so strongly felt in the factory for an outlet to his sudden and furious bursts of energy, his overmastering desire to prove that he could do things "without being bossed all the time," finds little chance for expression, for he discovers that in whatever really active pursuit he tries to engage, he is promptly suppressed by the police. . . .

The unjustifiable lack of educational supervision during the first years of factory work makes it quite impossible for the modern educator to offer any real assistance to young people during that trying transitional period between school and industry. The young people themselves who fail to conform can do little but rebel against the entire situation.

There are many touching stories by which this might be illustrated. One of them comes from a large steel mill of a boy of fifteen whose business it was to throw a lever when a small tank became filled with molten metal. During the few moments when the tank was filling it was his foolish custom to catch the reflection of the metal upon a piece of looking-glass, and to throw the bit of light into the eyes of his fellow workmen. Although an exasperated foreman had twice dispossessed him of his mirror, with a third fragment he was one day flicking the gloom of the shop when the neglected tank overflowed, almost instantly burning off both his legs. Boys working in the stock yards, during their moments of wrestling and rough play, often slash each other painfully with the short knives which they use in their work, but in spite of this the play impulse is too irrepressible to be denied. . . .

The discovery of the labor power of youth was to our age like the discovery of a new natural resource, although it was merely incidental to the invention of modern machinery and the consequent subdivision of labor. In utilizing it thus ruthlessly we are not only in danger of quenching the divine fire of youth, but we are imperiling industry itself when we venture to ignore these very sources of beauty, of variety and of suggestion.

22

✧

THE WAR FOR DEMOCRACY

Woodrow Wilson won the presidency in 1912 on behalf of a "new freedom," a program involving lower tariffs, banking reform, antitrust legislation, and, in foreign policy, the repudiation of Theodore Roosevelt's gunboat diplomacy. Even after sending troops to various Caribbean countries and to Mexico, Wilson claimed that his main concern was to promote peace and democracy in the world. When World War I erupted in Europe, Wilson saw the war as the result of imperialistic rivalries ("a war with which we have nothing to do") and urged, despite personal sympathy with Great Britain, that the United States stay neutral so as to influence the peace negotiations. Wilson won reelection in 1916 largely on a promise to keep the country out of war. But a combination of pro-British propaganda in American newspapers and German submarine attacks on American ships proved formidable, and in April 1917, Wilson finally requested a declaration of war in the following address to Congress. The sweeping, visionary arguments of this remarkable speech shaped not only America's expectations about the war itself but also attitudes about the proper U.S. role in international affairs for years to come.

Born in 1856 in Virginia, Woodrow Wilson grew up in the South; his father was a Presbyterian minister. He attended Princeton and Johns Hopkins, where he earned a doctorate, and began to write and teach in the field of constitutional government and politics. He gained national stature while president of Princeton from 1902 until 1910; he became the Democratic governor of New Jersey in 1911 and, two years later, president of the United States. Wilson's main objective at the peace conference after World War I was to create a League of Nations to help keep the peace. In 1919 during an intensive speechmaking campaign to arouse public support for the League, Wilson suffered a debilitating stroke. He died in Washington, D.C., in 1924.

Questions to Consider. Note, in reading the following message, that although Woodrow Wilson believed in the unique and superior character of American institutions, he was willing to enter into alliances with European powers. What were the four principal grounds on which

Wilson was willing to reverse the American diplomatic tradition? Which of these did he seem to take most seriously? Were there other American interests that he might have stressed but did not? What reasons might Wilson have had for stressing so strongly America's attachment to Germany's people as opposed to its government? Might Wilson's arguments and rhetoric have served to prolong rather than to shorten the war?

✧

Address to Congress (1917)

WOODROW WILSON

I have called the Congress into extraordinary session because there are serious, very serious choices of policy to be made, and made immediately, which it was neither right nor constitutionally permissible that I should assume the responsibility of making.

On the third of February last I officially laid before you the extraordinary announcement of the Imperial German Government that on and after the first day of February it was its purpose to put aside all restraints of law or of humanity and use its submarines to sink every vessel that sought to approach either the ports of Great Britain and Ireland or the western coasts of Europe or any of the ports controlled by the enemies of Germany within the Mediterranean. . . .

I was for a little while unable to believe that such things would in fact be done by any government that had hitherto subscribed to the humane practices of civilized nations. International law had its origin in the attempt to set up some law which would be respected and observed upon the seas, where no nation had right of dominion and where lay the free highways of the world. . . . This minimum of right the German Government has swept aside under the plea of retaliation and necessity and because it had no weapons which it could use at sea except these which it is impossible to employ as it is employing them without throwing to the winds all scruples of humanity or of respect for all understandings that were supposed to underlie the intercourse of the world. I am not now thinking of the loss of property involved, immense and serious as that is, but only of the wanton and wholesale destruction of the lives of non-combatants, men, women, and children, engaged in pursuits which have always, even in the darkest periods of modern history, been deemed innocent and legitimate. Property can be paid for; the lives of peaceful and innocent people cannot

From *The New York Times*, April 3, 1917.

be. The present German submarine warfare against commerce is a warfare against mankind.

It is a war against all nations. American ships have been sunk, American lives taken, in ways which it has stirred us very deeply to learn of, but the ships and people of other neutral and friendly nations have been sunk and overwhelmed in the waters in the way. There has been no discrimination. The challenge is to all mankind. Each nation must decide for itself how it will meet it. The choice we make for ourselves must be made with a moderation of counsel and a temperateness of judgement befitting our character and our motives as a nation. We must put excited feeling away. Our motive will not be revenge or the victorious assertion of the physical might of the nation, but only the vindication of right, of human right, of which we are only a single champion. . . .

With a profound sense of the solemn and even tragical character of the step I am taking and of the grave responsibilities which it involves, but in unhesitating obedience to what I deem my constitutional duty, I advise that the Congress declare the recent course of the Imperial German Government to be in fact nothing less than war against the government and people of the United States; that it formally accept the status of belligerent which has thus been thrust upon it; and that it take immediate steps not only to put the country in a more thorough state of defense but also to exert all its power and employ all its resources to bring the Government of the German Empire to terms and end the war. . . .

We have no quarrel with the German people. We have no feeling towards them but one of sympathy and friendship. It was not upon their impulse that their government acted in entering this war. It was not with their previous knowledge or approval. It was a war determined upon as wars used to be determined upon in the old, unhappy days when peoples were nowhere consulted by their rulers and wars were provoked and waged in the interest of dynasties or of little groups of ambitious men who were accustomed to use their fellow men as pawns and tools. . . .

We are accepting this challenge of hostile purpose because we know that in such a Government, following such methods, we can never have a friend; and that in the presence of its organized power, always lying in wait to accomplish we know not what purpose, there can be no assured security for the democratic Governments of the world. We are now about to accept gauge of battle with this natural foe to liberty and shall, if necessary, spend the whole force of the nation to check and nullify its pretensions and its power. We are glad, now that we see the facts with no veil of false pretense about them, to fight thus for the ultimate peace of the world and for the liberation of its peoples, the German peoples included: for the rights of nations great and small and the privilege of men everywhere to choose their way of life and of obedience. The world must be made safe for democracy. Its peace must be planted upon the tested foundations of political liberty. We have no selfish ends to serve. We desire no conquest, no dominion. We seek no indemnities for ourselves, no material compensation for the sacrifices we shall freely make. We are but one of the champions of the rights of mankind. We shall be satisfied when those rights have been made as secure as the faith and the freedom of nations can make them. . . .

It will be all the easier for us to conduct ourselves as belligerents in a high spirit of right and fairness because we act without animus, not in enmity towards a people or with the desire to bring any injury or disadvantage upon them, but only in armed opposition to an irresponsible government which has thrown aside all considerations of humanity and of right and is running amuck. We are, let me say again, the sincere friends of the German people, and shall desire nothing so much as the early reestablishment of intimate relations of mutual advantage between us,—however hard it may be for them, for the time being, to believe that this is spoken from our hearts. We have borne with their present Government through all these bitter months because of that friendship,—exercising a patience and forbearance which would otherwise have been impossible. We shall, happily, still have an opportunity to prove that friendship in our daily attitude and actions towards the millions of men and women of German birth and native sympathy who live amongst us and share our life, and we shall be proud to prove it towards all who are in fact loyal to their neighbors and to the Government in the hour of test. They are, most of them, as true and loyal Americans as if they had never known any other fealty of allegiance. They will be prompt to stand with us in rebuking and restraining the few who may be of a different mind and purpose. If there should be disloyalty, it will be dealt with with a firm hand of stern repression; but, if it lifts its head at all, it will lift it only here and there and without countenance except from a lawless and malignant few.

It is a distressing and oppressive duty, Gentlemen of the Congress, which I have performed in thus addressing you. There are, it may be, many months of fiery trial and sacrifice ahead of us. It is a fearful thing to lead this great peaceful people into war, into the most terrible and disastrous of all wars, civilization itself seeming to be in the balance. But the right is more precious than peace, and we shall fight for the things which we have always carried nearest our hearts,—for democracy, for the right of those who submit to authority to have a voice in their own Governments, for the rights and liberties of small nations, for a universal dominion of right by such a concert of free peoples as shall bring peace and safety to all nations and make the world itself at last free. To such a task we can dedicate our lives and our fortunes, everything that we have, with the pride of those who know that the day has come when America is privileged to spend her blood and her might for the principles that gave her birth and happiness and the peace which she has treasured. God helping her, she can do no other.

23

✧

SKEPTICS

Many Americans found great glory in World War I. After all, the dough-boys, as the American infantrymen were called, had turned the tide against Germany, and John ("Black Jack") Pershing, commander of the U.S. forces, emerged from the conflict a national hero. But the human price had been stiff: 100,000 Americans dead and 200,000 wounded. American casualties in World War I were low compared with European casualties (almost 2 million Germans and 1 million British died) or with U.S. losses in the Civil War (600,000) or in World War II (400,000). But the American losses were hardly insignificant, particularly since the country was in the war for only eighteen months and mobilized only about 4 million men. Much of the dying occurred in the appalling conditions of the Argonne Forest, where years of trenching and shelling had created a veritable wasteland of death.

Justifying such remarkable carnage would have taken remarkable results—something on the order of the new international order that Woodrow Wilson had promised. But this, of course, the president had not been able to deliver, not even his own country's membership in the League of Nations. So the skepticism that had attended U.S. entry into the war persisted, engendering a somber, even cynical mood beneath the boisterous patriotic surface. One source of this dark mood was the *Chicago Tribune,* which was the most influential newspaper in the Midwest and contained persistent editorials criticizing Wilsonian interventionism. The *Tribune* editorial of November 13, 1921, reprinted below, is in response to a wave of recrimination, social unrest, and small-scale military skirmishes in Europe and also the growing European calls for U.S. financial aid. This editorial is an expression of characteristic midwestern Republican views on the foolishness of idealism, the evils of European politics, and the folly of war.

A variant of these views also pervaded the major fiction of the period. Many writers of the early twentieth century were probably predisposed to skepticism about the war effort because they felt alienated and estranged from "bourgeois" America, with its perpetual striving for status and possessions, and some had pacifist leanings even before the United States entered World War I in 1917. Actual participation in the war confirmed the pacifist inclinations of several writers. Such books as E.E. Cummings's *The Enormous Room,* John Dos Passos's *Three Soldiers,* William Faulkner's *Soldier's Pay,* and Ernest Hemingway's *A Farewell to Arms* depicted the war as murderous and meaningless. Hemingway worked the war most deeply into his fiction. The excerpts below come from *In Our Time,* a collection of stories both about the war and about life in upstate Michigan strung together with brief mood-setting paragraphs; all the paragraphs reprinted here are this kind of paragraph, each with its own characters and locale. Hemingway wrote in a spare, detached style that was widely imitated in the postwar years and won him almost as much acclaim as his plots and characters. The disillusionment that pervaded his work was imitated, too, so much so that finally it seemed almost incredible that the United States could have participated in the war. Americans who sought an explanation for U.S. entry in World War I increasingly found some mixture of self-righteousness, bumbling stupidity, and the machinations of the arms dealers, and resolved never to go to war again—and did not until Pearl Harbor.

The editor and publisher of the *Chicago Tribune* when the editorial below was published was Robert R. McCormick, a graduate of Yale University and Northwestern University's law school and nephew of Cyrus H. McCormick of mechanical reaper fame. Forty-one years old in 1921, Robert McCormick had already held political office in Chicago and served as both a *Tribune* war correspondent and an artillery officer in France. Under McCormick's direction the *Tribune* company had a fivefold increase in newspaper circulation and also had acquired vast nonnewspaper business holdings. McCormick died in Illinois in 1955, with his formidable suspicions of idealists and Europeans still intact. His fellow Chicagoan, Ernest Hemingway, was born in 1899 into a middle-class family. Having skipped college to become a newspaper reporter, he spent the war years with a volunteer ambulance unit in Italy and after the war joined the growing colony of expatriate Americans in Paris. Hemingway received the Nobel Prize for Literature in 1954. He died at his home in Ketchum, Idaho, in 1961.

Questions to Consider. The 1921 *Tribune* editorial painted a gloomy picture of European conditions three years after the end of the war. Does the editorial seem to express surprise at this state of affairs? What or whom did the writer hold most responsible? Had the war, then, been utterly futile and valueless? What actions did the writer advise the United States to take, or not to take? With whom was the editorial arguing? In the Hemingway paragraphs, does the dominant mood seem to be anger, pity, or sarcasm? Are there any common features in these Hemingway scenes? Why might people of the 1920s have found them startling, even shocking? Do they still have shock power?

❖

Unregenerate Europe (1921)

THE CHICAGO TRIBUNE

It is natural that pacifists and excited humanitarians should stress the evil consequences of the world war at this time. It is equally natural that foreign statesmen and public agencies should join them in keeping this phase of the European situation [of famine and insurrections] before us. It gives a tremendous momentum to the pacifist propaganda, and it relieves the governments and peoples of Europe of a large part of their responsibility for the present condition of their affairs.

One the western front. American machine gunners searching out pockets of resistance in the German defenses during the costly U.S. offensive of summer 1918. (Bilderdienst Suddeutscher Verlag)

But the American mind should clear itself on this point. No one will deny that the war is responsible directly for a vast wastage of life and property. But what needs recognition and emphasis at this moment . . . is that had common sense and self-control governed the policies of the governments and the sentiments of the peoples of Europe their affairs would not be tottering now on the rim of chaos.

On the contrary, were there wisdom and courage in the statesmanship of Europe, were there the same selfless devotion in chancelleries and parliaments as was exhibited on the battlefield, Europe would have been today well on the way to recovery.

The expenditures of the war and the intensification of long existing animosities and jealousies undoubtedly have complicated the problems of statecraft and of government. Undoubtedly the temporary depletion of man power and the temporary exhaustion of body and spirit among the war worn peoples were a burden which recovery has had to assume. Undoubtedly the wastage of wealth and diversion of productive agencies were a handicap to expeditious restoration.

But that these are chiefly responsible for the present state of Europe we do not admit and the future judgment of history, we are confident, will deny.

It is chiefly the folly which has been persistently demonstrated by governments and people since the war that is responsible for Europe's condition today. It is because the moment hostilities ceased and the enemy was disarmed, victors and vanquished turned their backs on the healing and constructive principles they had solemnly asserted from time to time when matters were going against them at the battle front, that the European nations almost without exception have been going down hill. There never in history has been a more perfect illustration of the ancient sarcasm: "When the devil is sick, the devil a monk would be; when the devil is well, the devil a monk is he."

If we wish to know why Europe is in the present state, we cannot do better than to draw a parallel between the assertions of purpose and principle of the allies and "associated" powers in 1916, '17, and '18, and what has actually happened since Nov. 11, 1918.

The war was a gigantic folly and waste. No one will deny that. But it was not so foolish nor so wasteful as the peace which has followed it. The European governments, those who come at our invitation and those who remain away, would have us believe they are mere victims of the war. They say nothing of what the war did for them. We might remind them that they profited as well as lost by the war. Many of them were freed from age long tyranny. They got rid of kaisers and saber clattering aristocracies. They were given freedom, and their present state shows how little they have known how to profit by it. They have been given new territories and new resources, and they have shown how little they deserve their good fortune. The last three years in Europe have been given not to sane efforts to heal wounds, remove hostilities, develop cooperation for the common economic restoration which is essential to the life of each. On the contrary, they have been marked by new wars and destruction, by new animosities and rivalries, by a refusal to face facts, make necessary sacrifices and compromises for financial and economic recovery, by greedy grabbing of territory and new adventures in the very imperialism which brought about the war.

It is well for Americans and their representatives to keep this in mind. The appeal to America's disinterestedness is unfairly fortified by the assumption that Europe is the innocent victim of one egotist's or one nation's ruthless ambition. We can take due account of the disastrous effects of the Prussian effort at dominance, but that should not overshadow the stubborn errors which began over again on the very threshold of peace, and which have made the peace more destructive than the war. When the European governments and peoples are ready to make a real peace, which cannot arrive until they give over the policies and attitudes that produced the world war, America will then not fail to give generous aid. But America would be foolish to contribute to the support of present methods or give any encouragement to the spirit which now prevails in the old world.

In Our Time (1925)

ERNEST HEMINGWAY

Minarets stuck up in the rain out of Adrianople [Turkey] across the mud flats. The carts were jammed for thirty miles along the Karagatch road. Water buffalo and cattle were hauling carts through the mud. There was no end and no beginning. Just carts loaded with everything they owned. The old men and women, soaked through, walked along keeping the cattle moving. The Maritza [River] was running yellow almost up to the bridge. Carts were jammed solid on the bridge with camels bobbing along through them. Greek cavalry herded along the procession. The women and children were in the carts, crouched with mattresses, mirrors, sewing machines, bundles. There was a woman having a baby with a young girl holding a blanket over her and crying. Scared sick looking at it. It rained all through the evacuation.

*

We were in a garden in Mons [Belgium]. Young Buckley came in with his patrol from across the river. The first German I saw climbed up over the garden wall. We waited till he got one leg over and then potted him. He had so much equipment on and looked awfully surprised and fell down into the garden. Then three more came over further down the wall. We shot them. They all came just like that.

*

It was a frightfully hot day. We'd jammed an absolutely perfect barricade across the bridge. It was simply priceless. A big old wrought-iron grating from the front of a house. Too heavy to lift and you could shoot through it and they would have to climb over it. It was absolutely topping. They tried to get over it, and we potted them from forty yards. They rushed it, and officers came out alone and worked on it. It was an absolutely perfect obstacle. Their officers were very fine. We were frightfully put out when we heard the flank had gone, and we had to fall back.

*

They shot the six cabinet ministers at half-past six in the morning against the wall of a hospital. There were pools of water in the courtyard. There were wet dead leaves on the paving of the courtyard. It rained hard. All the shutters of the hospital were nailed shut. One of the ministers was sick with typhoid. Two soldiers carried him downstairs and out into the rain. They tried to hold him up against the wall but he sat down in a puddle of water. The other five stood very quietly against the wall. Finally the officer told the soldiers it was no good trying to make him stand up. When they fired the first volley he was sitting down in the water with his head on his knees.

*

Nick sat against the wall of the church where they had dragged him to be clear of machine gun fire in the street. Both legs stuck out awkwardly. He had been hit in the spine. His face was sweaty and dirty. The sun shone on his face. The day was very hot. Rinaldi, big backed, his equipment sprawling, lay face downward against the wall. Nick looked straight ahead brilliantly. The pink wall of the house opposite had fallen out from the roof, and an iron bedstead hung twisted toward the street. Two Austrian dead lay in the rubble in the shade of the house. Up the street were other dead. Things were getting forward in the town. It was going well. Stretcher bearers would be along any time now. Nick turned his head and looked down at Rinaldi. "Senta Rinaldo; Senta. You and me we've made a separate peace." Rinaldi lay still in the sun, breathing with difficulty. "We're not patriots." Nick turned his head away, smiling sweatily. Rinaldi was a disappointing audience.

*

While the bombardment was knocking the trench to pieces at Fossalta [Italy], he lay very flat and sweated and prayed, "Oh Jesus Christ get me out of here. Dear Jesus, please get me out. Christ, please, please, please, Christ. If you'll only keep me from getting killed I'll do anything you say. I believe in you and I'll tell everybody in the world that you are the only thing that matters. Please, please, dear Jesus." The shelling moved further up the line. We went to work on the trench and in the morning the sun came up and the day was hot and muggy and cheerful and quiet. The next night back at Mestre he did not tell the girl he went upstairs with at the Villa Rossa about Jesus. And he never told anybody.

24

✦

SALESMANSHIP

In the conclusion of *The Great Gatsby,* F. Scott Fitzgerald summed up the dissipation, extravagance, and spiritual sterility of the post–World War I generation:

They were careless people, Tom and Daisy—they smashed up things and creatures and then retreated back into their money or their vast carelessness, or whatever it was that kept them together, and let other people clean up the mess they had made. . . .

Gatsby believed in the green light, the orgiastic future that year by year recedes before us. It eluded us then, but that's no matter—tomorrow we will run faster, stretch out our arms farther. . . . And one fine morning—

Other great novelists and poets wrote about the "sad young men" and women of the Jazz Age, and though each looked at life through a unique lens, they shared a similar disenchantment with society's obsession with business, money, and material success. "The business of America is business," Calvin Coolidge declared, but he struck a responsive chord in the citizenry with that statement and was an extremely popular president.

Obsession with business was all but "orgiastic" in the 1920s. Beginning in 1922 the United States experienced an era of tremendous economic expansion and unprecedented prosperity. The country's industrial output more than doubled, per capita income increased by one-third, and there was almost no inflation. The use of labor-saving devices such as refrigerators, vacuum cleaners, and washing machines became widespread, and millions of Americans purchased automobiles on readily available credit. The United States had become a "consumer culture."

Nevertheless, production levels were so high that consumers were unable to buy all the products that industry produced, and new markets had to be created. It was in this climate that the advertising industry came of age. Among the most successful "ad men" of the era was Bruce Barton, chairman of the board of the New York advertising agency Batten, Barton, Durstine & Osborne, and author of an immensely popular book, part of which is reproduced below. In *The Man Nobody Knows,* Barton portrayed Jesus Christ as a salesman—not an ordinary salesman, but the world's greatest salesman—and exhorted his readers to profit by his example. Barton wrote:

Only strong magnetic men inspire great enthusiasm and build great organizations. Yet Jesus built the greatest organization of all. . . . He picked up twelve men from the bottom ranks of business and forged them into an organization that conquered the world.

The story of the carpenter from Nazareth, Barton added, is "the story of the founder of modern business."

Barton was hardly alone in his sentiments. A contemporary observed:

The sanest religion is business. Any relationship that forces a man to follow the Golden Rule rightfully belongs amid the ceremonials of the church. A great business enterprise includes and presupposes this relationship.

Meanwhile, by the time he died in 1925, Russell H. Conwell, a Baptist minister, had delivered his lecture, "Acres of Diamonds," more than six thousand times and had touched millions of readers. "Money is power, and you ought to be reasonably ambitious to have it," he preached. "If you can honestly attain unto riches . . . it is your Christian and godly duty to do so."

Barton would have agreed. After all, as the head of a successful ad agency and the author of eight books with titles like *More Power to You* and *It's a Good Old World,* he had accumulated a small fortune. Having served as congressman from Tennessee, he died in 1967 at age eighty-one.

Questions to Consider. Is the author respectful of Jesus? Billy Sunday was a popular evangelist of the time. A church historian noted that "accompanying his contortions, furniture smashing, and partial undressing was an unbroken torrent of words. What the church needed . . . was fighting men of God, not 'hog-jowled, weasel-eyed, sponge-columned, mushy-fisted, jelly-spined, pussy-footing, four-flushing, Charlotte-russe Christians.' " Do you see a relationship between the approach of "vaudeville evangelists" like Sunday and the sales philosophy of Bruce Barton?

———————— ✦ ————————

The Man Nobody Knows (1925)

BRUCE BARTON

Jesus was, as we say, many-sided, and every man sees the side of His nature which appeals most to himself.

The doctor thinks of the great Physician whose touch never failed, who by the genius that remains a mystery to man preceded modern science in a knowledge of the relation of the spirit to health, a knowledge still incomplete. The preacher studies the Sermon on the Mount and marvels that truths so profound should be expressed in words so clear and simple. The politically active man remembers best His courage in opposing the most powerful elements in His community and is awed by His capacity to speak honestly without loss of loyalty. Lawyers have written in praise of His pleading at His trial; and the literary critics of every age have cheerfully acknowledged His mastery as a storyteller.

Each man, it is plain, understands that part of His universal genius which with his own abilities and skills he can most nearly approach. I am not a doctor or lawyer or critic but an advertising man. That means that I am and have been concerned with the ways in which words, design and color may carry conviction to people, with the art-science of bringing others to your point of view.

I propose in this chapter to consider some words and deeds of Jesus which persuaded and still persuade men of the wisdom and justice in His teaching. So I have, I hope, seen Jesus as a man who lived and worked, and not as the symbol conventionally displayed.

Let us begin by asking why He could command public attention and why, in contrast, His churches have not done so well. The answer is twofold. His mission was to teach men. But before even He could teach, He must get men to listen. He was never trite; He had no single method. The Gospels show clearly that no one could predict what He would say or do; His actions and words were always new, arresting, challenging and meaningful to the men among whom He lived. . . .

He was known by His service, not by His sermons; this is the noteworthy fact. His preaching seems in the light of such events almost incidental. On only one occasion did He deliver a long discourse, and that was probably interrupted often by questions and debates. He did not come to establish a theology but to lead a good life. Living more healthfully than any of His contemporaries, He spread health wherever He went. Thinking more daringly, more divinely, than anyone before Him, He expressed Himself in words of great beauty. His sermons, if they may be called sermons, were chiefly explanatory of His service. He healed a lame man, gave sight to a blind man, fed the hungry, cheered the poor; and by these works He was known.

The church, which hopes to spread widely the news of good work, often receives little attention. Yet it is much more fruitful in such good works than the uninformed suspect. . . .

These are Jesus' works, done in Jesus' name. If He lived again now, He would be known by His service, not merely by His sermons. One thing is certain: He would not neglect the market place. Few of His sermons were delivered in synagogues. For the most part He was in the crowded places— the Temple court, the city squares, the centers where goods were bought and sold. I emphasized this fact once to a group of preachers.

"You mean that we ought to do street preaching!" one of them exclaimed. . . .

No. Few ideas gain currency unless they may be presented simultaneously to hundreds of thousands. Magazines, newspapers, and radio networks are now the street in Capernaum. Here our goods are sold; here voices are raised to win our loyalty to ideas, to causes—to faiths. That the voice of Jesus should be still in our market place is an omission which He could soon find a way to correct. . . .

Benjamin Franklin in his autobiography tells the process which he went through in acquiring an effective style. He would read a passage from some great master of English, then lay the book aside and attempt to reproduce the thought in his own words. Comparing his version with the original, he discovered wherein he had obscured the thought or wasted words or failed to drive straight to the point. Every man who wishes to know a little more of Jesus should study the parables in the same fashion, schooling himself in their language and learning the elements of their power.

1. First of all they are marvelously condensed. . . .

Jesus had no introductions. A single sentence grips attention; three or four more tell the story; one or two more and both the thought and its application are clear. And this is true of ideas that reformed the moral structure of the world! When He wanted a new disciple, He said simply "Follow me." . . .

Two men spoke on the battleground of Gettysburg nearly a century ago. The first delivered an oration of more than two hours in length; not one person in ten who reads this page can even recall his name; certainly not one in a thousand can quote a single sentence from his masterly effort. The second speaker uttered two hundred and fifty words, and those words, Lincoln's Gettysburg Address, are a part of the mental endowment of almost every American. . . .

Jesus hated prosy dullness. He praised the Centurion who was anxious not to waste His time; the only prayer which He publicly commended was uttered by a poor publican who merely cried out, "God, be merciful to me a sinner." A seven-word prayer, and Jesus called it a good one. A sixty-six word prayer, He said, contained all that men needed to say or God to hear. What would be His verdict on most of our prayers and our speeches and our writing?

2. His language was marvelously simple—a second great essential. There is hardly a sentence in His teaching which a child cannot understand. His illustrations were all drawn from the commonest experiences of life: "a sower went forth to sow"; "a certain man had two sons"; "a man built his house on the sands"; "the kingdom of heaven is like a grain of mustard seed." . . .

Jesus used few qualifying words and no long ones. We referred a minute ago to those three literary masterpieces. The Lord's Prayer, The Twenty-third Psalm, The Gettysburg Address. Recall their phraseology:

Our Father which art in Heaven, hallowed be they name

The Lord is my shepherd; I shall not want

Four score and seven years ago

Not a single three-syllable word; hardly any two-syllable words. All the greatest things in human life are one-syllable things—love, joy, hope, home, child, wife, trust, faith, God—and the great pieces of writing, generally speaking, use the small word in place of the large if meaning permits.

3. Sincerity illuminates strongly every word, every sentence He uttered; sincerity is the third essential. Many wealthy men have purchased newspapers with the idea of advancing their personal fortunes or bringing about some political action in which they have a private interest. Such newspapers almost invariably fail. No matter how much money is spent on them, no matter how zealously the secret of their ownership is guarded, readers eventually become conscious that something is wrong. They come to feel that the voice of the editor is not his own.

It was the way Jesus looked at men, and the life He led among them, that gave His words transforming power. What He was and what He said were one and the same thing. Nobody could stand at His side for even a minute without being persuaded that here was a man who loved people and considered even the humblest of them worthy of the best He had to give. There is no presupposition more deadening to a writer than the idea that he can "write down" to his readers. . . .

Persuasion depends on respect for the listeners, and in Jesus great respect coupled with great love.

4. Finally Jesus knew that any idea may have to be repeated. . . .

It has been said that "reputation is repetition." No important truth can be impressed on the minds of any large number of people by being said only once. The thoughts which Jesus had to give the world were revolutionary, but they were few in number. "God is your father," He said, "caring more for the welfare of every one of you than any human father can possibly care for his children. His Kingdom is happiness! His rule is love." This is what He had to teach, and He knew the necessity of driving it home from every possible angle. So in one of His stories God is the Shepherd searching the wilds for one wandering sheep; in another the Father welcoming home a prodigal boy; in another a King who forgives his debtors large amounts and expects them to be forgiving in turn—many stories but the same big Idea.

Because the stories were unforgettable, the idea lived and is today one of the most powerful influences on human action and thought. To be sure the work is far from complete. The idea that God is the Father of all men—not merely of a specially selected few—has still to reach some areas and to establish its dominance in society. More or less unconsciously a lot of us share the feeling of the French nobleman in Saint Simon's immortal story, who was sure that God would "think twice before damning a person of his quality." . . .

Whoever feels an impulse to make his own life count in the grand process of human betterment can have no surer guide for his activities than Jesus. Let him learn the lesson of the parables: that in teaching people you first capture their interest; that your service rather than your sermons must be your claim on their attention; that what you say must be simple and brief and above all *sincere*.

25

✧

A PROGRESSIVE SPIRIT

The campaign for women's rights, which had begun before the Civil War, made painfully slow progress after the war. Most Americans continued to hold fast to the idea that a woman is weaker than a man and that her place is in the home caring for her husband and children. Age-old handicaps persisted: educational deprivation, legal discrimination, economic exploitation, and political disfranchisement. But veteran women's rights leaders like Elizabeth Cady Stanton carried on the struggle for equal rights undaunted, and energetic new reformers like Anna Howard Shaw joined their ranks. There was some progress in education: women's colleges appeared and the new state universities opened their doors to women. There was also some improvement in the legal status of married women. Yet the inequalities remained great. The number of women entering professions like law and medicine remained minuscule, and whenever women did obtain work outside the home they were vastly underpaid.

Some feminists argued that, with the ballot in their hands, American women would have a powerful weapon with which to fight for all their other rights. The suffragists sought action at both the federal and the state levels. Congress began considering suffrage proposals as early as 1868 but failed to adopt any of them. The states did somewhat better. In 1890 Wyoming entered the Union with woman suffrage, and a few years later Colorado, Utah, and Idaho followed suit. By 1914, eleven states, all but one in the West, had given women the right to vote, and in 1916 Montana sent the first woman, Jeannette Rankin, to Congress. By this time, Carrie Chapman Catt, successor to Susan B. Anthony as president of the National Woman Suffrage Association, and other suffragists had renewed their struggle for federal action. In 1919, at long last, Congress passed an amendment to the Constitution stating that the right of citizens to vote could not "be denied or abridged by the United States or by any state on account of sex." Ratification of the Nineteenth Amendment by the states was complete by August 1920, and American women were able to vote in the presidential election that November.

Meanwhile, the struggle for women's economic and social, as well as political, rights continued. The General Federation of Women's Clubs, founded in 1889, devoted considerable energy toward improving working conditions for women and children in industry. At the same time radical feminists like Margaret H. Sanger and Emma Goldman began sponsoring unrestricted dissemination of birth-control information. The birth-control advocates at first stressed economics: the gradual reduction in the size of the working class by means of birth control, they insisted, would increase labor's ability to bargain with the capitalists. But the birth-control movement took root among middle-class rather than working-class women and centered on individual self-fulfillment rather than social reconstruction. It would, they realized, liberate them from many restrictions of the traditional American home. But it was not until after the adoption of the Nineteenth Amendment that feminists began devoting major energies to the birth-control crusade.

From almost the crusade's beginning, the name of Margaret Sanger and the cause of birth control were synonymous. Sanger and her friends, in fact, invented the term *birth control.* Sanger was not the first advocate of planned parenthood, nor was she the only influential leader in the movement. But her effectiveness, both as speaker and writer, soon won her fame both in the United States and abroad.

Margaret Sanger, the sixth of eleven children, was born in Corning, New York, in 1883. She studied nursing as a young woman and became a maternity nurse serving in New York City's crowded Lower East Side. There she became aware of the poverty, misery, illness, and even death produced by involuntary pregnancies and self-induced abortions. She gave up nursing in 1912 to devote her full attention to the cause of birth control. In 1914 she founded the National Birth Control League and began publishing a magazine called *Woman Rebel,* which had the slogan "No Gods, No Masters" on the masthead. In 1915 she was indicted for sending birth-control literature through the mails and in 1916 arrested for operating a birth-control clinic in Brooklyn. During her brief prison stay she started a new magazine called the *Birth Control Review,* which was dedicated to the scientific control of human reproduction. After World War I, with the relaxation of laws forbidding doctors to prescribe contraceptives and give instruction in birth-control methods, she was able to open a birth-control clinic in Manhattan and to encourage the formation of similar clinics in other cities. She sponsored numerous national and international birth-control conferences and published many articles and books on birth control and sex education. She died in Tucson, Arizona, in 1966.

Questions to Consider. Among Sanger's many writings was a book entitled *Happiness in Marriage,* published in 1926 and centered on transforming marriage into a voluntary association. In the excerpt from the book reprinted below, Sanger expanded on the ways in which "premature parenthood" could wreck marriage. How did she think the "position of womanhood" had changed in the past few years? What did she mean by saying that social equality complicates as well as ennobles the marriage relationship? What objectives did she seek for American women, and why did she think birth control would help them achieve those objectives? How convincing do you think her argument was for people (and there were still many in the early twentieth century) who thought birth-control literature was obscene? Sanger was considered a radical in her day. Would she be called one today?

✦

Happiness in Marriage (1926)

MARGARET H. SANGER

We must recognize that the whole position of womanhood has changed today. Not so many years ago it was assumed to be a just and natural state of affairs that marriage was considered as nothing but a preliminary to motherhood. A girl passed from the guardianship of her father or nearest male relative to that of her husband. She had no will, no wishes of her own. Hers not to question why, but merely to fulfil duties imposed upon her by the man into whose care she was given.

Marriage was synonymous with maternity. But the pain, the suffering, the wrecked lives of women and children that such a system caused, show us that it did not work successfully. Like all other professions, motherhood must serve its period of apprenticeship.

Today women are on the whole much more individual. They possess as strong likes and dislikes as men. They live more and more on the plane of social equality with men. They are better companions. We should be glad that there is more enjoyable companionship and real friendship between men and women.

This very fact, it is true, complicates the marriage relation, and at the same time ennobles it. Marriage no longer means the slavish subservience of the woman to the will of the man. It means, instead, the union of two strong and highly individualized natures. Their first problem is to find out just what the terms of this partnership are to be. Understanding full and complete cannot come all at once, in one revealing flash. It takes time to arrive at a full and sympathetic understanding of each other, and mutually to arrange lives to increase this understanding. Out of the mutual adjustments, harmony must grow and discords gradually disappear.

From Margaret Sanger, *Happiness in Marriage* (Blue Ribbon Books, New York, 1926), 83–97. Reprinted by permission.

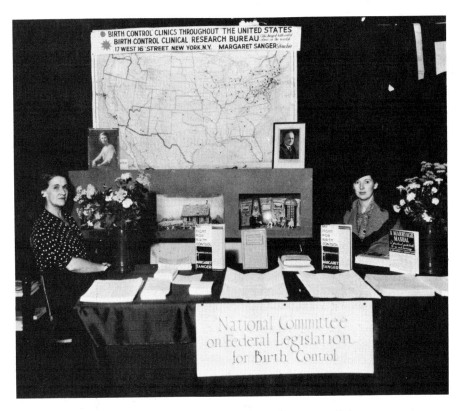

Margaret Sanger. Activists like Margaret Sanger provided a major impetus to social reform between 1900 and 1925. In these years, government spending on education and welfare at all levels rose by 1,000 percent to approximately $5 billion. The biggest increase came at the local level, and of this local increase, the bulk went for schooling. The number of child workers shrank drastically. So, too, did the burglary rate and the consumption of alcohol. Contraceptive use spread most rapidly among America's middle classes, whose symbol of the liberated woman became not the social activist but the flapper. This photograph shows Margaret Sanger (left) at the booth of the National Committee on Federal Legislation for Birth Control. (Library of Congress)

These results cannot be obtained if the problem of parenthood is thrust upon the young husband and wife before they are spiritually and economically prepared to meet it. For naturally the coming of the first baby means that all other problems must be thrust aside. That baby is a great fact, a reality that must be met. Preparations must be made for its coming. The layette must be prepared. The doctor must be consulted. The health of the wife may need consideration. The young mother will probably prefer to go to the hospital. All of these preparations are small compared to the regime after the coming of the infant.

Now there is a proper moment for every human activity, a proper season for every step in self-development. The period for cementing the bond of love is no exception to this great truth. For only by the full and glorious living through these years of early marriage are the foundations of an enduring and happy married life rendered possible. By this period the woman attains a spiritual freedom. Her womanhood has a chance to bloom. She wins a mastery over her destiny; she acquires self-reliance, poise, strength, a youthful maturity. She abolishes fear. Incidentally, few of us realize, since the world keeps no record of this fact, how many human beings are conceived in fear and even in repugnance by young mothers who are the victims of undesired maternity. Nor has science yet determined the possibilities of a generation conceived and born of conscious desire.

In the wife who has lived through a happy marriage, for whom the bonds of passionate love have been fully cemented, maternal desire is intensified and matured. Motherhood becomes for such a woman not a penalty or a punishment, but the road by which she travels onward toward completely rounded self-development. Motherhood thus helps her toward the unfolding and realization of her higher nature.

Her children are not mere accidents, the outcome of chance. When motherhood is a mere accident, as so often it is in the early years of careless or reckless marriages, a constant fear of pregnancy may poison the days and nights of the young mother. Her marriage is thus converted into a tragedy. Motherhood becomes for her a horror instead of a joyfully fulfilled function.

Millions of marriages have been blighted, not because of any lack of love between the young husband and wife, but because children have come too soon. Often these brides become mothers before they have reached even physical maturity, before they have completed the period of adolescence. This period in our race is as a rule complete around the age of twenty-three. Motherhood is possible after the first menstruation. But what is physically possible is very often from every other point of view inadvisable. A young woman should be fully matured from every point of view—physically, mentally and psychically—before maternity is thrust upon her.

Those who advise early maternity neglect the spiritual foundation upon which marriage must inevitably be built. This takes time. They also ignore the financial responsibility a family brings.

The young couple begin to build a home. They may have just enough to get along together. The young wife, as in so many cases of early marriage these days, decides to continue her work. They are partners in every way—a commendable thing. The young man is just beginning his career—his salary is probably small. Nevertheless, they manage to get along, their hardships are amusing, and are looked upon as fun. Then suddenly one day, the young wife announces her pregnancy. The situation changes immediately. There are added expenses. The wife must give up her work. The husband must go into debt to pay the expenses of the new and joyfully received arrival. The novelty lasts for some time. The young wife assumes the household duties and the ever growing care of the infant. For a time the child seems to bring the couple closer together. But more often there ensues a concealed resentment on the part of the immature mother at the constant drudgery and slavery to the unfortunate child who has arrived too early upon the scene, which has interfered with her love life.

Two brothers I know married practically at the same time. They were both carpenters, living in the same neighborhood. The wife of the one gave birth to six children in a period of ten years. In spite of the efforts of the man to sustain the family, they were forced at the end of ten years to accept outside charity. The wife became a household drudge, nervous, broken, spiritless, neglected by her husband, despised by her children. The wife of the other brother did not become a mother until three years after marriage. This man remained throughout the ten years of my observation, clean, alert, honest, kind to his wife and two children. The wife kept up neat, tidy looks and was able to help her husband and children to advance themselves. Yet at the time of marriage both girls were equally attractive and intelligent. . . .

For the unthinking husband, the "proud papa," the blushing bride is converted at once into the "mother of my children." It is not an unusual occurrence to find that three months after the birth of the baby, the parents are thinking and speaking to each other as "mumsy" and "daddy." The lover and sweetheart relation has disappeared forever and the "mama-papa" relation has taken its place.

Instead of being a self-determined and self-directing love, everything is henceforward determined by the sweet tyranny of the child. I have known of several young mothers, despite a great love for the child, to rebel against this intolerable situation. Vaguely feeling that this new maternity has rendered them unattractive to their husbands, slaves to a deadly routine of bottles, baths and washing, they have revolted. I know of innumerable marriages which have been wrecked by premature parenthood. . . .

For these reasons, in order that harmonious and happy marriage may be established as the foundation for happy homes and the advent of healthy and desired children, premature parenthood must be avoided. Birth Control is the instrument by which this universal problem may be solved.

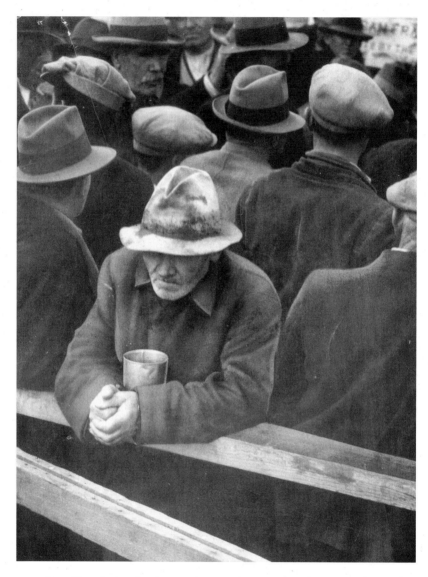

Breadline during the Depression. (Culver Pictures)

CHAPTER FIVE

Crisis and Hope

26

✧

AMERICAN EARTHQUAKE

American industrialization meant not only surging production but also periodic business "busts"—in the 1870s, the 1890s, 1907, and 1919–21. In each of these cases, prices, profits, and employment all plunged and remained low until the economy's basic strength pushed them again to higher levels. But no previous bust matched the Great Depression, which descended on the nation in the early 1930s. From 1929, when Herbert Hoover became the third consecutive Republican president since World War I, until 1933, when Franklin D. Roosevelt, a Democrat, succeeded him, the economy all but collapsed. Stocks and bonds lost three-fourths of their value, bank failures increased from five hundred to four thousand a year, farm income fell by half, and unemployment rose from 4 percent to almost 25 percent.

It was this last figure that most stunned and terrified ordinary Americans. There had been unemployment before, but never so much or for so long. And this joblessness was not limited to minorities or factory workers, as so often had been the case. The ranks of the destitute now included hundreds of thousands of white-collar workers, small businesspeople, and sharecroppers. Most disturbing of all, millions of women were now jobless and impoverished; many were homeless, with nowhere to turn. The country found it disquieting in the extreme.

People were aware of the massive human suffering of the Great Depression both because it was so widespread and because it was reported with such immediacy and attention to stark detail. Great fiction appeared, from Jack Conroy's *The Disinherited* at the beginning of the period to *The Grapes of Wrath,* John Steinbeck's epic of displaced Okies, at its end. Gripping photography and murals and innovative drama and poetry, glittering with unprecedented concreteness of detail, all depicted facets of the American ordeal. Journalism followed a similar path. Meridel LeSueur's article on Minnesota women, excerpted below, appeared in *New Masses,* a lively, irreverent Communist party literary journal that attracted and published much excellent social writing. In this case, the editors—staunch Stalinists—praised LeSueur's writing but also reproached her for defeatism and lack of "true revolutionary spirit."

Meridel LeSueur was born in 1900 in Iowa. Her grandfather was a Protestant fundamentalist temperance zealot; her father helped found

the Industrial Workers of the World. After high school LeSueur attended
the American Academy of Dramatic Art and worked in Hollywood as
an actress and stuntwoman in the 1920s. During the 1930s she lived
with her two children in Minneapolis while writing what a critic called
"luminous short stories" as well as articles on farmers and the unemployed, especially women. Hailed in the 1930s as a major writer, she
was blacklisted during the 1940s as a Communist sympathizer and
lived by writing children's books and women's articles under a pseud-
onym. One of the first writers to examine the lives of poor women,
her literary career revived during the 1970s with the emergence of
feminism. Between 1971 and 1985 twelve of her books, new and old,
appeared. She is currently working on three more—"my best writing,
the most living images, and a real chorale of my whole life and my
time."

Questions to Consider.   Who were the poor women LeSueur described
in "Women on the Breadlines"? What did they have in common besides
their poverty? Were they equally poor? Were their aspirations the same?
How did their gender affect their condition and behavior during the
Great Depression? How did they relate to one another, to authority
figures, and to men? In later years conservatives would attack LeSueur
for her radicalism. Can the reasons for these attacks be seen in this
article? When Stalinists of the 1930s attacked her for being too negative
and defeatist, were the attacks justified?

———————✧———————

Women on the Breadlines (1932)

MERIDEL LESUEUR

I am sitting in the city free employment bureau. It's the woman's section.
We have been sitting here now for four hours. We sit here every day,
waiting for a job. There are no jobs. Most of us have had no breakfast.
Some have had scant rations for over a year. Hunger makes a human being
lapse into a state of lethargy, especially city hunger. Is there any place else
in the world where a human being is supposed to go hungry amidst plenty
without an outcry, without protest, where only the boldest steal or kill for
bread, and the timid crawl the streets, hunger like the beak of a terrible
bird at the vitals?

We sit looking at the floor. No one dares think of the coming winter.
There are only a few more days of summer. Everyone is anxious to get

From *New Masses* (January 1932), 5–7.

A Dorothea Lange photograph of a country woman who had lost her home in the early years of the Great Depression. One of the foremost photographers of her time, Lange captured the pathos of the 1930s on film as brilliantly as Meridel LeSueur captured it in prose. (Dorothea Lange/Magnum Photos)

work to lay up something for that long siege of bitter cold. But there is no work. Sitting in the room we all know it. That is why we don't talk much. We look at the floor dreading to see that knowledge in each other's eyes. There is a kind of humiliation in it. We look away from each other. We look at the floor. It's too terrible to see this animal terror in each other's eyes.

So we sit hour after hour, day after day, waiting for a job to come in. There are many women for a single job. A thin sharp woman sits inside the wire cage looking at a book. For four hours we have watched her looking at that book. She has a hard little eye. In the small bare room there are half a dozen women sitting on the benches waiting. Many come and go. Our faces are all familiar to each other, for we wait here everyday.

This is a domestic employment bureau. Most of the women who come here are middle-aged, some have families, some have raised their families and are now alone, some have men who are out of work. Hard times and the man leaves to hunt for work. He doesn't find it. He drifts on. The woman probably doesn't hear from him for a long time. She expects it. She isn't surprised. She struggles alone to feed the many mouths. Sometimes she gets help from the charities. If she's clever she can get herself a good living from the charities, if she's naturally a lick-spittle, naturally a little docile and cunning. If she's proud then she starves silently, leaving her children to find work, coming home after a day's searching to wrestle with her house, her children.

Some such story is written on the faces of all these women. There are young girls too, fresh from the country. Some are made brazen too soon by the city. There is a great exodus of girls from the farms into the city now. Thousands of farms have been vacated completely in Minnesota. The girls are trying to get work. The prettier ones can get jobs in the stores when there are any, or waiting on table, but these jobs are only for the attractive and the adroit, the others, the real peasants, have a more difficult time. . . .

A young girl who went around with Ellen [a poor, attractive young woman] tells about seeing her last evening back of a cafe downtown outside the kitchen door, kicking, showing her legs so that the cook came out and gave her some food and some men gathered in the alley and threw small coin on the ground for a look at her legs. And the girl says enviously that Ellen had a swell breakfast and treated her to one too, that cost two dollars.

A scrub woman whose hips are bent forward from stooping with hands gnarled like water soaked branches clicks her tongue in disgust. No one saves their money, she says, a little money and these foolish young things buy a hat, a dollar for breakfast, a bright scarf. And they do. If you've ever been without money, or food, something very strange happens when you get a bit of money, a kind of madness. You don't care. You can't remember that you had no money before, that the money will be gone. You can remember nothing but that there is the money for which you have been suffering. Now here it is. A lust takes hold of you. You see food in the windows. In imagination you eat hugely; you taste a thousand meals. You look in windows. Colours are brighter; you buy something to dress up in. An excitement takes hold of you. You know it is suicide but you can't help it. You must have food, dainty, splendid food and a bright hat so once again you feel blithe, rid of that ratty gnawing shame.

"I guess she'll go on the street now," a thin woman says faintly and no one takes the trouble to comment further. Like every commodity now the body is difficult to sell and the girls say you're lucky if you get fifty cents. . . .

It's one of the great mysteries of the city where women go when they are out of work and hungry. There are not many women in the bread line. There are no flop houses for women as there are for men, where a bed can be had for a quarter or less. You don't see women lying on the floor at the mission in the free flops. They obviously don't sleep in the jungle or under newspapers in the park. There is no law I suppose against their being in these places but the fact is they rarely are.

Yet there must be as many women out of jobs in cities and suffering extreme poverty as there are men. What happens to them? Where do they go? Try to get into the Y.W. without any money or looking down at heel. Charities take care of very few and only those that are called "deserving." The lone girl is under suspicion by the virgin women who dispense charity.

I've lived in cities for many months broke, without help, too timid to get in bread lines. I've known many women to live like this until they simply faint on the street from privations, without saying a word to anyone. A woman will shut herself up in a room until it is taken away from her, and eat a cracker a day and be as quiet as a mouse so there are no social statistics concerning her. . . .

Sometimes a girl facing the night without shelter will approach a man for lodging. A woman always asks a man for help. Rarely another woman. I have known girls to sleep in men's rooms for the night, on a pallet without molestation, and given breakfast in the morning. . . .

Mrs. Grey, sitting across from me is a living spokesman for the futility of labour. She is a warning. Her hands are scarred with labour. Her body is a great puckered scar. She has given birth to six children, buried three, supported them all alive and dead, bearing them, burying them, feeding them. Bred in hunger they have been spare, susceptible to disease. For seven years she tried to save her boy's arm from amputation, diseased from tuberculosis of the bone. It is almost too suffocating to think of that long close horror of years of child bearing, child feeding, rearing, with the bare suffering of providing a meal and shelter.

Now she is fifty. Her children, economically insecure, are drifters. She never hears of them. She doesn't know if they are alive. She doesn't know if she is alive. Such subtleties of suffering are not for her. For her the brutality of hunger and cold, the bare bone of life. That is enough. These will occupy a life. Not until these are done away with can those subtle feelings that make a human being be indulged.

She is lucky to have five dollars ahead of her. That is her security. She has a tumour that she will die of. She is thin as a worn dime with her tumour sticking out of her side. She is brittle and bitter. Her face is not the face of a human being. She has born more than it is possible for a human being to bear. She is reduced to the least possible denominator of human feelings.

It is terrible to see her little bloodshot eyes like a beaten hound's, fearful in terror.

We cannot meet her eyes. When she looks at any of us we look away. She is like a woman drowning and we turn away. . . .

The young ones know though. I don't want to marry. I don't want any children. So they all say. No children. No marriage. They arm themselves alone, keep up alone. The man is helpless now. He cannot provide. If he propagates he cannot take care of his young. The means are not in his hands. So they live alone. Get what fun they can. The life risk is too horrible now. Defeat is too clearly written on it.

It is appalling to think that these women sitting so listless in the room may work as hard as it is possible for a human being to work, may labour night and day, like Mrs. Gray wash street cars from midnight to dawn and offices in the early evening, scrubbing for fourteen and fifteen hours a day, sleeping only five hours or so, doing this their whole lives, and never earn one day of security, having always before them the pit of the future. The endless labour, the bending back, the water soaked hands, earning never more than a week's wages, never having in their hands more life than that.

27

✦

THE POLITICS OF UPHEAVAL

There are cycles in American presidential politics. Of the first nine presidential elections, for instance, Jefferson's Democratic Republicans won seven, the Federalists two. The Democrats also won six of the next nine elections. Then a new cycle began in which the Republicans won seven of nine elections from 1860 to 1892 (versus just two for the once-mighty Democrats) and also won seven of the next nine, with their only setbacks coming at the hands of Woodrow Wilson in 1912 and 1916. At this point, the cataclysm of the Great Depression and the charisma of Franklin D. Roosevelt returned the Democrats to dominance. They won, often by landslide margins, every election from 1932 to 1964, except for two losses to Dwight Eisenhower in the 1950s. Since then, however, they have reverted to their post–Civil War form, enabling the Nixon-Reagan-Bush GOP to post a five-to-one score through 1988.

Given the magnitude of the Great Depression and Franklin D. Roosevelt's role in triggering so massive a political realignment, his inaugural address in 1933 might appear moderate. It calls for confidence, honest labor, the protection of agriculture and land, organized relief, and a bit of economic planning. Only Roosevelt's castigation of the "money changers" and his plea for executive authority to meet the crisis seemed to prefigure the sweeping liberalism that many observers instinctively associate with the Roosevelt years. Nevertheless, the address was charged with emotion and a sense of mission. Its moderation reflected both the confusion of the times, when few people understood the nation's problems and still fewer had solutions, and the personal conservatism of the speaker, who was ultimately American capitalism's savior as well as its reformer.

Franklin Delano Roosevelt, a distant cousin of Theodore Roosevelt, was born in 1882 to a wealthy New York family. He attended exclusive schools and colleges and practiced law in New York City. He married his cousin Eleanor in 1905, entered Democratic politics—serving in the state senate from 1910 to 1913—and became assistant secretary of the navy in 1913. After running (and losing) as the Democrats' vice-presidential candidate in 1920, he contracted polio, which left him permanently crippled. Remaining active in politics, he served as governor of New York from 1928 to 1932, when he defeated Hoover for the presidency. During the 1932 campaign Roosevelt criticized Hoover for excessive government spending and an unbalanced budget. Nevertheless, after entering the White House, Roosevelt also was obliged to adopt a spending policy to help those who were starving, put people to work, and revive the economy. His New Deal stressed economic recovery as well as relief and reform. Roosevelt's programs, backed by the great Democratic majorities that he forged, mitigated many of the effects of the Great Depression, though the slump never actually ended until the advent of World War II. Roosevelt achieved reelection in 1936, 1940, and 1944, a record unequaled then and unconstitutional since 1951. He died in office in Warm Springs, Georgia, in 1945.

Questions to Consider. Why, in his first inaugural address, did Roosevelt place great emphasis on candor, honesty, and truth. Did he display these qualities himself in discussing the crisis? In what ways did he try to reassure the American people? What reasons did he give for the Great Depression? What values did he think were important for sustaining the nation in a time of trouble? What solutions did he propose for meeting the economic crisis? How did he regard his authority to act under the Constitution? How would you have reacted to his address if you had been an unemployed worker, a hard-pressed farmer, or a middle-class citizen who had lost a home through foreclosure?

---◆---

First Inaugural Address (1933)

FRANKLIN D. ROOSEVELT

This is a day of national consecration, and I am certain that my fellow-Americans expect that on my induction into the Presidency I will address them with a candor and a decision which the present situation of our nation impels. This is pre-eminently the time to speak the truth, the whole truth, frankly and boldly. Nor need we shrink from honestly facing conditions in our country today. This great nation will endure as it has endured, will revive and will prosper.

So first of all let me assert my firm belief that the only thing we have to fear is fear itself—nameless, unreasoning, unjustified terror which paralyzes needed efforts to convert retreat into advance. In every dark hour of

From *The New York Times,* March 5, 1933.

our national life a leadership of frankness and vigor has met with that understanding and support of the people themselves which is essential to victory. I am convinced that you will again give that support to leadership in these critical days.

In such a spirit on my part and on yours we face our common difficulties. They concern, thank God, only material things. Values have shrunken to fantastic levels; taxes have risen; our ability to pay has fallen; government of all kinds is faced by serious curtailment of income; the means of exchange are frozen in the currents of trade; the withered leaves of industrial enterprise lie on every side; farmers find no markets for their produce; the savings of many years in thousands of families are gone.

More important, a host of unemployed citizens face the grim problem of existence, and an equally great number toil with little return. Only a foolish optimist can deny the dark realities of the moment.

Yet our distress comes from no failure of substance. We are stricken by no plague of locusts. Compared with the perils which our forefathers conquered because they believed and were not afraid, we have still much to be thankful for. Nature still offers her bounty and human efforts have multiplied it. Plenty is at our doorstep, but a generous use of it languishes in the very sight of the supply. Primarily, this is because the rulers of the exchange of mankind's goods have failed through their own stubbornness and their own incompetence, have admitted their failure and abdicated. Practices of the unscrupulous money changers stand indicted in the court of public opinion, rejected by the hearts and minds of men.

True, they have tried, but their efforts have been cast in the pattern of an outworn tradition. Faced by failure of credit, they have proposed only the lending of more money. Stripped of the lure of profit by which to induce our people to follow their false leadership, they have resorted to exhortations, pleading tearfully for restored confidence. They know only the rules of a generation of self-seekers. They have no vision, and when there is no vision the people perish.

The money changers have fled from their high seats in the temple of our civilization. We may now restore that temple to the ancient truths. The measure of the restoration lies in the extent to which we apply social values more noble than mere monetary profit.

Happiness lies not in the mere possession of money; it lies in the joy of achievement, in the thrill of creative effort. The joy and moral stimulation of work no longer must be forgotten in the mad chase of evanescent profits. These dark days will be worth all they cost us if they teach us that our true destiny is not to be ministered unto but to minister to ourselves and to our fellow-men.

Recognition of the falsity of material wealth as the standard of success goes hand in hand with the abandonment of the false belief that public office and high political position are to be valued only by the standards of pride of place and personal profit; and there must be an end to a conduct in banking and in business which too often has given to a sacred trust the likeness of callous and selfish wrongdoing. Small wonder that confidence languishes, for it thrives only on honesty, on honor, on the sacredness of obligations, on faithful protection, on unselfish performance. Without them it cannot live.

Restoration calls, however, not for changes in ethics alone. This nation asks for action, and action now.

Our greatest primary task is to put people to work. This is no unsolvable problem if we face it wisely and courageously. It can be accomplished in part by direct recruiting by the Government itself, treating the task as we would treat the emergency of war, but at the same time, through this employment, accomplishing greatly needed projects to stimulate and reorganize the use of our natural resources.

Hand in hand with this, we must frankly recognize the overbalance of population in our industrial centers and, by engaging on a national scale in the redistribution, endeavor to provide a better use of the land for those best fitted for the land. The task can be helped by definite efforts to raise the values of agricultural products and with this the power to purchase the output of our cities. It can be helped by preventing realistically the tragedy of the growing loss, through foreclosure, of our small homes and our farms. It can be helped by insistence that the Federal, State and local governments act forthwith on the demand that their cost be drastically reduced. It can be helped by the unifying of relief activities which today are often scattered, uneconomical and unequal. It can be helped by national planning for a supervision of all forms of transportation and of communications and other utilities which have a definitely public character. There are many ways in which it can be helped, but it can never be helped merely by talking about it. We must act, and act quickly. . . .

This I propose to offer, pledging that the larger purposes will bind upon us all as a sacred obligation with a unity of duty hitherto evoked only in the time of armed strife.

With this pledge taken, I assume unhesitatingly the leadership of this great army of our people, dedicated to a disciplined attack upon our common problems.

Action in this image and to this end is feasible under the form of government which we have inherited from our ancestors. Our Constitution is so simple and practical that it is possible always to meet extraordinary needs by changes in emphasis and arrangement without loss of essential form. That is why our constitutional system has proved itself the most superbly enduring political mechanism the modern world has produced. It has met every stress of vast expansion of territory, of foreign wars, of bitter internal strife, of world relations.

It is to be hoped that the normal balance of executive and legislative authority may be wholly adequate to meet the unprecedented task before us. But it may be that an unprecedented demand and need for undelayed action may call for temporary departure from that normal balance of public procedure.

I am prepared under my constitutional duty to recommend the measures that a stricken nation in the midst of a stricken world may require. These measures, or such other measures as the Congress may build out of its experience and wisdom, I shall seek, within my constitutional authority, to bring to speedy adoption.

But in the event that the Congress shall fail to take one of these two courses, and in the event that the national emergency is still critical, I shall not evade the clear course of duty that will then confront me. I shall ask the Congress for the one remaining instrument to meet the crisis—broad Executive power to wage a war against the emergency as great as the power that would be given me if we were in fact invaded by a foreign foe.

For the trust reposed in me I will return the courage and the devotion that befit the time. I can do no less. . . .

28

✧

ORGANIZING THE MASSES

Economic conditions in the 1930s had a tremendous impact on American labor. The Great Depression wreaked havoc with the lives of
working people. By 1932, New York had a million jobless and Chicago
another 600,000; 50 percent of Cleveland's workforce was unemployed, as was 60 percent of Akron's and 80 percent of Toledo's. Even
those who still had jobs saw their wages and hours decline dramatically,
and things did not greatly improve as the decade wore on.

The New Deal gave labor unions an opportunity to replenish their
membership, which had plummeted to half of its World War I strength.
The chief piece of legislation affecting unions was the Labor Relations
Act of 1935, which established a national board to keep employers
from interfering with labor organizers or union members and to super-
vise union elections. Thus encouraged, leaders of several large unions
bolted the conservative American Federation of Labor (AFL) to form
the Committee for Industrial Organization, which soon became the
Congress of Industrial Organizations (CIO). The AFL emphasized craft
unions (which were made up of workers in a given trade); the CIO
insisted that industrial unions (which included all industrial workers,
skilled and unskilled, in an industry) were essential in the great mass-
production industries in which labor previously had been unorganized.
In 1936 and 1937 the CIO, led by John L. Lewis, president of the
United Mine Workers, mounted successful, though bloody, organizing
campaigns to establish unions in the steel, rubber, electrical, automobile, and other basic industries. The AFL soon responded with organizing drives of its own. Thus, total union membership had tripled by
1940. The New Deal facilitated the rise of Big Labor as it did the
welfare state, all the while preserving the country's basic economic
system.

John L. Lewis, the forceful CIO leader, was born near Lucas, Iowa,
in 1880 to a Welsh immigrant family. Leaving school after the seventh
grade, Lewis worked briefly with his father in the coal fields and then
wandered across the West for several years before returning to the
mines in about 1905. He soon became active in union affairs and in
1920 was elected president of the United Mine Workers. Although he

was originally associated with the AFL, Lewis spearheaded the formation of the CIO after the passage of the Labor Relations Act of 1935
and presided vigorously and dramatically for the next few years over
the violent struggle for industrial unionism. In the 1940s he repeatedly
quarreled with leaders of the CIO, the AFL, and the federal government,
called several bitter coal strikes, and was twice held in contempt of
court for ignoring antistrike injunctions. He nonetheless remained a
revered labor spokesman. He was president of the United Mine Workers
until 1960 and chairman of its retirement fund until his death in Washington, D.C., in 1969.

Questions to Consider. John L. Lewis had great gifts as an orator. ("He
can use his voice like a policeman's billy," said one commentator, "or
like a monk at orisons"). His physical appearance was also striking—he
had a mass of reddish hair, bushy eyebrows, and piercing blue eyes.
But his effectiveness as a speaker depended on his choice of words.
In the 1936 radio speech reprinted below, he was trying to justify the
CIO to an American public still not particularly friendly to organized
labor. Do you think his style of speech was likely to win the understanding and sympathy of middle-class Americans? How "radical" was the
position taken in his speech? How did he link the CIO to traditional
American values and institutions? How extensive, according to Lewis,
was resistance to the CIO's organizing drive in the big unorganized
industries of the country? How did he implicate the federal government
in this resistance? In what ways did he distinguish the CIO's philosophy
from that of "alien" doctrines like Communism? What did he have to
say about politics?

---------------◆---------------

The Steelworkers Organization Campaign (1936)

JOHN L. LEWIS

Out of the agony and travail of economic America, the Committee for
Industrial Organization was born. To millions of Americans, exploited
without stint by corporate industry and socially debased beyond the understanding of the fortunate, its coming was as welcome as the dawn to the

From *John L. Lewis and the International Union, United Mine Workers of America: The Story from
1917 to 1952* (United Mine Workers of America, Washington, D.C., 1952), 43–49. Reprinted by
permission of the United Mine Workers of America.

Strike pickets. During the winter of 1936–1937 the Congress of Industrial Organizations climaxed its drive to unionize America's basic industries with a series of strikes that caused conflict in some communities and tensions in many others. In this artwork, workers picket for bargaining rights and higher wages in late 1937. A year later, total union membership had zoomed to almost 8 million. Workers were responding to CIO organizers who sang, "You'll win. What I mean. . . . Take it easy. . . . but take it!" ("We Demand!" by Joe Jones; The Butler Institute of American Art)

night watcher. To a lesser group of Americans, infinitely more fortunately situated, blessed with larger quantities of the world's goods and insolent in their assumption of privilege, its coming was heralded as a harbinger of ill, sinister of purpose, of unclean methods and nonvirtuous objectives.

The workers of the nation were tired of waiting for corporate industry to right their economic wrongs, to alleviate their social agony and to grant them their political rights. Despairing of fair treatment, they resolved to do something for themselves. They, therefore, have organized a new labor movement, conceived within the principles of the national Bill of Rights and committed to the proposition that the workers are free to assemble in their own forums, voice their own grievances, declare their own hopes, and contract on even terms with modern industry, for the sale of their only material possession—their labor.

The Committee for Industrial Organization has a numerical enrollment of 3,718,000 members. It has thirty-two affiliated national and international unions. Of this number, eleven unions account for 2,765,000 members. This group is organized in the textile, auto, garment, lumber, rubber, electrical manufacturing, power, steel, coal and transport industries. The remaining membership exists in the maritime, oil production and refining, ship-building, leather, chemical, retail, meat packing, vegetable canning, metal-liferous mining, miscellaneous manufacturing, agricultural labor, and service and miscellaneous industries. Some 200 thousand workers are organized into 506 chartered local unions not yet attached to a national industrial union. Much of this progress was made in the face of violent and deadly opposition which reached its climax in the slaughter of workers paralleling the massacres of Ludlow [Colorado, 1914] and Homestead [Pennsylvania, 1892].

In the steel industry, the corporations generally have accepted collective bargaining and negotiated wage agreements with the Committee for Industrial Organization. Eighty-five per cent of the industry is thus under contract and a peaceful relationship exists between the management and the workers. Written wage contracts have been negotiated with 399 steel companies covering 510 thousand men. One thousand thirty-one local lodges in 700 communities have been organized.

Five of the corporations in the steel industry elected to resist collective bargaining and undertook to destroy the steel workers' union. These companies filled their plants with industrial spies, assembled depots of guns and gas bombs, established barricades, controlled their communities with armed thugs, leased the police power of cities and mobilized the military power of a state to guard them against the intrusion of collective bargaining within their plants.

During this strike, eighteen steel workers were either shot to death or had their brains clubbed out by police or armed thugs in the pay of the steel companies. In Chicago, Mayor [Edward V.] Kelly's police force was successful in killing ten strikers before they could escape the fury of the police, shooting eight of them in the back. One hundred sixty strikers were maimed and injured by police clubs, riot guns and gas bombs and were hospitalized. Hundreds of strikers were arrested, jailed, treated with brutality while incarcerated and harassed by succeeding litigation. None but strikers were murdered, gassed, injured, jailed or maltreated. No one had to die except the workers who were standing for the right guaranteed them by the Congress and written in the law.

The infamous Governor [Martin L.] Davey of Ohio, successful in the last election because of his reiterated promises of fair treatment to labor, used the military power of the commonwealth on the side of the Republic Steel Co. and the Youngstown Sheet and Tube Co. Nearly half of the staggering military expenditure incident to the crushing of this strike in Ohio was borne by the federal government through the allocation of financial aid to the military establishment of the state.

The steel workers have now buried their dead, while the widows weep and watch their orphaned children become objects of public charity. The murder of these unarmed men has never been publicly rebuked by any authoritative officer of the state or federal government. Some of them, in extenuation, plead lack of jurisdiction, but murder as a crime against the moral code can always be rebuked without regard to the niceties of legalistic jurisdiction by those who profess to be the keepers of the public conscience.

Shortly after Kelly's police force in Chicago had indulged in their bloody orgy, Kelly came to Washington looking for political patronage. That patronage was forthcoming and Kelly must believe that the killing of the strikers is no liability in partisan politics.

The men in the steel industry who sacrificed their all were not merely aiding their fellows at home but were adding strength to the cause of their comrades in all industry. Labor was marching toward the goal of industrial democracy and contributing constructively toward a more rational arrangement of our domestic economy.

Labor does not seek industrial strife. It wants peace, but a peace with justice. In the long struggle for labor's rights, it has been patient and forebearing. Sabotage and destructive syndicalism have had no part in the American labor movement. Workers have kept faith in American institutions. Most of the conflicts which have occurred have been when labor's right to live has been challenged and denied.

Fascist organizations have been launched and financed under the shabby pretext that the CIO movement is communistic. The real breeders of discontent and alien doctrines of government and philosophies subversive of good citizenship are such as these who take the law into their own hands.

No tin-hat brigade of goose-stepping vigilantes or Bible-babbling mob of blackguarding and corporation-paid scoundrels will prevent the onward march of labor, or divert its purpose to play its natural and rational part in the development of the economic, political and social life of our nation.

Unionization, as opposed to Communism, presupposes the relation of employment; it is based upon the wage system and it recognizes fully and unreservedly the institution of private property and the right to investment profit.

The organized workers of America, free in their industrial life, conscious partners in production, secure in their homes and enjoying a decent standard of living, will prove the finest bulwark against the intrusion of alien doctrines of government.

Do those who have hatched this foolish cry of Communism in the CIO fear the increased influence will be cast on the side of shorter hours, a better system of distributed employment, better homes for the underprivileged, social security for the aged, a fairer distribution of the national income?

Certainly labor wants a fairer share in the national income. Assuredly labor wants a larger participation in increased productivity efficiency. Obviously the population is entitled to participate in the fruits of the genius of our men of achievement in the field of the material sciences.

Under the banner of the Committee for Industrial Organization, American labor is on the march. Its objectives today are those it had in the beginning: to strive for the unionization of our unorganized millions of workers and for the acceptance of collective bargaining as a recognized American institution.

The objectives of this movement are not political in a partisan sense. Yet it is true that a political party which seeks the support of labor and makes pledges of good faith to labor must, in equity and good conscience, keep that faith and redeem those pledges.

The spectacle of august and dignified members of the Congress, servants of the people and agents of the republic, skulking in hallways and closets, hiding their faces in a party caucus to prevent a quorum from acting upon a labor measure, is one that emphasizes the perfidy of politicians and blasts the confidence of labor's millions in politicians' promises and statesmen's vows.

Labor next year cannot avoid the necessity of a political assay of the work and deeds of its so-called friends and its political beneficiaries. It must determine who are its friends in the arena of politics as elsewhere. It feels that its cause is just and that its friends should not view its struggle with neutral detachment or intone constant criticism of its activities.

Those who chant their praises of democracy, but who lose no chance to drive their knives into labor's defenseless back, must feel the weight of labor's woe even as its open adversaries must ever feel the thrust of labor's power.

Labor, like Israel, has many sorrows. Its women weep for their fallen and they lament for the future of the children of the race. It ill behooves one who has supped at labor's table and who has been sheltered in labor's house to curse with equal fervor and fine impartiality both labor and its adversaries when they become locked in deadly embrace.

29

✦

WAR AIMS

Circumstances change, said Franklin D. Roosevelt, and so did he as president, from (in other words) "Mr. New Deal" facing the dangers of the Great Depression in the 1930s to "Mr. Win-the-War" facing the dangers of the Axis Powers in the 1940s. Historians have sometimes seen the coming of war as a discontinuity in his administration.

But the break was not so sharp as it might have been. One thread providing continuity was that Roosevelt was never disinterested in world affairs, even during the most urgent days of the Depression. As the Nazi threat to France and England and the Japanese threat to China grew in the late 1930s, so did Roosevelt's determination to help—if he could do so without declaring war. Another thread was that Roosevelt perceived the looming conflict partly in ideological terms—as a struggle, with the forces of authoritarianism and social reaction pitted against the forces of democracy and social progress. To some extent, Roosevelt's view of the conflict resembled Woodrow Wilson's goal in World War I of making the world "safe for democracy." It also followed logically from the nature of the enemy, which most people regarded as nothing but a coalition of racist, militaristic tyrants. Opposing such an enemy meant, by extension, opposing what the enemy stood for.

In his "Four Freedoms" address, delivered to Congress and broadcast to the public in January 1941—prior to America's formal entry into the war—Roosevelt went beyond Woodrow Wilson in his statement of war goals. In this speech, as in others he delivered over the next four years, the president made it clear that he considered this war to be not just about freedom of speech, press, and religion, as his predecessors might have it. This was also a war about freedom from want, the philosophy underlying many of the New Deal programs. And it was about freedom from fear, a sentiment that had filled his first inaugural address eight years before. At least in this 1941 statement, "Mr. Win-the-War" continued to be "Mr. New Deal."

Questions to Consider. Isolationist, antiwar feelings were still very strong in the country in early 1941. How did Roosevelt try at the beginning of his speech to neutralize antiwar sentiment? At what point in the address did he introduce what might be considered progressive political ideas of the kind that characterized the New Deal? According to Roosevelt, what were the foundations of "a healthy and strong democracy"? Would all Americans have agreed with his list of democratic "foundations"? Why did the president demand individual sacrifice and warn people not to try to get rich from his programs? Of the "four freedoms" Roosevelt eventually enumerated, which do you think would have been most popular in the 1940s?

————————✧————————

The Four Freedoms (1941)

FRANKLIN D. ROOSEVELT

I address you, the Members of the Seventy-seventh Congress, at a moment unprecedented in the history of the Union. I use the word "unprecedented," because at no previous time has American security been as seriously threatened from without as it is today. . . .

Every realist knows that the democratic way of life is at this moment being directly assailed in every part of the world—assailed either by arms, or by secret spreading of poisonous propaganda by those who seek to destroy unity and promote discord in nations still at peace.

During sixteen months this assault has blotted out the whole pattern of democratic life in an appalling number of independent nations, great and small. The assailants are still on the march, threatening other nations, great and small.

Therefore, as your President, performing my constitutional duty to "give to the Congress information on the state of the Union," I find it necessary to report that the future and the safety of our country and of our democracy are overwhelmingly involved in events far beyond our borders.

Armed defense of democratic existence is now being gallantly waged in four continents. If that defense fails, all the population and all the resources of Europe, Asia, Africa, and Australasia will be dominated by the conquerors. The total of those populations and their resources greatly exceeds the sum total of the population and resources of the whole of the Western Hemisphere—many times over. . . .

No realistic American can expect from a dictator's peace international generosity, or return of true independence, or world disarmament, or freedom of expression, or freedom of religion—or even good business.

From *The New York Times* January 7, 1941.

Such a peace would bring no security for us or for our neighbors. Those who would give up essential liberty to purchase a little temporary safety deserve neither liberty nor safety. . . .

There is much loose talk of our immunity from immediate and direct invasion from across the seas. Obviously, as long as the British Navy retains its power, no such danger exists. Even if there were no British Navy, it is not probable that any enemy would be stupid enough to attack us by landing troops in the United States from across thousands of miles of ocean, until it had acquired strategic bases from which to operate.

But we learn much from the lessons of the past years in Europe— particularly the lesson of Norway, whose essential seaports were captured by treachery and surprise built up over a series of years. . . .

As long as the aggressor nations maintain the offensive, they, not we, will choose the time and the place and the method of their attack. . . .

Let us say to the democracies, "We Americans are vitally concerned in your defense of freedom. We are putting forth our energies, our resources, and our organizing powers to give you the strength to regain and maintain a free world. We shall send you, in ever-increasing numbers, ships, planes, tanks, guns. This is our purpose and our pledge."

In fulfillment of this purpose we will not be intimidated by the threats of dictators that they will regard as a breach of international law and as an act of war our aid to the democracies which dare to resist their aggression. Such aid is not an act of war, even if a dictator should unilaterally proclaim it so to be.

When the dictators are ready to make war upon us, they will not wait for an act of war on our part. They did not wait for Norway or Belgium or The Netherlands to commit an act of war.

Their only interest is in a new one-way international law, which lacks mutuality in its observance and, therefore, becomes an instrument of oppression. . . .

As men do not live by bread alone, they do not fight by armaments alone. Those who man our defenses, and those behind them who build our defenses, must have the stamina and courage which come from an unshakable belief in the manner of life which they are defending. The mighty action which we are calling for cannot be based on a disregard of all things worth fighting for.

There is nothing mysterious about the foundations of a healthy and strong democracy. The basic things expected by our people of their political and economic systems are simple.

They are:

Equality of opportunity for youth and for others.
Jobs for those who can work.
Security for those who need it.
The ending of special privilege for the few.

The preservation of civil liberties for all.

The enjoyment of the fruits of scientific progress in a wider and constantly rising standard of living.

These are the simple and basic things that must never be lost sight of in the turmoil and unbelievable complexity of our modern world. The inner and abiding strength of our economic and political systems is dependent upon the degree to which they fulfill these expectations. . . .

I have called for personal sacrifice. I am assured of the willingness of almost all Americans to respond to that call.

A part of the sacrifice means the payment of more money in taxes. . . . No person should try, or be allowed to get rich out of this program. . . .

In the future days, which we seek to make secure, we look forward to a world founded upon four essential human freedoms.

The first is freedom of speech and expression, everywhere in the world.

The second is freedom of every person to worship God in his own way, everywhere in the world.

The third is freedom from want, which, translated into world terms, means economic understandings which will secure to every nation a healthy peacetime life for its inhabitants, everywhere in the world.

The fourth is freedom from fear—which, translated into world terms, means a worldwide reduction of armaments to such a point and in such a thorough fashion that no nation will be in a position to commit an act of physical aggression against any neighbor—anywhere in the world.

That is no vision of a distant millennium. It is a definite basis for a kind of world attainable in our own time and not the so-called new order of tyranny which the dictators seek to impose. That kind of world is the very antithesis of the kind created with the crash of a bomb.

To that new order we oppose the greater conception—the moral order. A good society is able to face schemes of world domination and foreign revolutions alike without fear.

Since the beginning of our American history we have been engaged in change—in a perpetual peaceful revolution—a revolution which goes on steadily, quietly adjusting itself to changing conditions—without the concentration camp or the quicklime in the ditch. The world order which we seek is the cooperation of free countries, working together in a friendly, civilized society.

This Nation has placed its destiny in the hands and heads and hearts of its millions of free men and women; and its faith in freedom under the guidance of God. Freedom means the supremacy of human rights everywhere. Our support goes to those who struggle to gain those rights or keep them. Our strength is in our unity of purpose.

To that high concept there can be no end save victory.

30

✧

DAY OF INFAMY

The United States did not completely isolate itself from other nations after the disillusionment of World War I. During the 1920s the U.S. government negotiated arms-limitations pacts, sought to preserve the Open Door in China, encouraged massive bank loans to a war-ravaged Europe, and maintained troops in Latin America. Yet throughout the 1920s and into the 1930s the United States held steady on two key matters. It refused to enter military or defense alliances with any nation and to spend heavily on armies and armaments. During the 1930s the American public was probably more opposed to war than at any other time in U.S. history.

The rise of aggressive governments in Nazi Germany, Fascist Italy and Imperial Japan gradually changed America's sense of detachment. But the shift to involvement was slow. Not until German forces subdued France in 1940 did President Franklin Roosevelt promise "everything short of war" to a beleaguered England. Roosevelt asked Congress for a declaration of war only when Japan, which saw America's presence in the Pacific as a threat to its own ambitions there, conducted devastating attacks on the American fleet and naval base at Pearl Harbor, Hawaii, and on the Philippines on December 7, 1941. The president's emphasis on the surprise element in this "day of infamy" and on the need henceforth to guard against "treachery" presaged not only the vast wartime military build-up to come but also the maintenance of a large military establishment after the war was over. Roosevelt's address in 1941 thus shaped America's perceptions of its international position just as Woodrow Wilson's had in 1917, though in a profoundly different direction.

Questions to Consider. Several questions arise from a reading of Roosevelt's announcement of war. How comparable was the sinking of American ships by Japanese airplanes in 1941 to the sinking of American ships by German submarines in 1917? Did this difference in the nature of the weaponry add to the impact of Roosevelt's announcement? Note, too, that Roosevelt did not attach a lengthy declaration of large goals for humanity to his message, as Wilson had done. Why not? Did the facts actually "speak for themselves," as Roosevelt stated?

How could the president assert that the American people had "already formed their opinion"? Did the notions of American exceptionalism and the redemption of humanity sneak into the message despite its brevity?

————————✧————————

Address to Congress (1941)

FRANKLIN D. ROOSEVELT

Yesterday, December 7, 1941—a date which will live in infamy—the United States of America was suddenly and deliberately attacked by naval and air forces of the Empire of Japan.

The United States was at peace with that nation and, at the solicitation of Japan, was still in conversation with its Government and its Emperor looking toward the maintenance of peace in the Pacific. Indeed, one hour after Japanese air squadrons had commenced bombing in Oahu, the Japanese Ambassador to the United States and his colleague delivered to the Secretary of State a formal reply to a recent American message. While this reply stated that it seemed useless to continue the existing diplomatic negotiations, it contained no threat or hint of war or armed attack.

It will be recorded that the distance of Hawaii from Japan makes it obvious that the attack was deliberately planned many days or even weeks ago. During the intervening time the Japanese Government has deliberately sought to deceive the United States by false statements and expressions of hope for continued peace.

The attack yesterday on the Hawaiian Islands has caused severe damage to American naval and military forces. Very many American lives have been lost. In addition American ships have been reported torpedoed on the high seas between San Francisco and Honolulu.

Yesterday the Japanese Government also launched an attack against Malaya. Last night Japanese forces attacked Hong Kong. Last night Japanese forces attacked Guam. Last night Japanese forces attacked the Philippine Islands. Last night the Japanese attacked Wake Island. This morning the Japanese attacked Midway Island.

Japan has, therefore, undertaken a surprise offensive extending throughout the Pacific area. The facts of yesterday speak for themselves. The people of the United States have already formed their opinions and well understand the implications to the very life and safety of our nation.

As Commander-in-Chief of the Army and Navy, I have directed that all measures be taken for our defense.

From *The New York Times,* December 9, 1941.

Magazine of USS Shaw explodes. This, one of the most remarkable combat photographs of all time, was taken at the exact moment the destroyer blew up during the Japanese attack on Pearl Harbor. (Brown Brothers)

Always will we remember the character of the onslaught against us.

No matter how long it may take us to overcome this premeditated invasion, the American people in their righteous might will win through to absolute victory.

I believe I interpret the will of the Congress and of the people when I assert that we will not only defend ourselves to the uttermost but will make very certain that this form of treachery shall never endanger us again.

Hostilities exist. There is no blinking at the fact that our people, our territory and our interests are in grave danger.

With confidence in our armed forces—with the unbounded determination of our people—we will gain the inevitable triumph—so help us God.

I ask that the Congress declare that since the unprovoked and dastardly attack by Japan on Sunday, December seventh, a state of war has existed between the United States and the Japanese Empire.

31

✧

DESTROYER OF WORLDS

American strategy in the Pacific war was to "island-hop" toward Japan, occupying undefended atolls where possible and taking others by amphibious assault where necessary. This oceanic march began in 1942 with a painful, costly victory at Guadalcanal, northeast of Australia. It culminated in 1945 at Okinawa, off southern Japan, in a gruesome fight that produced 150,000 casualties. Meanwhile, the United States had proved its new air capability with the victory of its carrier-based planes at Midway in 1942 and with long-range bombing of the Japanese mainland after 1943. Finally, as American soldiers grouped to invade Japan in mid-1945, President Harry S Truman warned the Japanese that unless they surrendered by August 3 they would face "prompt and utter destruction." When they did not surrender, he ordered that an atomic bomb be dropped on Hiroshima on August 6 and another on Nagasaki on August 9.

The concept of the atomic bomb was brought to the United States by scientists fleeing Nazi Germany and Fascist Italy. In 1939, after suggestions from scientist Albert Einstein that the Germans might develop nuclear weapons, President Roosevelt authorized a National Defense Research Committee, which in turn led to the top-secret Manhattan Project for developing the bomb. By 1945, nuclear plants in Tennessee and Washington had produced enough fissionable material to construct a test bomb, which was exploded spectacularly in the New Mexico desert in July. One of the first decisions that President Truman faced upon succeeding Roosevelt in office concerned using the bomb against Japan. Why he ordered the use of the bomb continues to be debated. He claimed he did so to avoid a bloody land assault that would have cost many lives—American and Japanese. Some historians suggest he did so to demonstrate U.S. power to the Russians. Nevertheless, the effects of the bomb itself were soon clear. More than 100,000 Japanese died from the two blasts.

While on assignment in late 1945 and 1946, John Hersey, a journalist covering the Far East for major American periodicals, prepared an account of how the bomb affected individual Japanese. Though most Allied leaders regarded the atomic bomb as just another big bomb, the excerpts from Hersey's *Hiroshima* reprinted below make clear that in its capacity for devastation the bomb dwarfed all other weapons of war.

John Hersey was born in 1914 in Tientsin, China, to American missionary parents, and became a journalist in the late 1930s after study at Yale University and Cambridge University in England. His first major work was *Men on Bataan* (1942), based on a series of interviews. A stream of books based on interviews and news clippings soon followed, including *Into the Valley* (1943), about a company of marines on Guadalcanal, and *Hiroshima* (1946). Hersey won the Pulitzer Prize for *A Bell for Adano* (1944), a story about the American occupation of Italy.

Questions to Consider. *Hiroshima* probably continues to be the most widely read and influential study of the effects of the dropping of the bomb. What clues in the excerpts below help explain this popularity? Is it strictly a consequence of Hersey's strategy of focusing on individuals? Might his style of writing also be a factor? Why does Hersey tell us about the blind soldiers? Is it the blindness that moves us, or the fact that these blind are soldiers? Why did Hersey choose to make two of his six main characters, Dr. Fujii and Dr. Sasaki, medical men? Why is one of the six, Father Kleinsorge, not Japanese? Some U.S. officials were upset, even angry, that *Hiroshima* was so popular. What passage in the excerpts do you think might have caused such official distress?

———— ✧ ————

Hiroshima (1946)

JOHN HERSEY

The lot of Drs. Fujii, Kanda, and Machii right after the explosion—and, as these three were typical, that of the majority of the physicians and surgeons of Hiroshima—with their offices and hospitals destroyed, their equipment scattered, their own bodies incapacitated in varying degrees, explained why so many citizens who were hurt went untended and why so many who might have lived died. Of a hundred and fifty doctors in the city, sixty-five were already dead and most of the rest were wounded. Of 1,780 nurses, 1,654 were dead or too badly hurt to work. In the biggest hospital, that of the Red Cross, only six doctors out of thirty were able to function, and only ten nurses out of more than two hundred. The sole uninjured

Hiroshima after the dropping of the atomic bomb. After three years and $2 billion invested in secret research, the United States exploded the first atomic device at Alamogordo, New Mexico, on the morning of July 16, 1945. A scientist who was there said it was as if "the earth had opened and the skies had split," or like the moment of creation when God said, "Let there be light." Although the catastrophic power of the weapon was clear, President Truman never really considered stopping its use. (The Bettmann Archive)

doctor on the Red Cross Hospital staff was Dr. Sasaki. After the explosion, he hurried to a storeroom to fetch bandages. This room, like everything he had seen as he ran through the hospital, was chaotic—bottles of medicines thrown off shelves and broken, salves spattered on the walls, instruments strewn everywhere. He grabbed up some bandages and an unbroken bottle of mercurochrome, hurried back to the chief surgeon, and bandaged his cuts. Then he went out into the corridor and began patching up the wounded patients and the doctors and nurses there. He blundered so without his glasses that he took a pair off the face of a wounded nurse, and although they only approximately compensated for the errors of his vision, they were better than nothing. (He was to depend on them for more than a month.)

Dr. Sasaki worked without method, taking those who were nearest him first, and he noticed soon that the corridor seemed to be getting more and more crowded. Mixed in with the abrasions and lacerations which most people in the hospital had suffered, he began to find dreadful burns. He realized then that casualties were pouring in from outdoors. There were so many that he began to pass up the lightly wounded; he decided that all he could hope to do was to stop people from bleeding to death. Before

long, patients lay and crouched on the floors of the wards and the labora-
tories and all the other rooms, and in the corridors, and on the stairs, and
in the front hall, and under the portecochère, and on the stone front steps,
and in the driveway and courtyard, and for blocks each way in the streets
outside. Wounded people supported maimed people; disfigured families
leaned together. Many people were vomiting. A tremendous number of
schoolgirls—some of those who had been taken from their classrooms to
work outdoors, cleaning fire lanes—crept into the hospital. In a city of two
hundred and forty-five thousand, nearly a hundred thousand people had
been killed or doomed at one blow; a hundred thousand more were hurt.
At least ten thousand of the wounded made their way to the best hospital
in town, which was altogether unequal to such a trampling, since it had
only six hundred beds, and they had all been occupied. The people in the
suffocating crowd inside the hospital wept and cried, for Dr. Sasaki to hear,
"*Sensei!* Doctor!" and the less seriously wounded came and pulled at his
sleeve and begged him to go to the aid of the worse wounded. Tugged
here and there in his stockinged feet, bewildered by the numbers, staggered
by so much raw flesh, Dr. Sasaki lost all sense of the profession and stopped working as a skillful surgeon and a sympathetic man; he became
an automaton, mechanically wiping, daubing, winding, wiping, daubing,
winding. . . .

The morning, again, was hot. Father Kleinsorge went to fetch water for
the wounded in a bottle and a teapot he had borrowed. He had heard that
it was possible to get fresh tap water outside Asano Park. Going through
the rock gardens, he had to climb over and crawl under the trunks of fallen
pine trees; he found he was weak. There were many dead in the gardens.
At a beautiful moon bridge, he passed a naked, living woman who seemed
to have been burned from head to toe and was red all over. Near the
entrance to the park, an Army doctor was working, but the only medicine
he had was iodine, which he painted over cuts, bruises, slimy burns,
everything—and by now everything he painted had pus on it. Outside the
gate of the park, Father Kleinsorge found a faucet that still worked—part
of the plumbing of a vanished house—and he filled his vessels and returned.
When he had given the wounded the water, he made a second trip. This
time, the woman by the bridge was dead. On his way back with the water,
he got lost on a detour around a fallen tree, and as he looked for his way
through the woods, he heard a voice ask from the underbrush, "Have you
anything to drink?" He saw a uniform. Thinking there was just one soldier,
he approached with the water. When he had penetrated the bushes, he
saw there were about twenty men, and they were all in exactly the same
nightmarish state: their faces were wholly burned, their eyesockets were
hollow, the fluid from their melted eyes had run down their cheeks. (They
must have had their faces upturned when the bomb went off; perhaps they
were anti-aircraft personnel.) Their mouths were mere swollen, pus-covered

wounds, which they could not bear to stretch enough to admit the spout of the teapot. So Father Kleinsorge got a large piece of grass and drew out the stem so as to make a straw, and gave them all water to drink that way. One of them said, "I can't see anything." Father Kleinsorge answered, as cheerfully as he could, "There's a doctor at the entrance to the park. He's busy now, but he'll come soon and fix your eyes, I hope." . . .

Early that day, August 7th, the Japanese radio broadcast for the first time a succinct announcement that very few, if any, of the people most concerned with its content, the survivors in Hiroshima, happened to hear: "Hiroshima suffered considerable damage as the result of an attack by a few B-29s. It is believed that a new type of bomb was used. The details are being investigated." Nor is it probable that any of the survivors happened to be tuned in on a short-wave rebroadcast of an extraordinary announcement by the president of the United States, which identified the new bomb as atomic: "That bomb had more power than twenty thousand tons of TNT. It had more than two thousand times the blast power of the British Grand Slam, which is the largest bomb ever yet used in the history of warfare." Those victims who were able to worry at all about what had happened thought of it and discussed it in more primitive, childish terms—gasoline sprinkled from an airplane, maybe, or some combustible gas, or a big cluster of incendiaries, or the work of parachutists; but, even if they had known the truth, most of them were too busy or too weary or too badly hurt to care that they were the objects of the first great experiment in the use of atomic power, which (as the voices on the short wave shouted) no country except the United States, with its industrial know-how, its willingness to throw two billion gold dollars into an important wartime gamble, could possibly have developed. . . .

Dr. Sasaki and his colleagues at the Red Cross Hospital watched the unprecedented disease unfold and at last evolved a theory about its nature. It had, they decided, three stages. The first stage had been all over before the doctors even knew they were dealing with a new sickness; it was the direct reaction to the bombardment of the body, at the moment when the bomb went off, by neutrons, beta particles, and gamma rays. The apparently uninjured people who had died so mysteriously in the first few hours or days had succumbed in this first stage. It killed ninety-five per cent of the people within a half-mile of the center, and many thousands who were farther away. The doctors realized in retrospect that even though most of these dead had also suffered from burns and blast effects, they had absorbed enough radiation to kill them. The rays simply destroyed body cells— caused their nuclei to degenerate and broke their walls. Many people who did not die right away came down with nausea, headache, diarrhea, malaise, and fever, which lasted several days. Doctors could not be certain whether some of these symptoms were the result of radiation or nervous shock. The second stage set in ten or fifteen days after the bombing. Its first symptom was falling hair. Diarrhea and fever, which in some cases went as high as 106, came next. Twenty-five to thirty days after the explosion, blood disorders appeared: gums bled, the white-blood-cell count dropped sharply, and *petechiae* [eruptions] appeared on the skin and mucous membranes. The drop in the number of white blood corpuscles reduced the patient's capacity to resist infection, so open wounds were unusually slow in healing and many of the sick developed sore throats and mouths. The two key symptoms, on which the doctors came to base their prognosis, were fever and the lowered white-corpuscle count. If fever remained steady and high, the patient's chances for survival were poor. The white count almost always dropped below four thousand; a patient whose count fell below one thousand had little hope of living. Toward the end of the second stage, if the patient survived, anemia, or a drop in the red blood count, also set in. The third stage was the reaction that came when the body struggled to compensate for its ills—when, for instance, the white count not only returned to normal but increased to much higher than normal levels. In this stage, many patients died of complications, such as infections in the chest cavity. Most burns healed with deep layers of pink, rubbery scar tissue, known as keloid tumors. The duration of the disease varied, depending on the patient's constitution and the amount of radiation he had received. Some victims recovered in a week; with others the disease dragged on for months.

As the symptoms revealed themselves, it became clear that many of them resembled the effects of overdoses of X-ray, and the doctors based their therapy on that likeness. They gave victims liver extract, blood transfusions, and vitimins, especially B_1. The shortage of supplies and instruments hampered them. Allied doctors who came in after the surrender found plasma and penicillin very effective. Since the blood disorders were, in the long run, the predominant factor in the disease, some of the Japanese doctors evolved a theory as to the seat of the delayed sickness. They thought that perhaps gamma rays, entering the body at the time of the explosion, made the phosphorus in the victims' bones radioactive, and that they in turn emitted beta particles, which, though they could not penetrate far through flesh, could enter the bone marrow, where blood is manufactured, and gradually tear it down. Whatever its source, the disease had some baffling quirks. Not all the patients exhibited all the main symptoms. People who suffered flash burns were protected, to a considerable extent, from radiation sickness. Those who had lain quietly for days or even hours after the bombing were much less liable to get sick than those who had been active. Gray hair seldom fell out. And, as if nature were protecting man against his own ingenuity, the reproductive processes were affected for a time; men became sterile, women had miscarriages, menstruation stopped. . . .

A surprising number of the people of Hiroshima remained more or less indifferent about the ethics of using the bomb. Possibly they were too terrified by it to want to think about it at all. Many citizens of Hiroshima, however, continued to feel a hatred for Americans which nothing could possibly erase. "I see," Dr. Sasaki once said, "that they are holding a trial for war criminals in Tokyo just now. I think they ought to try the men who decided to use the bomb and they should hang them all."

Father Kleinsorge and the other German Jesuit priests, who as foreigners, could be expected to take a relatively detached view, often discussed the ethics of using the bomb. One of them, Father Siemes, who was out at Nagatsuka [Hiroshima suburb] at the time of the attack, wrote in a report to the Holy See in Rome: "Some of us consider the bomb in the same category as poison gas and were against its use on a civilian population. Others were of the opinion that in total war, as carried on in Japan, there was no difference between civilians and soldiers, and that the bomb itself was an effective force tending to end the bloodshed, warning Japan to surrender and thus to avoid total destruction. It seems logical that he who supports total war in principle cannot complain of a war against civilians. The crux of the matter is whether total war in its present form is justifiable, even when it serves a just purpose. Does it not have material and spiritual evil as its consequences which far exceed whatever good might result? When will our moralists give us a clear answer to this question?"

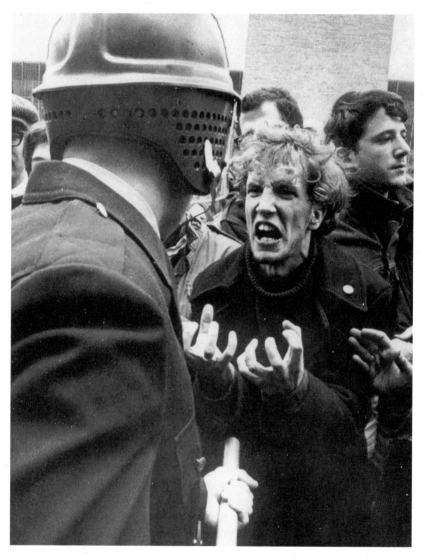

An anti-Vietnam Riot. Confrontations during the Vietnam era were often emotional and violent. (UPI/Bettmann)

CHAPTER SIX

◆

Protracted Conflict

32

❖

CONTAINMENT

When Germany invaded Poland in September 1939, Britain and France came to Poland's aid, and World War II began. But the surrender of Germany in May 1945 did not mean a free and independent Poland. Instead, when the war ended, the Soviet Union took over most of eastern Europe, including Poland, and installed regimes of its own choosing, backed by military force. The Russians had suffered severely in both World War I and World War II from invasions from the West and were determined to surround themselves with a ring of friendly states after the war. But American policy makers, shocked by the ruthlessness with which the Russians had accomplished their purpose, interpreted Soviet policy as expansionist rather than defensive in nature and began to fear that the Soviet Union had designs on western Europe as well. The United States therefore sponsored economic aid (the Marshall Plan) as well as military aid (the Truman Doctrine) to nations in Europe that seemed threatened by Soviet aggression; it also persuaded the nations of western Europe to organize the North Atlantic Treaty Organization (NATO). Thus was born the cold war between the Soviet Union and the United States.

In July 1947 an article entitled "The Sources of Soviet Conduct" appeared in *Foreign Affairs,* an influential journal published in New York. The author, identified only as "X," was later revealed to be George F. Kennan, head of the policy-planning staff of the State Department, so the article may have reflected official American views on Soviet foreign policy. Pointing out that the Soviet Union based its policies on a firm belief in the "innate antagonism between capitalism and socialism," Kennan warned that the Russians were going to be difficult to deal with for a long time. He added that the Kremlin was "under no ideological compulsion to accomplish its purposes in a hurry" and that the only wise course for the United States to follow was that of "a long-term, patient but firm and vigilant containment of Russian expansionist tendencies." Kennan's article, which is excerpted below, shaped as well as reflected American policy.

George F. Kennan was born in Milwaukee, Wisconsin, in 1904. After graduating from Princeton University in 1925, he joined the foreign service, in which he specialized in Russian affairs while serving in minor European posts. In 1933, he went to Moscow when the United States extended diplomatic recognition to the Soviet Union and opened an embassy there. Kennan served elsewhere in the late 1930s, but he returned to the Soviet Union during World War II and was appointed U.S. ambassador there in 1952. Kennan continued to write extensively on Russian and American diplomacy even after leaving the foreign service in the late 1950s. He came to deplore the excessively military application of the containment doctrine he had outlined in 1947, and in his later books and articles he made various proposals for demilitarization and disengagement that might diminish cold war tensions and lessen the chances of nuclear war.

Questions to Consider. In assigning responsibility for the cold war to a combination of Marxist ideology, the Kremlin's desire for power, and the world Communist movement, Kennan was also arguing, of course, that the West was largely defensive and even innocent. What evidence from twentieth-century history might be introduced to counter this argument? Kennan argued, similarly, that the Soviet threat was likely to last, practically speaking, forever. Given his views on Soviet objectives, were social or political changes conceivable that might alter these objectives or the Soviet capacity to pursue them? Did changes of this type in fact occur? Again, Kennan's article outlined his notions of Soviet society clearly enough. What assumptions, according to the evidence of the article, was Kennan making about American society? Finally, Kennan wrote his essay to mold American policy. One can imagine, however, various policies flowing from this analysis: an effort to roll back Russian power in Europe, an armed "garrison" state in the United States, intense economic or propaganda competition, and even a pre-emptive nuclear strike. Which of these did Kennan himself hope to see?

The Sources of Soviet Conduct (1947)

GEORGE F. KENNAN

The political personality of Soviet power as we know it today is the product of ideology and circumstances: ideology inherited by the present Soviet leaders from the movement in which they had their political origin, and

From *Foreign Affairs* (July 1947), 25:566–582. Reprinted by permission of *Foreign Affairs,* July 1947. Copyright 1947 by the Council on Foreign Relations, Inc.

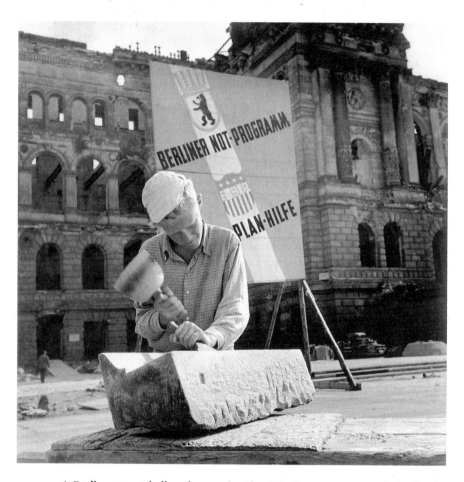

A Berlin concert hall under repair. The U.S. Congress approved the first $5 billion for the European Recovery Program (as the Marshall Plan was officially called) in 1948 with the stipulation that most of the funds would go to purchase American-made products. Goods began to arrive in Europe soon afterward. Much of the early aid went for agricultural assistance and housing construction to stave off the malnutrition and homelessness that had haunted Europe after World War I. (UPI/Bettmann)

circumstances of the power which they now have exercised for nearly three decades in Russia. . . .

Marxian ideology, in its Russian-Communist projection, has always been in process of subtle evolution. The materials on which it bases itself are extensive and complex. But the outstanding features of Communist thought as it existed in 1916 may perhaps be summarized as follows: (a) that the central factor in the life of man, the fact which determines the character of public life and the "physiognomy of society," is the system by which material goods are produced and exchanged; (b) that the capitalist system of production is a nefarious one which inevitably leads to the exploitation of the working class by the capital-owning class and is incapable of developing adequately the economic resources of society or of distributing fairly the material goods produced by human labor; (c) that capitalism contains the seeds of its own destruction and must, in view of the inability of the capital-owning class to adjust itself to economic change, result eventually and inescapably in a revolutionary transfer of power to the working class; and (d) that imperialism, the final phase of capitalism, leads directly to war and revolution.

The rest may be outlined in Lenin's own words: "Unevenness of economic and political development is the inflexible law of capitalism. It follows from this that the victory of Socialism may come originally in a few capitalist countries or even in a single capitalist country. The victorious proletariat of that country, having expropriated the capitalists and having organized Socialist production at home, would rise against the remaining capitalist world, drawing to itself in the process the oppressed classes of other countries." It must be noted that there was no assumption that capitalism would perish without proletarian revolution. A final push was needed from a revolutionary proletariat movement in order to tip over the tottering structure. But it was regarded as inevitable that sooner or later that push be given. . . .

Now the outstanding circumstance concerning the Soviet regime is that down to the present day this process of political consolidation has never been completed and the men in the Kremlin have continued to be predominantly absorbed with the struggle to secure and make absolute the power which they seized in November 1917. They have endeavored to secure it primarily against forces at home, within Soviet society itself. But they have also endeavored to secure it against the outside world. For ideology, as we have seen, taught them that the outside world was hostile and that it was their duty eventually to overthrow the political forces beyond their borders. The powerful hands of Russian history and tradition reached up to sustain them in this feeling. . . .

Now it lies in the nature of the mental world of the Soviet leaders, as well as in the character of their ideology, that no opposition to them can be officially recognized as having any merit or justification whatsoever. Such opposition can flow, in theory, only from the hostile and incorrigible forces of dying capitalism. As long as remnants of capitalism were officially recognized as existing in Russia, it was possible to place on them, as an internal element, part of the blame for the maintenance of a dictatorial form of society. But as these remnants were liquidated, little by little, this justification fell away; and when it was indicated officially that they had been finally destroyed, it disappeared altogether. And this fact created one of the most basic of the compulsions which came to act upon the Soviet regime: since capitalism no longer existed in Russia and since it could not be admitted that there could be serious or widespread opposition to the Kremlin springing spontaneously from the liberated masses under its authority, it became necessary to justify the retention of the dictatorship by stressing the menace of capitalism abroad. . . .

As things stand today, the rulers can no longer dream of parting with these organs and suppression. The quest for absolute power, pursued now for nearly three decades with a ruthlessness unparalleled (in scope at least) in modern times, has again produced internally as it did externally, its own reaction. The excesses of the police apparatus have fanned the potential opposition to the regime into something far greater and more dangerous than it could have been before those excesses began. . . .

So much for the historical background. What does it spell in terms of the political personality of Soviet power as we know it today?

Of the original ideology, nothing has been officially junked. Belief is maintained in the basic badness of capitalism, in the inevitability of its destruction, in the obligation of the proletariat to assist in that destruction and to take power into its own hands. But stress has come to be laid primarily on those concepts which relate most specifically to the Soviet regime itself: to its position as the sole truly Socialist regime in a dark and misguided world, and to the relationships of power within it.

The first of these concepts is that of the innate antagonism between capitalism and Socialism. . . . It means that there can never be on Moscow's side any sincere assumption of a community of aims between the Soviet Union and powers which are regarded as capitalism. It must invariably be assumed in Moscow that the aims of the capitalist world are antagonistic to the Soviet regime and, therefore, to the interests of the peoples it controls. If the Soviet Government occasionally sets its signature to documents which would indicate the contrary, this is to be regarded as a tactical maneuver permissible in dealing with the enemy (who is without honor) and should be taken in the spirit of *caveat emptor* [let the buyer beware]. Basically, the antagonism remains. It is postulated. And from it flow many of the phenomena which we find disturbing in the Kremlin's conduct of foreign policy: the secretiveness, the lack of frankness, the duplicity, the war suspiciousness, and the basic unfriendliness of purpose. These phenomena are there to stay, for the foreseeable future. . . .

This means that we are going to continue for a long time to find the Russians difficult to deal with. It does not mean that they should be considered as embarked upon a do-or-die program to overthrow our society by a given date. The theory of the inevitability of the eventual fall of capitalism has the fortunate connotation that there is no hurry about it. The forces of progress can take their time in preparing the final *coup de grace*. Meanwhile, what is vital is that the "Socialist fatherland"—that oasis of power which has been already won for Socialism in the person of the Soviet Union— should be cherished and defended by all good Communists at home and abroad, its fortunes promoted, its enemies badgered and confounded. The promotion of premature, "adventuristic" revolutionary projects abroad which might embarrass Soviet power in any way would be an inexcusable, even a counter-revolutionary act. The cause of Socialism is the support and promotion of Soviet power, as defined in Moscow.

This brings us to the second of the concepts important to contemporary Soviet outlook. This is the infallibility of the Kremlin. The Soviet concept of power, which permits no focal points of organization outside the Party itself, requires that the Party leadership remain in theory the sole repository of truth. For if truth were to be found elsewhere, there would be justification for its expression in organized activity. But it is precisely that which the Kremlin cannot and will not permit.

The leadership of the Communist Party is therefore always right, and has been always right ever since in 1929 Stalin formalized his personal power by announcing that decisions of the Politburo were being taken unanimously.

On the principle of infallibility there rests the iron discipline of the Communist Party. In fact, the two concepts are mutually self-supporting. Perfect discipline requires recognition of infallibility. Infallibility requires the observance of discipline. And the two together go far to determine the behaviorism of the entire Soviet apparatus of power. But their effect cannot be understood unless a third factor be taken into account: namely, the fact that the leadership is at liberty to put forward for tactical purposes any particular thesis which it finds useful to the cause at any particular moment and to require the faithful and unquestioning acceptance of that thesis by the members of the movement as a whole. This means that truth is not a constant but is actually created, for all intents and purposes, by the Soviet leaders themselves. It may vary from week to week, from month to month. It is nothing absolute and immutable—nothing which flows from objective reality. . . . Once a given party line has been laid down on a given issue of current policy, the whole Soviet governmental machine, including the mechanism of diplomacy, moves inexorably along the prescribed path, like a persistent toy automobile wound up and headed in a given direction, stopping only when it meets with some unanswerable force. The individuals who are the components of this machine are unamenable to argument or reason which comes to them from outside sources. . . . Since there can be no appeal to common purposes, there can be no appeal to common mental approaches. For this reason, facts speak louder than words to the ears of the Kremlin; and words carry the greatest weight when they have the ring of reflecting, or being backed up by, facts of unchallengeable validity.

But we have seen that the Kremlin is under no ideological compulsion to accomplish its purposes in a hurry. Like the Church, it is dealing in ideological concepts which are of long-term validity, and it can afford to be patient. It has no right to risk the existing achievements of the revolution for the sake of vain baubles of the future. The very teachings of Lenin himself require great caution and flexibility in the pursuit of Communist purposes. Again, these precepts are fortified by the lessons of Russian history: of centuries of obscure battles between nomadic forces over the stretches of a vast unfortified plain. Here caution, circumspection, flexibility and deception are the valuable qualities; and their value finds natural appreciation in the Russian or the oriental mind. Thus the Kremlin has no compunction about retreating in the face of superior force. And being under the compulsion of no timetable, it does not get panicky under the necessity for such a retreat. Its political action is a fluid stream which moves constantly, wherever it is permitted to move, toward a given goal. Its main concern is to make sure that it has filled every nook and cranny available to it in the basin of world power. But if it finds unassailable barriers in its path, it accepts these philosophically and accommodates itself to them. . . .

These considerations make Soviet diplomacy at once easier and more difficult to deal with than the diplomacy of individual aggressive leaders like Napoleon and Hitler. On the one hand it is more sensitive to contrary force, more ready to yield on individual sectors of the diplomatic front when that force is felt to be too strong, and thus more rational in the logic and rhetoric of power. On the other hand it cannot be easily defeated or discouraged by a single victory on the part of its opponents. And the patient persistence by which it is animated means that it can be effectively countered not by sporadic acts which represent the momentary whims of democratic opinion but only by intelligent long-range policies on the part of Russia's adversaries—policies no less steady in their purpose, and no less variegated and resourceful in their application, than those of the Soviet Union itself.

In these circumstances it is clear that the main element of any United States policy toward the Soviet Union must be that of a long-term, patient but firm and vigilant containment of Russian expansive tendencies. It is important to note, however, that such a policy has nothing to do with outward histrionics: with threats or blustering or superfluous gestures of outward "toughness." While the Kremlin is basically flexible in its reaction to political realities, it is by no means unamenable to considerations of prestige. Like almost any other government, it can be placed by tactless and threatening gestures in a position where it cannot afford to yield even though this might be dictated by its sense of realism. The Russian leaders are keen judges of human psychology, and as such they are highly conscious that loss of temper and of self-control is never a source of strength in political affairs. They are quick to exploit such evidence of weakness. For these reasons, it is a *sine qua non* of successful dealing with Russia that the foreign government in question should remain at all times cool and collected and that its demands on Russian policy should be put forward in such a manner as to leave the way open for a compliance not too detrimental to Russian prestige. . . .

It is clear that the United States cannot expect in the foreseeable future to enjoy political intimacy with the Soviet regime. It must continue to regard the Soviet Union as a rival, not a partner, in the political arena. It must continue to expect that Soviet policies will reflect no abstract love of peace and stability, no real faith in the possibility of a permanent happy coexistence of the Socialist and capitalist worlds, but rather a cautious, persistent pressure toward the disruption and weakening of all rival influence and rival power.

Balanced against this are the fact that Russia, as opposed to the Western world in general, is still by far the weaker party, that Soviet policy is highly flexible, and that Soviet society may well contain deficiencies which will eventually weaken its own total potential. This would of itself warrant the United States entering with reasonable confidence upon a policy of firm containment, designed to confront the Russians with unalterable counterforce at every point where they show signs of encroaching upon the interests of a peaceful and stable world.

But in actuality the possibilities for American policy are by no means limited to holding the line and hoping for the best. It is entirely possible for the United States to influence by its actions the internal developments, both within Russia and throughout the international Communist movement, by which Russian policy is largely determined. This is not only a question of the modest measure of informational activity which this government can conduct in the Soviet Union and elsewhere, although that, too, is important. It is rather a question of the degree to which the United States can create among the peoples of the world generally the impression of a country which knows what it wants, which is coping successfully with the problems of its internal life and with the responsibilities of a World Power, and which has a spiritual vitality capable of holding its own among the major ideological currents of the time. . . .

By the same token, exhibitions of indecision, disunity and internal disintegration within this country have an exhilarating effect on the whole Communist movement. At each evidence of these tendencies, a thrill of hope and excitement goes through the Communist world; a new jauntiness can be noted in the Moscow tread; now groups of foreign supporters climb on to what they can only view as the band wagon of international politics; and Russian pressure increases all along the line in international affairs.

It would be an exaggeration to say that American behavior unassisted and alone could exercise a power of life and death over the Communist movement and bring about the early fall of Soviet power in Russia. But the United States has it in its power to increase enormously the strains under which Soviet policy must operate, to force upon the Kremlin a far greater degree of moderation and circumspection than it has had to observe in recent years, and in this way to promote tendencies which must eventually find their outlet in either the breakup or the gradual mellowing of Soviet power. . . .

Thus the decision will really fall in large measure in this country itself. The issue of Soviet-American relations is in essence a test of the overall worth of the United States as a nation among nations. To avoid destruction the United States need only measure up to its own best traditions and prove itself worthy of preservation as a great nation.

Surely, there was never a fairer test of national quality than this. In the light of these circumstances, the thoughtful observer of Russian-American relations will find no cause for complaint in the Kremlin's challenge to American society. He will rather experience a certain gratitude to a Providence which, by providing the American people with this implacable challenge, has made their entire security as a nation dependent on their pulling themselves together and accepting the responsibilities of moral and political leadership that history plainly intended them to bear.

33

✧

SEEING REDS

In 1946 Joseph R. McCarthy defeated Progressive Senator Robert M. La Follette, Jr., in the Republican primary in Wisconsin and went on to win election to the U.S. Senate that fall. During the primary contest he was supported by Wisconsin Communists who were infuriated by La Follette's pre–Pearl Harbor anti-interventionism and by his criticisms of Soviet dictator Joseph Stalin. Asked about the support the Communists were giving him against La Follette, McCarthy said airily, "The Communists have votes, too, don't they?" Four years later he became the leader of an impassioned crusade against Communism, and the word "McCarthyism" came to mean a reckless and demagogic assault on domestic dissent.

McCarthyism did not operate in a vacuum. Revelations of Communist spy activity in Canada, England, and the United States after World War II produced demands for counterespionage measures, and in 1947 President Truman inaugurated a loyalty program to ferret out Communists in government. Meanwhile, a series of "spy" cases hit the headlines: the trial and conviction of eleven Communist leaders under the Smith Act for conspiring to advocate the violent overthrow of the government; the conviction of former State Department official Alger Hiss, denounced as a Communist spy, for perjury; and the trial and execution of Julius and Ethel Rosenberg, government workers charged with passing atomic secrets to the Russians. For many Americans, the distinction between the expression of unpopular ideas and deliberate conspiratorial activity on behalf of a foreign power became increasingly blurred. In 1950, Senator McCarthy obliterated the distinction.

In a radio speech (excerpted below) given in Wheeling, West Virginia, in February 1950, McCarthy announced that he had in his hand a list of Communists in the State Department "known to the Secretary of State" and "still working and making policy." Overnight McCarthy became a national figure. Although he never showed anyone his famous "list" and was increasingly vague about the precise number of names it contained (205 or 81 or 57 or "a lot"), he came to exercise great influence in the U.S. Senate and in the nation. In July 1950, a Senate subcommittee headed by Maryland's Millard Tydings dismissed

McCarthy's charges as "a fraud and a hoax." But when Tydings, a conservative Democrat, ran for reelection that fall, McCarthy's insinuations that he was pro-Communist helped defeat him. Similar accusations helped defeat Connecticut Democrat William Benton in 1952.

Not every Republican admired Senator McCarthy or approved his tactics, even when they benefited Republican candidates. Margaret Chase Smith of Maine, the only woman in the U.S. Senate in 1950, had served with McCarthy on the Permanent Investigations Subcommittee of the Senate and had become perturbed by his lack of concern for the unfair damage the subcommittee might do to individuals' reputations. Smith became still more perturbed following McCarthy's West Virginia speech in February 1950 about Communists in the State Department. Conscious that she was a first-term senator and believing that the initial challenge to McCarthy should come from the Democrats (the majority party in the Senate), she delayed speaking her mind for some time. When the Democrats failed to rebut McCarthy's charges effectively, she determined to speak out and did so on June 1, 1950. Six other Republican senators endorsed Smith's "Declaration of Conscience," as it soon came to be called. But she was the one who made the speech, which became one of the most famous of its time.

It would take more than a statement by a handful of Senate Republicans to halt Joe McCarthy. In 1951 McCarthy charged that George C. Marshall, President Truman's former secretary of state and of defense, was part of "a conspiracy so immense and infamy so black as to dwarf any previous venture in the history of man." During the 1952 presidential campaign McCarthy talked ominously of "twenty years of treason" under the Democrats. His followers identified Roosevelt's New Deal, Truman's Fair Deal, and, indeed, all efforts for social reform since the Great Depression as Communist inspired. In 1953, as chairman of the Senate Committee on Government Operations, McCarthy launched a series of investigations of federal agencies, including the Voice of America, the International Information Agency, and the Army Signal Corps installation at Fort Monmouth, New Jersey. When the army decided to fight back, McCarthyism reached its climax in a series of televised Senate hearings in the spring of 1954. During these hearings, the Wisconsin senator's accusations and defamations of character gradually alienated all but his most devoted followers. On July 30, Republican Senator Ralph Flanders of Vermont, who had not endorsed Margaret Chase Smith's 1950 Declaration, introduced a resolution of censure. In December, the Senate voted, 67 to 32, to censure McCarthy for his behavior.

Joseph R. McCarthy was born in Grand Chute, Wisconsin, in 1908 to middle-class Roman Catholic parents. He graduated from Marquette University and entered the legal profession in Wisconsin in 1935. Originally a Democrat, he won his first political race (for a local judgeship) as a Republican in 1939. After serving as a Marine from 1942 to 1944, he became a state Republican power with his defeat of La Follette in the 1946 senatorial race. McCarthy's strongest bases of support were Wisconsin's small business owners and voters of German heritage; they reelected him in 1952 and largely continued their support even after his fall from national popularity. He died at the Bethesda Naval Hospital in Maryland in 1957.

Margaret Chase was born in 1897 in Skowhegan, Maine, where, after graduating from high school, she taught school, worked for the telephone company, and was circulation manager for a local newspaper. In 1930 she married Clyde Harold Smith, who served in Congress from 1936 to 1940. When he died in 1940, Margaret Chase Smith was elected to fill his seat, and in 1949 she became the first woman ever elected to the U.S. Senate. Following her 1950 "Declaration of Conscience," she became a target of the McCarthyites, who in 1954 ran a "proxy" candidate against her in the Maine Republican primary. Smith won by a five-to-one margin and later lodged a successful million-dollar lawsuit against two reporters who had labeled her a Communist. Liberal on race and civil liberties issues, conservative in foreign policy, Smith was one of the most senior members of the U.S. Senate and the ranking Republican on the Armed Services Committee when she finally lost a reelection bid in 1972 at age 75. She died in 1995.

Questions to Consider. Why did McCarthy launch his attack in 1950 rather than in 1949 or 1951? What area of the world most concerned him and what had happened there to give his message impact? Why did he attack from an out-of-the-way place (Wheeling, West Virginia) rather than from Washington or even his home state, Wisconsin, and why, moreover, on the radio? What reasons might McCarthy have had for singling out the State Department for attack, rather than, for example, the Department of Defense or the Department of Justice? In view of the fact that seven twentieth-century presidents and even more secretaries of state had attended just four private colleges (Yale, Harvard, Princeton, and Amherst) was there a certain logic in men such as McCarthy trying to link a Communist conspiracy with a conspiracy of "those who have had all the benefits"?

Margaret Chase Smith's Declaration began with a reference to "national suicide" and ineffectual legislative and executive leadership. Why did Smith begin a speech designed to thwart a Republican senator in this way? How did Smith define "Americanism"? Would most Americans have agreed with her in 1950? Why was it considered courageous for Smith to oppose the political tactics of "Fear, Ignorance, Bigotry, and Smear"? Did Smith believe that Communists might in fact be in the federal government? Did she believe they should remain there if discovered? What two reasons did she give for opposing McCarthy?

———————◇———————

Lincoln Day Address (1950)

JOSEPH R. MCCARTHY

Ladies and gentlemen, tonight as we celebrate the one hundred and forty-first birthday of one of the greatest men in American history, I would like to be able to talk about what a glorious day today is in the history of the world. As we celebrate the birth of this man who with his whole heart and soul hated war, I would like to be able to speak of peace in our time, of war being outlawed, and of worldwide disarmament. These would be truly appropriate things to be able to mention as we celebrate the birthday of Abraham Lincoln.

Five years after a world war has been won, men's hearts should anticipate a long peace, and men's minds should be free from the heavy weight that comes with war. But this is not such a period—for this is not a period of peace. This is a time of the "cold war." This is a time when all the world is split into two vast, increasingly hostile armed camps—a time of a great armaments race.

Today we are engaged in a final, all-out battle between Communistic atheism and Christianity. The modern champions of Communism have selected this as the time. And, ladies and gentlemen, the chips are down—they are truly down.

Six years ago, at the time of the first conference to map out the peace—Dumbarton Oaks—there was within the Soviet orbit 180 million people. Lined up on the antitotalitarian side there were in the world roughly 1,625 million people. Today, only six years later, there are 800 million people under the absolute domination of soviet Russia—an increase of over 400 percent. On our side, the figure has shrunk to around 500 million. In other words, in less than six years the odds have changed from 9 to 1 in our favor to 8 to 5 against us. This indicates the swiftness of the tempo of Communist victories and American defeats in the cold war. As one of our outstanding historical figures once said, "When a great democracy is destroyed, it will not be because of enemies from without, but rather because of enemies from within."

The truth of this statement is becoming terrifyingly clear as we see this country each day losing on every front. . . .

The reason why we find ourselves in a position of impotency is not because our only powerful potential enemy has sent men to invade our shores, but rather because of the traitorous actions of those who have been treated so well by this Nation. It has not been the less fortunate or members

From *The Congressional Record*, 81st Congress, v. 96, part 2 (February 20, 1950).

of minority groups who have been selling this Nation out, but rather those who have had all the benefits that the wealthiest nation on earth has had to offer—the finest homes, the finest college education, and the finest jobs in Government we can give.

This is glaringly true in the State Department. There the bright young men who are born with silver spoons in their mouths are the ones who have been worst. . . .

When Chiang Kai-shek was fighting our war, the State Department had in China a young man named John S. Service. His task, obviously, was not to work for the Communization of China. Strangely, however, he sent official reports back to the State Department urging that we torpedo our ally Chiang Kai-shek and stating, in effect, that Communism was the best hope for China.

Later, this man—John Service—was picked up by the Federal Bureau of Investigation for turning over to the Communists secret State Department information. Strangely, however, he was never prosecuted. However, Joseph Grew, the Under Secretary of State, who insisted on his prosecution, was forced to resign. Two days after Grew's successor, Dean Acheson, took over as Under Secretary of State, this man—John Service—who had been picked up by the FBI and who had previously urged that Communism was the best hope of China, was not only reinstated in the State Department but promoted. And finally, under Acheson, placed in charge of all placements and promotions.

Today, ladies and gentlemen, this man Service is on his way to represent the State Department and Acheson in Calcutta—by far and away the most important listening post in the Far East. . . .

This, ladies and gentlemen, gives you somewhat of a picture of the type of individuals who have been helping to shape our foreign policy. In my opinion the State Department, which is one of the most important government departments, is thoroughly infested with Communists.

I have in my hand 57 cases of individuals who would appear to be either card carrying members or certainly loyal to the Communist Party, but who nevertheless are still helping to shape our foreign policy.

One thing to remember in discussing the Communists in our Government is that we are not dealing with spies who get 30 pieces of silver to steal the blueprints of a new weapon. We are dealing with a far more sinister type of activity because it permits the enemy to guide and shape our policy. . . .

As you hear this story of high treason, I know that you are saying to yourself, "Well, why doesn't the Congress do something about it?" Actually, ladies and gentlemen, one of the important reasons for the graft, the corruption, the dishonesty, the disloyalty, the treason in high Government positions—one of the most important reasons why this continues is a lack of moral uprising on the part of the 140 million American people. In the light of history, however, this is not hard to explain.

It is the result of an emotional hangover and a temporary moral lapse which follows every war. It is the apathy to evil which people who have been subjected to the tremendous evils of war feel. As the people of the world see mass murder, the destruction of defenseless and innocent people, and all of the crime and lack of morals which go with war, they become numb and apathetic. It has always been thus after war.

However, the morals of our people have not been destroyed. They still exist. This cloak of numbness and apathy has only needed a spark to rekindle them. Happily, this spark has finally been supplied.

As you know, very recently the Secretary of State [Dean Acheson] proclaimed his loyalty to a man [Alger Hiss] guilty of what has always been considered as the most abominable of all crimes—of being a traitor to the people who gave him a position of great trust. The Secretary of State in attempting to justify his continued devotion to the man who sold out the Christian world to the atheistic world, referred to Christ's Sermon on the Mount as a justification and reason therefor, and the reaction of the American people to this would have made the heart of Abraham Lincoln happy.

When this pompous diplomat in striped pants, with a phony British accent, proclaimed to the American people that Christ on the Mount endorsed Communism, high treason, and betrayal of a sacred trust, the blasphemy was so great that it awakened the dormant indignation of the American people.

He has lighted the spark which is resulting in a moral uprising and will end only when the whole sorry mess of twisted, warped thinkers are swept from the national scene so that we may have a new birth of national honesty and decency in Government.

Declaration of Conscience (1950)

MARGARET CHASE SMITH

I would like to speak briefly and simply about a serious national condition. It is a national feeling of fear and frustration that could result in national suicide and the end of everything that we Americans hold dear. It is a condition that comes from the lack of effective leadership in either the Legislative Branch or the Executive Branch of our Government.

That leadership is so lacking that serious and responsible proposals are being made that national advisory commissions be appointed to provide such critically needed leadership. . . .

From *The New York Times* June 2, 1950.

I speak as a Republican. I speak as a woman. I speak as a United States Senator. I speak as an American. . . .

I think that it is high time that we remembered that we have sworn to uphold and defend the Constitution. I think that it is high time that we remembered that the Constitution, as amended, speaks not only of the freedom of speech but also of trial by jury instead of trial by accusation. . . .

Those of us who shout the loudest about Americanism in making character assassinations are all too frequently those who, by our own words and acts, ignore some of the basic principles of Americanism:

The right to criticize;

The right to hold unpopular beliefs;

The right to protest;

The right of independent thought.

The exercise of these rights should not cost one single American citizen his reputation or his right to a livelihood nor should he be in danger of losing his reputation or livelihood merely because he happens to know someone who holds unpopular beliefs. Who of us doesn't? Otherwise none of us could call our souls our own. Otherwise thought control would have set in.

The American people are sick and tired of being afraid to speak their minds lest they be politically smeared as "Communists" or "Fascists" by their opponents. Freedom of speech is not what it used to be in America. It has been so abused by some that it is not exercised by others. . . .

Today our country is being psychologically divided by the confusion and the suspicions that are bred in the United States Senate to spread like cancerous tentacles of "know nothing, suspect everything" attitudes. Today we have a Democratic Administration that has developed a mania for loose spending and loose programs. History is repeating itself—and the Republican Party again has the opportunity to emerge as the champion of unity and prudence.

The record of the present Democratic Administration has provided us with sufficient campaign issues without the necessity of resorting to political smears. America is rapidly losing its position as leader of the world simply because the Democratic Administration has pitifully failed to provide effective leadership. . . .

Yet to displace it with a Republican regime embracing a philosophy that lacks political integrity or intellectual honesty would prove equally disastrous to this nation. The nation sorely needs a Republican victory. But I don't want to see the Republican Party ride to political victory on the Four Horsemen of Calumny—Fear, Ignorance, Bigotry, and Smear.

I doubt if the Republican Party could—simply because I don't believe the American people will uphold any political party that puts political exploitation above national interest. Surely we Republicans aren't that desperate for victory. . . .

As a United States Senator, I am not proud of the way in which the Senate has been made a publicity platform for irresponsible sensationalism. I am not proud of the reckless abandon in which unproved charges have been hurled from this side of the aisle. I am not proud of the obviously staged, undignified countercharges that have been attempted in retaliation from the other side of the aisle.

I don't like the way the Senate has been made a rendezvous for vilification, for selfish political gain at the sacrifice of individual reputations and national unity. I am not proud of the way we smear outsiders from the Floor of the Senate and hide behind the cloak of congressional immunity and still place ourselves beyond criticism on the Floor of the Senate.

As an American, I am shocked at the way Republicans and Democrats alike are playing directly into the Communist design of "confuse, divide, and conquer." As an American, I don't want a Democratic Administration "whitewash" or "cover-up" any more than I want a Republican smear or witch hunt.

As an American, I condemn a Republican "Fascist" just as much as I condemn a Democrat "Communist." I condemn a Democrat "Fascist" just as much as I condemn a Republican "Communist." They are equally dangerous to you and me and to our country. As an American, I want to see our nation recapture the strength and unity it once had when we fought the enemy instead of ourselves.

It is with these thoughts that I have drafted what I call a "Declaration of Conscience." I am gratified that [six Republican senators] have concurred in that declaration and have authorized me to announce their concurrence.

34

❖

A QUESTION OF COMMAND

In 1950 the cold war between the United States and the Soviet Union turned suddenly hot in Korea, a peninsula abutting China near Japan. Korea had been freed from Japanese rule at the end of World War II, divided at the 38th parallel, and occupied by Russian troops in the north and American troops in the south. The Russians installed a friendly regime in North Korea and then withdrew; the United Nations, at U.S. urging, did the same in South Korea. On June 25, 1950, North Korean armies suddenly crossed the 38th parallel and launched a full-scale invasion of South Korea. President Truman, seeing the hand of China and therefore of the Soviet Union behind this move, promptly committed American troops to the defense of South Korea. He won the backing of the United Nations for his action and announced American determination to support anticommunist governments throughout East Asia. The Korean War lasted from June 1950 until the armistice of July 1953. Under United Nations auspices, sixteen nations participated in the conflict against North Korea. South Korea remained independent, but the Korean War cost the United States $22 billion and 34,000 dead.

The Korean War also prompted a major reassertion of the constitutional primacy of civilian rule in the U.S. government. The United Nations commander in the Korean theater was General Douglas MacArthur, one of the greatest U.S. heroes of World War II and the American proconsul in charge of transforming postwar Japanese society. Against the advice of the American joint chiefs of staff, MacArthur launched a brilliant amphibious landing behind Communist lines. He then recaptured the capital city of Seoul and moved far enough into North Korea to reach the border with China.

MacArthur had gambled that China would not commit troops to the conflict; President Truman's advisers feared it would. MacArthur was wrong. Massive Chinese forces poured across the border, pushing U.N. forces back down the peninsula. Embarrassed, MacArthur publicly called for President Truman to order massive air strikes on China. The President, fearing a long and costly land war with China, refused the general's request and asked him not to argue U.S. policy in the newspapers. MacArthur again called for air attacks on China, took a swipe at the American doctrine of limited (non-nuclear and geographically restricted) war, and implied that Truman was practicing appeasement. President Truman had had enough: On April 10, 1951, he fired MacArthur for insubordination. On April 11 he gave the following radio address to the American public. MacArthur returned home to an enormous ticker-tape parade, an invitation to address a joint session of Congress, and a brief flirtation with Republican party kingpins. But Matthew Ridgway now commanded U.N. forces in Korea, Harry Truman was still president and commander in chief—and the long-established constitutional subordination of military to civilian authority again held firm.

Harry S Truman was born on a farm near Independence, Missouri, in 1884. After graduating from high school, he worked as a farmer and a bank clerk and, during World War I, saw action in France as a captain in the field artillery. On his return from the war he entered the clothing business and in 1922 went into politics. After serving as county judge and presiding judge of Jackson County, Missouri, he was elected senator in 1934 and served in the Senate until his election as vice-president in 1944. As a senator he supported Roosevelt's New Deal policies and won a national reputation as an enemy of favoritism and waste in defense spending. His presidency from 1945 to 1953 was characterized by futile efforts to ram progressive Fair Deal legislation through a conservative Congress and, increasingly, by an anticommunist domestic and foreign policy. He is popularly remembered for his integrity, combativeness, and sense of responsibility—"The buck," he said, "stops here." Truman never made a more politically risky decision than to fire Douglas MacArthur. He died at his home in Independence, Missouri, in 1972.

Questions to Consider. Americans of Truman's era, it has been said, had two overwhelming fears: Communism and war. How did Truman attempt to balance these two fears in his 1950 address? On which side did he finally come down most strongly? American policy makers of the 1950s have been accused of exaggerating the scope and unity of international Communism. Did Truman fall into this habit? Did the confrontation with MacArthur perhaps drive Truman to overcompensate? Truman's action preserved the primacy of civilian control of war policy; why did he not defend his actions on these grounds?

—————————❖—————————

Address on Korea and MacArthur (1951)

HARRY S TRUMAN

In the simplest terms, what we are doing in Korea is this:

We are trying to prevent a third world war.

I think most people in this country recognized that fact last June. And they warmly supported the decision of the Government to help the Republic of Korea against the Communist aggressors. Now, many persons, even some who applauded our decision to defend Korea, have forgotten the basic reason for our action. . . .

The aggression against Korea is the boldest and most dangerous move the Communists have yet made.

The attack on Korea was part of a greater plan for conquering all of Asia. . . .

They want to control all Asia from the Kremlin.

This plan of conquest is in flat contradiction to what we believe. We believe that Korea belongs to the Koreans. We believe that India belongs to the Indians. We believe that all the nations of Asia should be free to work out their affairs in their own way. This is the basis of peace in the Far East and it is the basis of peace everywhere else.

The whole Communist imperialism is back of the attack on peace in the Far East. It was the Soviet Union that trained and equipped the North Koreans for aggression. The Chinese Communists massed forty-four well-trained and well-equipped divisions on the Korean frontier. These were the troops they threw into battle when the North Korean Communists were beaten.

The question we have had to face is whether the Communist plan of conquest can be stopped without general war. Our Government and other countries associated with us in the United Nations believe that the best chance of stopping it without general war is to meet the attack in Korea and defeat it there.

That is what we have been doing. It is a difficult and bitter task.

But so far it has been successful.

So far, we have prevented World War III.

So far, by fighting a limited war in Korea, we have prevented aggression from succeeding, and bringing on a general war. And the ability of the whole free world to resist Communist aggression has been greatly improved. . . .

We do not want to see the conflict in Korea extended. We are trying to prevent a world war—not to start one. The best way to do that is to make

From *The New York Times*, April 12, 1951.

General Douglas MacArthur. On June 29, 1950, the American government ordered combat troops into Korea under the command of General MacArthur. Three months later, MacArthur's forces engineered a brilliant landing behind North Korean lines and quickly overran the northern half of the country. This position proved untenable because, contrary to MacArthur's prediction, Chinese troops entered the war and pushed the Americans far into the south— one of the longest retreats in U.S. history. Here MacArthur, left, receives a decoration from President Harry S Truman—who would soon strip him of his command for insubordination. (UPI/Bettmann Newsphoto)

it plain that we and the other free countries will continue to resist the attack.

But you may ask why can't we take other steps to punish the aggressor. Why don't we bomb Manchuria and China itself? Why don't we assist Chinese Nationalist troops to land on the mainland of China?

If we were to do these things we would be running a very grave risk of starting a general war. If that were to happen, we would have brought about the exact situation we are trying to prevent.

If we were to do these things, we would become entangled in a vast conflict on the continent of Asia and our task would become immeasurably more difficult all over the world.

What would suit the ambitions of the Kremlin better than for our military forces to be committed to a full-scale war with Red China?

It may well be that, in spite of our best efforts, the Communists may spread the war. But it would be wrong—tragically wrong—for us to take the initiative in extending the war.

The dangers are great. Make no mistake about it. Behind the North Koreans and Chinese Communists in the front lines stand additional millions of Chinese soldiers. And behind the Chinese stand the tanks, the planes, the submarines, the soldiers, and the scheming rulers of the Soviet Union.

Our aim is to avoid the spread of the conflict. . . .

If the Communist authorities realize that they cannot defeat us in Korea, if they realize it would be foolhardy to widen the hostilities beyond Korea, then they may recognize the folly of continuing their aggression. A peaceful settlement may then be possible. The door is always open.

Then we may achieve a settlement in Korea which will not compromise the principles and purposes of the United Nations.

I have thought long and hard about this question of extending the war in Asia. I have discussed it many times with the ablest military advisers in the country. I believe with all my heart that the course we are following is the best course.

I believe that we must try to limit the war to Korea for these vital reasons: To make sure that the precious lives of our fighting men are not wasted, to see that the security of our country and the free world is not needlessly jeopardized, and to prevent a third world war.

A number of events have made it evident that General MacArthur did not agree with that policy. I have, therefore, considered it essential to relieve General MacArthur so that there would be no doubt or confusion as to the real purpose and aim of our policy.

It was with the deepest personal regret that I found myself compelled to take this action. General MacArthur is one of our greatest military commanders. But the cause of world peace is more important than any individual.

The change in commands in the Far East means no change whatever in the policy of the United States. We will carry on the fight in Korea with vigor and determination in an effort to bring the war to a speedy and successful conclusion. . . .

Real peace can be achieved through a settlement based on the following factors:

One: The fighting must stop.

Two: Concrete steps must be taken to insure that the fighting will not break out again.

Three: There must be an end to the aggression.

A settlement founded upon these elements would open the way for the unification of Korea and the withdrawal of all foreign forces.

35

✧

THE MILITARY-INDUSTRIAL COMPLEX

During Dwight D. Eisenhower's eight years as president, the United States ended the Korean War and moved to replace expensive conventional armaments with "cheap" nuclear weapons. Moreover, though the Eisenhower administration landed troops briefly in Lebanon, sent military aid to Indochina, and helped overthrow radical governments in Iran and Guatemala, the United States managed to stay out of war in other parts of the world. There was intense cold war. But there was also peace.

Despite all the years of peace under Eisenhower, the United States in 1960 still kept 2,500,000 military personnel on active duty, poured $51 billion into the defense budget—10 percent of the entire gross national product—and threw every scientific resource into creating sophisticated weapons systems. So striking was this development that President Eisenhower, himself a former general and a probusiness Republican, felt compelled in his 1961 farewell address to warn the public against the rise of a "military-industrial complex" in the land. Since military spending never in fact receded after Eisenhower, the concept and the phrase entered permanently into the political vocabulary, thus becoming somewhat ironic Eisenhower legacies to the people.

Born in Texas in 1890, Dwight D. Eisenhower grew up in Kansas in modest circumstances. A West Point graduate of 1915, he served at various army posts in the United States and Asia and under General Douglas MacArthur during the 1930s; his abilities were also perceived by General George Marshall, and he won promotion to brigadier general in 1941. Commander of the Allied forces in western Europe, he oversaw Allied invasions of North Africa, Italy, and France during World War II, demonstrating impressive diplomatic and administrative skills, and returned to America in late 1945 as a five-star general and a vastly popular hero. It was largely these skills and this reputation, plus his disarming grin and the irresistible slogan "I like Ike," that propelled him to landslide presidential victories in 1952 and 1956. After 1961, Eisenhower eased quickly into retirement and discovered that, much like his nemesis Harry Truman, he had become one of

America's beloved political figures. He died in Washington, D.C., in 1969.

Questions to Consider. Two aspects of President Eisenhower's striking address deserve special attention. First, Eisenhower was warning not only against the influence of the military and the arms industry, as represented by huge military budgets, but also against the rise of a scientific-technological elite, as symbolized by the growing control of scholarship by Washington. Of these two tendencies, which did he seem to see as the greater threat? Second, although Eisenhower said plainly that these forces—the military-industrial and the scientific-technological—represented a danger to our liberties and democratic processes, he was vague about how exactly the forces did endanger them and especially about what might, in a concrete way, be done to prevent such threats. Was Eisenhower, a former general, perhaps tacitly urging that soldiers and defense contractors be restricted in their political activities—in campaign contributions, for example, or lobbying efforts—or that defense budgets be scrutinized and slimmed down with special rigor? How realistic were these hints? What connection, if any, was he making at the end of his speech between disarmament and democracy?

---------------◆---------------

Farewell Address (1961)

DWIGHT D. EISENHOWER

A vital element in keeping the peace is our military establishment. Our arms must be mighty, ready for instant action, so that no potential aggressor may be tempted to risk his own destruction.

Our military organization today bears little relation to that known by any of my predecessors in peacetime, or indeed by the fighting men of World War II or Korea.

Until the latest of our world conflicts, the United States had no armaments industry. American makers of plowshares could, with time and as required, make swords as well. But now we can no longer risk emergency improvisation of national defense; we have been compelled to create a permanent armaments industry of vast proportions. Added to this, three and a half million men and women are directly engaged in the defense

From *The New York Times,* January 18, 1961.

establishment. We annually spend on military security more than the net income of all United States corporations.

This conjunction of an immense military establishment and a large arms industry is new in the American experience. The total influence—economic, political, even spiritual—is felt in every city, every statehouse, every office of the federal government. We recognize the imperative need for this development. Yet we must not fail to comprehend its grave implications. Our toil, resources, and livelihood are all involved; so is the very structure of our society.

In the councils of government, we must guard against the acquisition of unwarranted influence, whether sought or unsought, by the military-industrial complex. The potential for the disastrous rise of misplaced power exists and will persist.

We must never let the weight of this combination endanger our liberties or democratic processes. We should take nothing for granted. Only an alert and knowledgeable citizenry can compel the proper meshing of the huge industrial and military machinery of defense with our peaceful methods and goals, so that security and liberty may prosper together.

Akin to, and largely responsible for the sweeping changes in our industrial-military posture, has been the technological revolution during recent decades.

In this revolution, research has become central; it also becomes more formalized, complex, and costly. A steadily increasing share is conducted for, by, or at the discretion of, the federal government. . . .

The prospect of domination of the nation's scholars by federal employment, project allocations, and the power of money is ever present—and is gravely to be regarded.

Yet, in holding scientific research and discovery in respect, as we should, we must also be alert to the equal and opposite danger that public policy could itself become the captive of a scientific-technological elite.

It is the task of statesmanship to mold, to balance, and to integrate these and other forces, new and old, within the principles of our democratic system—ever aiming toward the supreme goals of our free society.

Another factor in maintaining balance involves the element of time. As we peer into society's future, we—you and I, and our government—must avoid the impulse to live only for today, plundering, for our own ease and convenience, the precious resources of tomorrow. We cannot mortgage the material assets of our grandchildren without risking the loss also of their political and spiritual heritage. We want democracy to survive for all generations to come, not to become the insolvent phantom of tomorrow.

Down the long lane of the history yet to be written America knows that this world of ours, ever growing smaller, must avoid becoming a community of dreadful fear and hate, and be, instead, a proud confederation of mutual trust and respect.

Such a confederation must be one of equals. The weakest must come to the conference table with the same confidence as do we, protected as we are by our moral, economic, and military strength. That table, though scarred by many past frustrations, cannot be abandoned for the certain agony of the battlefield.

Disarmament, with mutual honor and confidence, is a continuing imperative. Together we must learn how to compose differences, not with arms, but with intellect and decent purpose. Because this need is so sharp and apparent I confess that I lay down my official responsibilities in this field with a definite sense of disappointment. As one who has witnessed the horror and the lingering sadness of war—as one who knows that another war could utterly destroy this civilization which has been so slowly and painfully built over thousands of years—I wish I could say tonight that a lasting peace is in sight.

Happily, I can say that war has been avoided. Steady progress toward our ultimate goal has been made. But, so much remains to be done. As a private citizen, I shall never cease to do what little I can to help the world advance along that road. . . .

36

THE DEFENSE OF FREEDOM

Although the New Frontier of President John F. Kennedy had a significant domestic component centering on civil rights and social welfare programs, Kennedy's primary emphasis, as his inaugural address, reprinted below, makes clear, was on the development of a vigorous foreign policy. Kennedy perceived the Soviet threat in much the same way that Richard M. Nixon, his Republican opponent, had perceived it during the 1960 presidential campaign: as ubiquitous and unremitting and therefore to be countered at every turn. But Kennedy's views held significant differences from the policy pursued by the Eisenhower administration.

Kennedy was more willing than Eisenhower to increase defense spending; he was also more skeptical about the value of responding to revolutions in the Third World by threatening thermonuclear war. Departing from the policies of his predecessor, Kennedy moved toward a doctrine of "flexible response" that stressed conventional forces over atomic weapons and emphasized international propaganda and public relations over armaments. At once idealistic and demanding, like the 1961 inaugural address itself, Kennedy's views led to the signing of treaties with the Soviet Union that banned atmospheric nuclear testing and to the establishment of emergency communications between the White House and the Kremlin. But these same views also led to the sending of more and more military personnel to South Vietnam, to prevent Ho Chi Minh, the Communist leader of North Vietnam, from unifying Vietnam under his rule.

John F. Kennedy was born in 1917 to a wealthy Irish-American family. After graduating with honors from Harvard in 1940, he served for a time as secretary to his father, who was then U.S. ambassador to Great Britain. *Why England Slept*—his best-selling book on British military policies during the 1930s—was published in 1940. During World War II he served in the U.S. Navy and won the Navy and Marine Corps Medal for his heroism. After the war he entered politics in Massachusetts, winning election to the House of Representatives in 1946 and to the Senate in 1952. His book *Profiles in Courage,* published in 1956, won the Pulitzer Prize, and in 1960 he narrowly bested

Richard Nixon in a contest for the presidency. The youngest man and the only Roman Catholic ever elected president, Kennedy projected an image of intelligence, vitality, and sophistication. Worldwide mourning occurred after he was assassinated in Dallas, Texas, on November 22, 1963.

Questions to Consider. Some historians have argued that in this address Kennedy formally shifted the focus of the cold war from Europe to the nonaligned or economically underdeveloped part of the world. Do you agree or disagree? If you agree, do you also believe there was a connection between this shift and Kennedy's emphasis on feeding and clothing the world—on winning by doing good? Was there also a connection between this shift and Kennedy's preference for invoking human rights instead of democracy? Historians have also read the address as an unprecedented fusion of "adversarialism" with "universalism." Again, do you agree or disagree? Was this fusion connected with Kennedy's sense of facing an "hour of maximum danger" in which Americans might have to "pay any price" for liberty?

———— ✧ ————

Inaugural Address (1961)

JOHN F. KENNEDY

We observe today not a victory of party but a celebration of freedom—symbolizing an end as well as a beginning—signifying renewal as well as change. For I have sworn before you and Almighty God the same solemn oath our forbears prescribed nearly a century and three-quarters ago.

The world is very different now. For man holds in his mortal hands the power to abolish all forms of human poverty and all forms of human life. And yet the same revolutionary beliefs for which our forbears fought are still at issue around the globe—the belief that the rights of man come not from the generosity of the state but from the hand of God.

We dare not forget today that we are the heirs of that first revolution. Let the word go forth from this time and place, to friend and foe alike, that the torch has been passed to a new generation of Americans—born in this century, tempered by war, disciplined by a hard and bitter peace, proud of our ancient heritage—and unwilling to witness or permit the slow undoing of those human rights to which this nation has always been

From *The New York Times*, January 21, 1961.

John F. Kennedy. Kennedy, with his wife Jacqueline sitting at his side, during the presidential inauguration, 1961. (© 1960 Paul Schutzer/LIFE Magazine, Time-Warner, Inc.)

committed, and to which we are committed today at home and around the world.

Let every nation know, whether it wishes us well or ill, that we shall pay any price, bear any burden, meet any hardship, support any friend, oppose any foe to assure the survival and the success of liberty.

This much we pledge—and more.

To those old allies whose cultural and spiritual origins we share, we pledge the loyalty of faithful friends. United, there is little we cannot do in a host of co-operative ventures. Divided, there is little we can do—for we dare not meet a powerful challenge at odds and split asunder.

To those new states whom we welcome to the ranks of the free, we pledge our word that one form of colonial control shall not have passed away merely to be replaced by a far more iron tyranny. We shall not always expect to find them supporting our view. But we shall always hope to find them strongly supporting their own freedom—and to remember that, in the past, those who foolishly sought power by riding the back of the tiger ended up inside.

To those people in the huts and villages of half the globe struggling to break the bonds of mass misery, we pledge our best efforts to help them help themselves, for whatever period is required—not because the Communists may be doing it, not because we seek their votes, but because it is right. If a free society cannot help the many who are poor, it cannot save the few who are rich.

To our sister republics south of our border, we offer a special pledge—to convert our good words into good deeds—in a new alliance for progress—to assist free men and free governments in casting off the chains of poverty. But this peaceful revolution of hope cannot become the prey of hostile powers. Let all our neighbors know that we shall join with them to oppose aggression or subversion anywhere in the Americas. And let every other power know that this hemisphere intends to remain the master of its own house.

To that world assembly of sovereign states, the United Nations, our last best hope in an age where the instruments of war have far outpaced the instruments of peace, we renew our pledge of support—to prevent it from becoming merely a forum for invective—to strengthen its shield of the new and the weak—and to enlarge the area in which its writ may run.

Finally, to those nations who would make themselves our adversary, we offer not a pledge but a request: that both sides begin anew the quest for peace, before the dark powers of destruction unleashed by science engulf all humanity in planned or accidental self-destruction.

We dare not tempt them with weakness. For only when our arms are sufficient beyond doubt can we be certain beyond doubt that they will never be employed.

But neither can two great and powerful groups of nations take comfort from our present course—both sides overburdened by the cost of modern weapons, both rigidly alarmed by the steady spread of the deadly atom, yet both racing to alter that uncertain balance of terror that stays the hand of mankind's final war.

So let us begin anew—remembering on both sides that civility is not a sign of weakness, and sincerity is always subject to proof. Let us never negotiate out of fear. But let us never fear to negotiate.

Let both sides explore what problems unite us instead of belaboring those problems which divide us.

Let both sides, for the first time, formulate serious and precise proposals for the inspection and control of arms—and bring the absolute power to destroy other nations under the absolute control of all nations.

Let both sides seek to invoke the wonders of science instead of its terror. Together let us explore the stars, conquer the deserts, eradicate disease, tap the ocean depths, and encourage the arts and commerce.

Let both sides unite to heed in all corners of the earth the command of Isaiah—to "undo the heavy burdens . . . [and] let the oppressed go free."

And if a beachhead of co-operation may push back the jungle of suspicion, let both sides join in creating a new endeavor, not a new balance of power, but a new world of law, where the strong are just and the weak secure and the peace preserved.

All this will not be finished in the first one hundred days. Nor will it be finished in the first one thousand days, nor in the life of this administration, nor even perhaps in our lifetime on this planet. But let us begin.

In your hands, my fellow citizens, more than mine, will rest the final success or failure of our course. Since this country was founded, each generation of Americans has been summoned to give testimony to its national loyalty. The graves of young Americans who answered the call to service surround the globe.

Now the trumpet summons us again—not as a call to bear arms, though arms we need—not as a call to battle, though embattled we are—but a call to bear the burden of a long twilight struggle, year in and year out, "rejoicing in hope, patient in tribulation"—a struggle against the common enemies of man: tyranny, poverty, disease, and war itself.

Can we forge against these enemies a grand and global alliance, North and South, East and West, that can assure a more fruitful life for all mankind? Will you join in that historic effort?

In the long history of the world, only a few generations have been granted the role of defending freedom in its hour of maximum danger. I do not shrink from this responsibility—I welcome it. I do not believe that any of us would exchange places with any other people or any other generation. The energy, the faith, the devotion which we bring to this endeavor will light our country and all who serve it—and the glow from that fire can truly light the world.

And so, my fellow Americans: ask not what your country can do for you—ask what you can do for your country.

My fellow citizens of the world: ask not what America will do for you, but what together we can do for the freedom of man.

Finally, whether you are citizens of America or citizens of the world, ask of us here the same high standards of strength and sacrifice which we ask of you. With a good conscience our only sure reward, with history the final judge of deeds, let us go forth to lead the land we love, asking His blessing and His help, but knowing that here on earth God's work must truly be our own.

37

✧

BLANK CHECK

American involvement in Vietnam began modestly enough with a promise in 1945 to help France restore colonial rule there. The United States backed France because Ho Chi Minh, the leader of the struggle for Vietnamese independence, was a Communist. American policy makers were more impressed by Ho's Communism than by his nationalism; they viewed him as a tool of the Kremlin, although he had the backing of many non-Communists in Indochina who wanted freedom from French control. In 1954, Ho's forces defeated the French, and the French decided to withdraw from Vietnam. At this point the United States stepped in, backed a partition of Vietnam, and gave aid to the South Vietnamese government in Saigon. American policy continued to be based on the belief that Communism in Vietnam was inspired by China or the Soviet Union, if not both. If Vietnam went Communist, Washington warned, other countries in Asia might topple like so many dominoes, and Communist influence in the world would grow at the expense of America's.

U.S. military personnel entered the Vietnamese conflict between North and South under presidents Eisenhower and Kennedy. American bombers began raiding North Vietnam in 1965, after the reelection of Kennedy's successor, Lyndon B. Johnson. By 1969, American troops in South Vietnam numbered around 550,000, and American planes had dropped more bombs in Vietnam than had been dropped on Germany and Japan during World War II. Yet the Vietcong (the South Vietnamese insurgents), aided by North Vietnamese military units, seemed stronger than ever. International opinion had now turned against the United States.

A key episode in Lyndon Johnson's escalation came with the so-called Tonkin Gulf incident. On August 2, 1964, the U.S.S. *Maddox,* an American destroyer supporting South Vietnamese commando raids against North Vietnam, came under attack by enemy patrol boats. The attackers suffered heavy damage; the *Maddox* was unharmed. Two days later the *Maddox* and another U.S. destroyer again moved into North Vietnamese waters. Although the weather was bad, sonar equipment indicated enemy torpedoes. When the captain of the *Maddox* later questioned members of his crew, no one could recall any enemy attacks, and subsequent investigations of the incident likewise turned up no evidence of hostile fire. The American destroyers nevertheless reportedly leveled heavy fire against North Vietnamese patrol boats. President Johnson, despite the questionable evidence and without admitting that U.S. ships were supporting raids against the North, ordered air strikes on North Vietnamese naval bases and announced on television that he was retaliating for "unprovoked" attacks. U.S. planes would now, he said, bomb North Vietnam.

On August 5, Johnson, in the address excerpted below, asked Congress to give him authority to repel "any armed attack against the forces of the United States and to prevent further aggression." The resolution passed the House by 466 to 0 and passed the Senate by 88 to 2. The resolution, as Johnson eventually argued, was tantamount to a declaration of war—which Congress has not voted against any country since December 1941. Under its auspices, the president authorized not only the carpet-bombing of North Vietnam but the American build-up to over a half-million combat troops. Its effect in 1964 was to preempt criticism from Republican presidential candidate Barry Goldwater, a hawk on foreign policy, help raise Johnson's approval rating in the polls from 42 percent to 72 percent, and contribute to a major victory in that fall's election.

Born in the poor hill country of central Texas in 1908, Lyndon Johnson worked his way through Southwest Texas State Teachers College in San Marcos and went to Washington as assistant to a local congressman in 1931. An intensely ambitious and ardent New Deal Democrat, Johnson began his political career with his election to fill a congressional vacancy in 1937. He was elected to the U.S. Senate in 1948. Unmatched at arranging the compromises and distributing the favors and money on which congressional politics rested, he became Senate minority leader in 1953 and majority leader in 1955, when the Democrats regained control of the Senate. As the vice-presidential nominee in 1960, he helped John F. Kennedy carry enough Southern states to become president; he became president himself upon Kennedy's assassination in 1963. As president, Johnson helped enact the most sweeping civil rights legislation of the century, but he also dramatically escalated a fundamentally unpopular war. Faced with widespread opposition to his policies, he declined to run for reelection in 1968. He died in San Antonio in 1973.

Questions to Consider. On what grounds did Johnson defend the American presence in Vietnam? How did he deal with the problematic nature of the evidence of North Vietnamese attacks on U.S. ships? Johnson wanted authorization not only for limited retaliation over this specific incident but to attack North Vietnam on a large scale over a long period of time. How did he move in this address from the particular incident to the general goal? What parts of the speech might have been especially effective in undercutting Barry Goldwater's criticism of the Democrats as "soft on Communism"? Was Johnson demanding, in effect, a declaration of war? If so, why didn't he ask for that?

Message to Congress on the Gulf of Tonkin (1964)

LYNDON B. JOHNSON

Last night I announced to the American people that the North Vietnamese regime had conducted further deliberate attacks against U.S. naval vessels operating in international waters, and that I had therefore directed air action against gun boats and supporting facilities used in these hostile operations. This air action has now been carried out with substantial damage to the boats and facilities. Two U.S. aircraft were lost in the action.

After consultation with the leaders of both parties in the Congress, I further announced a decision to ask the Congress for a Resolution expressing the unity and determination of the United States in supporting freedom and in protecting peace in Southeast Asia.

These latest actions of the North Vietnamese regime have given a new and grave turn to the already serious situation in Southeast Asia. Our commitments in that area are well known to the Congress. They were first made in 1954 by President Eisenhower. They were further defined in the Southeast Asia Collective Defense Treaty approved by the Senate in February 1955.

This Treaty with its accompanying protocol obligates the United States and other members to act in accordance with their Constitutional processes to meet Communist aggression against any of the parties or protocol states.

Our policy in Southeast Asia has been consistent and unchanged since 1954. I summarized it on June 2 in four simple propositions:

1. *America keeps her word.* Here as elsewhere, we must and shall honor our commitments.

2. *The issue is the future of Southeast Asia as a whole.* A threat to any nation in that region is a threat to all, and a threat to us.

3. *Our purpose is peace.* We have no military, political or territorial ambitions in the area.

From *The New York Times,* August 6, 1964.

4. *This is not just a jungle war, but a struggle for freedom on every front of human activity.* Our military and economic assistance to South Vietnam and Laos in particular has the purpose of helping these countries to repel aggression and strengthen their independence.

The threat to the free nations of Southeast Asia has long been clear. The North Vietnamese regime has constantly sought to take over South Vietnam and Laos. This Communist regime has violated the Geneva Accords for Vietnam. It has systematically conducted a campaign of subversion, which includes the direction, training, and supply of personnel and arms for the conduct of guerrilla warfare in South Vietnamese territory. In Laos, the North Vietnamese regime has maintained military forces, used Laotian territory for infiltration into South Vietnam, and most recently carried out combat operations—all in direct violation of the Geneva Agreements of 1962.

In recent months, the actions of the North Vietnamese regime have become steadily more threatening. In May, following new acts of Communist aggression in Laos, the United States undertook reconnaissance flights over Laotian territory, at the request of the Government of Laos. These flights had the essential mission of determining the situation in territory where Communist forces were preventing inspection by the International Control Commission. When the Communists attacked these aircraft, I responded by furnishing escort fighters with instructions to fire when fired upon. Thus, these latest North Vietnamese attacks on our naval vessels are not the first direct attack on armed forces of the United States.

As President of the United States I have concluded that I should now ask the Congress, on its part, to join in affirming the national determination that all such attacks will be met, and that the U.S. will continue in its basic policy of assisting the free nations of the area to defend their freedom.

As I have repeatedly made clear, the United States intends no rashness, and seeks no wider war. We must make it clear to all that the United States is united in its determination to bring about the end of Communist subversion and aggression in the area. We seek the full and effective restoration of the international agreements signed in Geneva in 1954, with respect to South Vietnam, and again in Geneva in 1962, with respect to Laos.

I recommend a Resolution expressing the support of the Congress for all necessary action to protect our armed forces and to assist nations covered by the SEATO Treaty. At the same time, I assure the Congress that we shall continue readily to explore any avenues of political solution that will effectively guarantee the removal of Communist subversion and the preservation of the independence of the nations of the area.

The Resolution could well be based upon similar resolutions enacted by the Congress in the past—to meet the threat to Formosa in 1955, to meet the threat to the Middle East in 1957, and to meet the threat in Cuba in 1962. It could state in the simplest terms the resolve and support of the

Congress for action to deal appropriately with attacks against our armed forces and to defend freedom and preserve peace in southeast Asia in accordance with the obligations of the United States under the southeast Asia Treaty. I urge the Congress to enact such a Resolution promptly and thus to give convincing evidence to the aggressive Communist nations, and to the world as a whole, that our policy in southeast Asia will be carried forward—and that the peace and security of the area will be preserved.

The events of this week would in any event have made the passage of a Congressional Resolution essential. But there is an additional reason for doing so at a time when we are entering on three months of political campaigning. Hostile nations must understand that in such a period the United States will continue to protect its national interests, and that in these matters there is no division among us.

38

✦

AGONY IN ASIA

The escalation of American involvement in Vietnam provoked perhaps the greatest wartime opposition in American history. By the end of 1965, the first draft card burnings had occurred. Students in major universities throughout the country had organized "teach-ins" (named after the civil rights "sit-ins") to discuss the nature of the war and had held the first antiwar march on Washington. By 1967, protest rallies were drawing hundreds of thousands, and evasion of the draft among middle-class students was widespread. Some of the country's most prominent leaders, including the Reverend Martin Luther King, Jr., were vehemently criticizing the Johnson administration for its Vietnam policy. The speech reprinted below, which King delivered at Riverside Church in New York City, stressed the links between international violence and domestic violence, war spending and social poverty, and the suppression of independence movements abroad and minority aspirations at home.

Martin Luther King's stance had special force because of his stature as an advocate of peace and human rights. Born in Atlanta, Georgia, in 1929, the son of a Baptist clergyman, King entered college at the age of fifteen. He eventually received a doctorate in theology from Boston University. In 1954 he was called to the ministry of a church in Montgomery, Alabama, and in 1955 he became a leader in the successful effort to integrate the local bus system. Calling on this experience and on his philosophy of nonviolence, King was soon promoting demonstrations against segregation throughout the South. In August 1963 he spoke to 250,000 people in the nation's capital on behalf of black voting rights, the first so-called March on Washington and a model for later antiwar protests. In 1964 he won the Nobel Peace Prize. In April 1968, having broken with the Johnson administration over the Vietnam war and on the eve of a vast "Poor People's Campaign" for economic justice, King was assassinated in Memphis, Tennessee. The death of the apostle of nonviolence triggered massive race riots in the nation's cities. His funeral attracted 150,000 mourners. The inscription on his tombstone, taken from his 1963 Washington speech, reads: "Free at Last, Free at Last, Thank God Almighty, I'm Free at Last."

Questions to Consider. Of the seven reasons King gave for deciding to "break silence" over Vietnam, which—as measurable by the rank and emphasis he gave them and by his rhetorical style—seem to have mattered most to him? Note how King inveighed first against racial injustice, then against violence, and finally against both issues. Was he right to link the two so closely? Would any perceptive critic of injustice have done so, or did this reflect King's particular way of seeing things and his personal experience in the civil rights movement? Many historians believe this speech marked a sharp political shift by King away from the struggle for civil rights and toward a broader struggle for economic justice and social transformation. Is there evidence for this interpretation in the speech? Why do you suppose King waited until 1967 to launch a public attack on American policy in Vietnam? Why was he careful to call his silence, rather than his attack, a "betrayal"?

A Time to Break Silence (1967)

MARTIN LUTHER KING, JR.

I come to this magnificent house of worship tonight because my conscience leaves me no other choice. I join with you in this meeting because I am in deepest agreement with the aims and work of the organization which has brought us together: Clergy and Laymen Concerned About Vietnam. The recent statement of your executive committee are the sentiments of my own heart and I found myself in full accord when I read its opening lines: "A time comes when silence is betrayal." That time has come for us in relation to Vietnam. . . .

Over the past two years, as I have moved to break the betrayal of my own silences and to speak from the burnings of my own heart, as I have called for radical departures from the destruction of Vietnam, many persons have questioned me about the wisdom of my path. At the heart of their concerns this query has often loomed large and loud: Why are you speaking about the war, Dr. King? Why are you joining the voices of dissent? Peace and civil rights don't mix, they say. Aren't you hurting the cause of your people, they ask? And when I hear them, though I often understand the source of their concern, I am nevertheless greatly saddened, for such questions mean that the inquirers have not really known me, my commitment

From *Freedomways* (Spring 1967), 103–117. Reprinted by permission of Joan Daves Agency.

Wartime remembrance. Another soldier returns from Vietnam. (© 1969 Constantine Manos/Magnum Photos)

or my calling. Indeed, their questions suggest that they do not know the world in which they live.

In the light of such tragic misunderstanding, I deem it of signal importance to try to state clearly, and I trust concisely, why I believe that the path from Dexter Avenue Baptist Church—the church in Montgomery,

Alabama, where I began my pastorate—leads clearly to this sanctuary tonight. . . .

Since I am a preacher by trade, I suppose it is not surprising that I have seven major reasons for bringing Vietnam into the field of my moral vision. There is at the outset a very obvious and almost facile connection between the war in Vietnam and the struggle I, and others, have been waging in America. A few years ago there was a shining moment in that struggle. It seemed as if there was a real promise of hope for the poor—both black and white—through the Poverty Program. There were experiments, hopes, new beginnings. Then came the build-up in Vietnam and I watched the program broken and eviscerated as if it were some idle political plaything of a society gone mad on war, and I knew that America would never invest the necessary funds or energies in rehabilitation of its poor so long as adventures like Vietnam continued to draw men and skills and money like some demonic destructive suction tube. So I was increasingly compelled to see the war as an enemy of the poor and to attack it as such.

Perhaps the more tragic recognition of reality took place when it became clear to me that the war was doing far more than devastating the hopes of the poor at home. It was sending their sons and their brothers and their husbands to fight and to die in extraordinarily high proportions relative to the rest of the population. We were taking the black young men who had been crippled by our society and sending them 8,000 miles away to guarantee liberties in Southeast Asia which they had not found in Southwest Georgia and East Harlem. So we have been repeatedly faced with the cruel irony of watching negro and white boys on TV screens as they kill and die together for a nation that has been unable to seat them together in the same schools. So we watch them in brutal solidarity burning the huts of a poor village, but we realize that they would never live on the same block in Detroit. I could not be silent in the face of such cruel manipulation of the poor.

My third reason moves to an even deeper level of awareness, for it grows out of my experience in the ghettos of the north over the last three years—especially the last three summers. As I have walked among the desperate, rejected and angry young men I have told them that Molotov cocktails and rifles would not solve their problems. I have tried to offer them my deepest compassion while maintaining my conviction that social change comes most meaningfully through nonviolent action. But they asked—and rightly so—what about Vietnam? They asked if our own nation wasn't using massive doses of violence to solve its problems, to bring about the changes it wanted. Their questions hit home, and I knew that I could never again raise my voice against the violence of the oppressed in the ghettos without having first spoken clearly to the greatest purveyor of violence in the world today—my own government. For the sake of those boys, for the sake of this government, for the sake of the hundreds of thousands trembling under our violence, I cannot be silent.

For those who ask the question, "Aren't you a Civil Rights leader?" and thereby mean to exclude me from the movement for peace, I have this further answer. In 1957 when a group of us formed the Southern Christian Leadership Conference, we chose as our motto: "To save the soul of America." We were convinced that we could not limit our vision to certain rights for black people, but instead affirmed the conviction that America would never be free or saved from itself unless the descendants of its slaves were loosed completely from the shackles they still wear. In a way we were agreeing with Langston Hughes, that black bard of Harlem, who had written earlier:

> *O, yes*
> *I say it plain,*
> *America never was America to me,*
> *And yet I swear this oath—*
> *America will be!*[1]

Now, it should be incandescently clear that no one who has any concern for the integrity and life of America today can ignore the present war. If America's soul becomes totally poisoned, part of the autopsy must read Vietnam. It can never be saved so long as it destroys the deepest hopes of men the world over. So it is that those of us who are yet determined that America will be are led down the path of protest and dissent, working for the health of our land.

As if the weight of such a commitment to the life and health of America were not enough, another burden of responsibility was placed upon me in 1964; and I cannot forget that the Nobel Prize for Peace was also a commission—a commission to work harder than I had ever worked before for "the brotherhood of man." This is a calling that takes me beyond national allegiances, but even if it were not present I would yet have to live with the meaning of my commitment to the ministry of Jesus Christ. To me the relationship of this ministry to the making of peace is so obvious that I sometimes marvel at those who ask me why I am speaking against the war. Could it be that they do not know that the good news was meant for all men—for Communists and capitalists, for their children and ours, for black and for white, for revolutionary and conservative? Have they forgotten that my ministry is in obedience to the one who loved his enemies so fully that he died for them? What can I say to the "Viet Cong" or to Castro or to Mao as a faithful minister of this one? Can I threaten them with death or must I not share with them my life?

---

1. Reprinted by permission of Harold Ober Associates Incorporated. Copyright 1938 by Langston Hughes. Copyright renewed 1965 by Langston Hughes.

Finally, as I try to delineate for you and for myself the road that leads from Montgomery to this place I would have offered all that was most valid if I simply said that I must be true to my conviction that I share with all men the calling to be a son of the Living God. Beyond the calling of race or nation or creed is this vocation of sonship and brotherhood, and because I believe that the Father is deeply concerned especially for his suffering and helpless and outcast children, I come tonight to speak for them. . . .

And as I ponder the madness of Vietnam and search within myself for ways to understand and respond to compassion my mind goes constantly to the people of that peninsula. I speak now not of the soldiers of each side, not of the junta in Saigon, but simply of the people who have been living under the curse of war for almost three continuous decades now. I think of them too because it is clear to me that there will be no meaningful solution there until some attempt is made to know them and hear their broken cries. . . .

They languish under our bombs and consider us—not their fellow Vietnamese—the real enemy. They move sadly and apathetically as we herd them off the land of their fathers into concentration camps where minimal social needs are rarely met. They know they must move or be destroyed by our bombs. So they go—primarily women and children and the aged.

They watch as we poison their water, as we kill a million acres of their crops. They must weep as the bulldozers roar through their areas preparing to destroy the precious trees. They wander into the hospitals, with at least twenty casualties from American firepower for one "Viet Cong"-inflicted injury. So far we may have killed a million of them—mostly children. They wander into the towns and see thousands of the children, homeless, without clothes, running in packs on the streets like animals. They see the children degraded by our soldiers as they beg for food. They see the children selling their sisters to our soldiers, soliciting for their mothers.

What do the peasants think as we ally ourselves with the landlords and as we refuse to put any action into our many words concerning land reform? What do they think as we test out our latest weapons on them, just as the Germans tested out new medicine and new tortures in the concentration camps of Europe? Where are the roots of the independent Vietnam we claim to be building? Is it among these voiceless ones?

We have destroyed their two most cherished institutions: the family and the village. We have destroyed their land and their crops. We have cooperated in the crushing of the nation's only non-communist revolutionary political force—the unified Buddhist Church. We have supported the enemies of the peasants of Saigon. We have corrupted their women and children and killed their men. What liberators! . . .

At this point I should make it clear that while I have tried in these last few minutes to give a voice to the voiceless on Vietnam and to understand the arguments of those who are called enemy, I am as deeply concerned about our own troops there as anything else. For it occurs to me that what we are submitting them to in Vietnam is not simply the brutalizing process that goes on in any war where armies face each other and seek to destroy. We are adding cynicism to the process of death, for they must know after a short period there that none of the things we claim to be fighting for are really involved. Before long they must know that their government has sent them into a struggle among Vietnamese, and the more sophisticated surely realize that we are on the side of the wealthy and the secure while we create a hell for the poor.

Somehow this madness must cease. We must stop now. I speak as a child of God and brother to the suffering poor of Vietnam. I speak for those whose land is being laid waste, whose homes are being destroyed, whose culture is being subverted. I speak for the poor of America who are paying the double price of smashed hopes at home and death and corruption in Vietnam. I speak as a citizen of the world, for the world as it stands aghast at the path we have taken. I speak as an American to the leaders of my own nation. The great initiative in this war is ours. The initiative to stop it must be ours. . . .

In 1957 a sensitive American official overseas said that it seemed to him that our nation was on the wrong side of a world revolution. During the past ten years we have seen emerge a pattern of suppression which now has justified the presence of U.S. military "advisers" in Venezuela. This need to maintain social stability for our investments accounts for the counterrevolutionary action of American forces in Guatemala. It tells why American helicopters are being used against guerrillas in Colombia and why American napalm and green beret forces have already been active against rebels in Peru. It is with such activity in mind that the words of the late John F. Kennedy come back to haunt us. Five years ago he said, "Those who make peaceful revolution impossible will make violent revolution inevitable."

Increasingly, by choice or by accident, this is the role our nation has taken—the role of those who make peaceful revolution impossible by refusing to give up the privileges and the pleasures that come from the immense profits of overseas investment.

I am convinced that if we are to get on the right side of the world revolution, we as a nation must undergo a radical revolution of values. We must rapidly begin the shift from a "thing-oriented" society to a "person-oriented" society. When machines and computers, profit motives and property rights are considered more important than people, the giant triplets of racism, materialism, and militarism are incapable of being conquered.

A true revolution of values will soon cause us to question the fairness and justice of many of our past and present policies. On the one hand we are called to play the Good Samaritan on life's roadside; but that will be only an initial act. One day we must come to see that the whole Jericho Road must be transformed so that men and women will not be constantly beaten and robbed as they make their journey on Life's highway. True compassion is more than flinging a coin to a beggar; it is not haphazard and superficial. It comes to see that an edifice which produces beggars needs restructuring. A true revolution of values will soon look uneasily on the glaring contrast of poverty and wealth. With righteous indignation, it will look across the seas and see individual capitalists of the West investing huge sums of money in Asia, Africa and South America, only to take the profits out with no concern for the social betterment of the countries, and say: "This is not just." It will look at our alliance with the landed gentry of Latin America and say: "This is not just." The Western arrogance of feeling that it has everything to teach others and nothing to learn from them is not just. A true revolution of values will lay hands on the world order and say of war: "This way of settling differences is not just."

Now let us begin. Now let us rededicate ourselves to the long and bitter—but beautiful—struggle for a new world. This is the calling of the sons of God, and our brothers wait eagerly for our response. Shall we say the odds are too great? Shall we tell them the struggle is too hard? Will our message be that the forces of American life militate against their arrival as full men, and we send our deepest regrets? Or will there be another message, of longing, of hope, of solidarity with their yearnings, of commitment to their cause, whatever the cost? The choice is ours, and though we might prefer it otherwise we must choose in this crucial moment of human history.

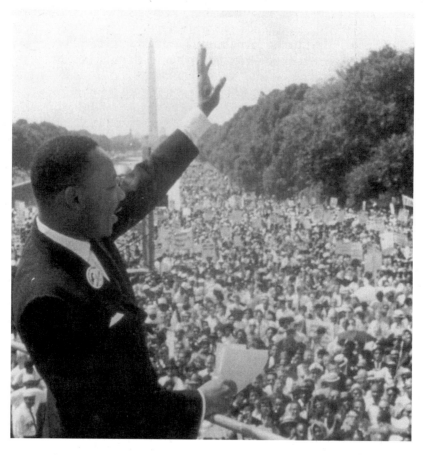

"I have a dream"—Dr. Martin Luther King, Jr. Dr. King spoke to over 200,000 people gathered at the Lincoln Memorial in August 1963 for the March on Washington. (UPI/Bettmann Newsphotos)

CHAPTER SEVEN

Uncertain Trumpets

39

✧

DESEGREGATION BEGINS

Racial segregation was a fact of life everywhere in the South until the middle of this century. Organizations such as the National Association for the Advancement of Colored People (NAACP) and the Congress of Racial Equality (CORE) fought hard against segregation and its hand-maiden, disfranchisement of blacks. But in 1896 the Supreme Court had ruled in *Plessy* v. *Ferguson* that separate facilities for blacks and whites were legal, and there seemed little recourse from this decree, especially given the unsympathetic racial views of the national government in this period. Only in 1947 did some tentative preliminary change come with the integration of major-league baseball for commercial reasons, the integration of the armed forces by presidential order, and the integration of Southern law schools by a Supreme Court decision that year arguing that such schools were inherently unequal because they denied opportunities to those excluded.

Then, in 1954, in an NAACP lawsuit entitled *Brown* v. *The Board of Education of Topeka,* the Supreme Court extended its reasoning from law schools to the entire segregated school system, thereby reversing the "separate-but-equal" doctrine some sixty years after its adoption. Written by Chief Justice Earl Warren on behalf of a unanimous Court, at first this momentous decision, reprinted below, was met with bitter resentment and resistance from most Southern whites. Yet it marked the beginning of the end for legally segregated schools in the nation. Together with the massive civil rights movement led by Martin Luther King, Jr., and others, it outlawed all segregated public facilities, whether buses, beaches, lunch counters, voting booths, or schools.

Earl Warren was born in Los Angeles in 1891. After he was graduated from the University of California at Berkeley, he practiced law in the San Francisco area until joining the army during World War I. In the 1920s Warren embarked on a successful political career in California, serving as district attorney, state attorney general, and governor. His only electoral defeat came as Republican vice-presidential candidate in 1948. When President Eisenhower appointed him chief justice in 1953, Warren was considered a rather traditional Republican moderate. His leadership of the Court, however, brought an unexpected burst of judicial activism that strengthened not only minority rights but also the rights of voters, trial defendants, and witnesses before congressional committees. Warren resigned from the Court in 1969 and died in Washington in 1974.

Questions to Consider. Compare Earl Warren's assumptions and reasoning in this case with those of Henry Billings Brown in *Plessy* v. *Ferguson* (1896). Note, for example, that Warren virtually disregarded what Brown had believed to be so crucial—the actual differences between the races. Note, too, that Warren read very large public purposes into the bountiful commitment of local governments to public education: good citizenship, values, training, and social adjustment. Were these two factors—colorblindness and purposeful public education—enough to account for the Court's 1954 decision? If so, why did Warren introduce psychological studies into his argument? Was it merely a reflection of the findings of modern social science? Or was it because Brown had already reasoned from psychological effects in *Plessy*? In what other areas besides education might modern courts attempt to use the equal protection clause of the Fourteenth Amendment as construed by the Warren Court?

------------------------◇------------------------

Brown v. *The Board of Education of Topeka* (1954)

EARL WARREN

These cases come to us from the States of Kansas, South Carolina, Virginia, and Delaware. They are premised on different facts and different local conditions, but a common legal question justifies their consideration together in this consolidated opinion.

In approaching this problem, we cannot turn the clock back to 1868 when the Amendment was adopted, or even to 1896 when *Plessy* v. *Ferguson* was written. We must consider public education in the light of its full development and its present place in American life throughout the Nation. Only in this way can it be determined if segregation in public schools deprives these plaintiffs of the equal protection of the laws.

Today, education is perhaps the most important function of state and local governments. Compulsory school attendance laws and the great expenditures for education both demonstrate our recognition of the importance of education to our democratic society. It is required in the

Brown v. *The Board of Education of Topeka*, 347 U.S. 483 (1954).

Resistance to desegregation. Federal troops escort black students into Central High School, Little Rock, Arkansas, in 1957 in obedience to a court order to desegregate the public schools "with all deliberate speed." President Eisenhower sent U.S. troops to the scene after the Arkansas governor vowed to resist the desegregation order. (© 1957 Burt Glinn/Magnum Photos)

performance of our most basic public responsibilities, even service in the armed forces. It is the very foundation of good citizenship. Today it is a principal instrument in awakening the child to cultural values, in preparing him for later professional training, and in helping him to adjust normally to his environment. In these days, it is doubtful that any child may reasonably be expected to succeed in life if he is denied the opportunity of an education. Such an opportunity, where the state has undertaken to provide it, is a right which must be made available to all on equal terms.

We come then to the question presented: Does segregation of children in public schools solely on the basis of race, even though the physical facilities and other "tangible" factors may be equal, deprive the children of the minority group of equal educational opportunities? We believe that it does.

In *Sweatt* v. *Painter*, . . . in finding that a segregated law school for Negroes could not provide them equal educational opportunities, this Court relied in large part on "those qualities which are incapable of objective measurement but which make for greatness in a law school." In *McLaurin* v. *Oklahoma State Regents*, . . . the Court, in requiring that a Negro admitted to a white graduate school be treated like all other students, again resorted to intangible considerations: " . . . his ability to study, to engage in discussions and exchange views with other students, and, in general, to learn his profession." Such considerations apply with added force to children in grade and high schools. To separate them from others of similar age and qualifications solely because of their race generates a feeling of inferiority as to their status in the community that may affect their hearts and minds in a way unlikely ever to be undone. The effect of this separation on their educational opportunities was well stated by a finding in the Kansas case by a court which nevertheless felt compelled to rule against the Negro plaintiffs:

> Segregation of white and colored children in public schools has a detrimental effect upon the colored children. The impact is greater when it has the sanction of the law; for the policy of separating the races is usually interpreted as denoting the inferiority of the Negro group. A sense of inferiority affects the motivation of a child to learn. Segregation with the sanction of the law, therefore, has a tendency to retard the educational and mental development of Negro children and to deprive them of some of the benefits they would receive in a racially integrated school system.

Whatever may have been the extent of psychological knowledge at the time of *Plessy* v. *Ferguson,* this finding is amply supported by modern authority. Any language in *Plessy* v. *Ferguson* contrary to this finding is rejected.

We conclude that in the field of public education the doctrine of "separate but equal" has no place. Separate educational facilities are inherently unequal. Therefore, we hold that the plaintiffs and others similarly situated for whom the actions have been brought are, by reason of the segregation complained of, deprived of the equal protection of the laws guaranteed by the Fourteenth Amendment. . . .

40

✧

NONVIOLENCE AND PROTEST

When the Supreme Court ordered public schools desegregated in 1954, the country's leading civil rights organizations—the NAACP, CORE, and the National Urban League—were all situated in the North. They drew their strength mainly from teachers, journalists, lawyers, students, businesspeople, and other persons who made up the tiny black middle class, and challenged racial oppression mostly through lawsuits and political lobbying. The initiatives of these organizations might affect Southern blacks and change the lives of black rural and urban workers, who made up most of the black population, because most blacks still lived in the South and did manual labor. But the organizations themselves were not based on this Southern black majority and so were unable to involve these blacks in the civil rights struggle or to mount direct challenges to racial injustice in the section of the country where it mattered most.

By the late 1950s the situation was changing. In part this resulted from efforts to implement the Brown decision, particularly in New Orleans, Louisiana, and Little Rock, Arkansas. There militant whites met black students with violence, prompting not only federal intervention but black demonstrations in support of desegregation. Southern NAACP chapters now grew rapidly, giving that organization a regional strength it had not enjoyed before. Even more important were the direct actions against segregated public facilities led by the Reverend Martin Luther King, Jr., and the civil rights group he founded in 1957, the Southern Christian Leadership Conference (SCLC). The first of these actions was precipitated by an incident in Montgomery, Alabama, in December 1955, when a woman named Rosa Parks refused to move to a seat at the back of the bus, where bus regulations required blacks to sit. When Parks was arrested, Montgomery blacks, acting under King's general leadership, began a boycott of the bus system that involved unprecedented mass meetings in local black churches and lasted until the city finally desegregated its public transportation a year later. This success spurred similar actions elsewhere against the racial caste system and propelled King and the SCLC to the forefront of civil rights protest.

In the early 1960s CORE sent "freedom riders" on bus trips into the South to find out whether interstate bus facilities were integrated. A new group, the Student Nonviolent Coordinating Committee (SNCC), organized sit-ins in segregated cafes, stand-ins at segregated theaters, and swim-ins at segregated beaches. Then in early 1963, King and the SCLC organized boycotts and marches in the industrial city of Birmingham, Alabama, during which thousands of black men, women, and children were beaten, shot at, attacked by dogs, sprayed with hoses, and imprisoned. Among the imprisoned was King; while in jail, in answer to an "open letter" by several white clergymen, he wrote a statement, reprinted below, on the goals and methods of the civil rights movement and SCLC's controversial philosophy of nonviolent protest. The Birmingham protests ended after important city business and civic leaders pledged to begin the process of local desegregation.

Questions to Consider. King organized his famous letter around points that local ministers had raised in an open letter critical of the demonstrations. Do you find his responses compelling? Is his explanation of the philosophy of nonviolence adequate? King himself acknowledged that many in the black community, especially in the North, found nonviolence too passive, deferential, and submissive. Were they likely to find his letter satisfactory? To defend lawbreaking, King divided laws into two categories and attempted to distinguish between why he advocated breaking unjust laws and opposed breaking just ones. Is his distinction valid? Finally, what evidence can you find in the style of the letter that it was written in jail by a minister?

Letter from Birmingham Jail (1963)

MARTIN LUTHER KING, JR.

My Dear Fellow Clergymen:

While confined here in the Birmingham city jail, I came across your recent statement calling my present activities "unwise and untimely." . . .

I think I should indicate why I am here in Birmingham, since you have been influenced by the view which argues against "outsiders coming in." I have the honor of serving as president of the Southern Christian Leadership Conference, an organization operating in every southern state, with headquarters in Atlanta, Georgia. We have some eighty-five affiliated organizations across the South, and one of them is the Alabama Christian Movement for Human Rights. Frequently we share staff, educational and financial resources with our affiliates. Several months ago the affiliate here in Birmingham asked us to be on call to engage in a nonviolent direct-action program if such were deemed necessary. We readily consented, and when the hour came we lived up to our promise. So I, along with several members of my staff, am here because I was invited here. I am here because I have organizational ties here.

But more basically, I am in Birmingham because injustice is here. Just as the prophets of the eighth century B.C. left their villages and carried their "thus saith the Lord" far beyond the boundaries of their home towns, and just as the Apostle Paul left his village of Tarsus and carried the gospel of Jesus Christ to the far corners of the Greco-Roman world, so am I compelled to carry the gospel of freedom beyond my own home town. Like Paul, I must constantly respond to the Macedonian call for aid.

Moreover, I am cognizant of the interrelatedness of all communities and states. I cannot sit idly by in Atlanta and not be concerned about what happens in Birmingham. Injustice anywhere is a threat to justice everywhere. We are caught in an inescapable network of mutuality, tied in a single garment of destiny. Whatever affects one directly, affects all indirectly. Never again can we afford to live with the narrow, provincial "outside agitator" idea. Anyone who lives inside the United States can never be considered an outsider anywhere within its bounds.

You deplore the demonstrations taking place in Birmingham. But your statement, I am sorry to say, fails to express a similar concern for the conditions that brought about the demonstrations. I am sure that none of you would want to rest content with the superficial kind of social analysis that deals merely with effects and does not grapple with underlying causes. It is unfortunate that demonstrations are taking place in Birmingham, but it is even more unfortunate that the city's white power structure left the Negro community with no alternative.

In any nonviolent campaign there are four basic steps: collection of the facts to determine whether injustices exist; negotiation; self-purification; and direct action. We have gone through all these steps in Birmingham. There can be no gainsaying the fact that racial injustice engulfs this community. Birmingham is probably the most thoroughly segregated city in the United States. Its ugly record of brutality is widely known. Negroes have experienced grossly unjust treatment in the courts. There have been more unsolved bombings of Negro homes and churches in Birmingham than in any other city in the nation. These are the hard, brutal facts of the case. On the basis of these conditions, Negro leaders sought to negotiate with the city fathers. But the latter consistently refused to engage in good-faith negotiation. . . .

As in so many past experiences, our hopes had been blasted, and the shadow of deep disappointment settled upon us. We had no alternative except to prepare for direct action, whereby we would present our very bodies as a means of laying our case before the conscience of the local and the national community. Mindful of the difficulties involved, we decided to undertake a process of self-purification. We began a series of workshops on nonviolence, and we repeatedly asked ourselves: "Are you able to accept blows without retaliating?" "Are you able to endure the ordeal of jail?" We decided to schedule our direct-action program for the Easter season, realizing that except for Christmas, this is the main shopping period of the year. . . .

You may well ask: "Why direct action? Why sit-ins, marches and so forth? Isn't negotiation a better path?" You are quite right in calling for negotiation. Indeed, this is the very purpose of direct action. Nonviolent direct action seeks to create such a crisis and foster such a tension that a community which has constantly refused to negotiate is forced to confront the issue. It seeks so to dramatize the issue that it can no longer be ignored. My citing the creation of tension as part of the work of the nonviolent resister may sound rather shocking. But I must confess that I am not afraid of the word "tension." I have earnestly opposed violent tension, but there is a type of constructive, nonviolent tension which is necessary for growth.

The purpose of our direct-action program is to create a situation so crisis-packed that it will inevitably open the door to negotiation. I therefore concur with you in your call for negotiation. Too long has our beloved Southland been bogged down in a tragic effort to live in monologue rather than dialogue. . . .

We know through painful experience that freedom is never voluntarily given by the oppressor; it must be demanded by the oppressed. Frankly, I have yet to engage in a direct-action campaign that was "well timed" in the view of those who have not suffered unduly from the disease of segregation. For years now I have heard the word "Wait!" It rings in the ear of every Negro with piercing familiarity. This "Wait" has almost always meant "Never." We must come to see, with one of our distinguished jurists, that "justice too long delayed is justice denied."

We have waited for more than 340 years for our constitutional and God-given rights. The nations of Asia and Africa are moving with jetlike speed toward gaining political independence, but we still creep at horse-and-buggy pace toward gaining a cup of coffee at a lunch counter. Perhaps it is easy for those who have never felt the stinging darts of segregation to say "Wait." But when you have seen vicious mobs lynch your mothers and fathers at will and drown your sisters and brothers at whim; when you have seen hate-filled policemen curse, kick and even kill your black brothers and sisters; when you see the vast majority of your twenty million Negro brothers smothering in an airtight cage of poverty in the midst of an affluent society; when you suddenly find your tongue twisted and your speech stammering as you seek to explain to your six-year-old daughter why she can't go to the public amusement park that has just been advertised on television, and see tears welling up in her eyes when she is told that Funtown is closed to colored children, and see ominous clouds of inferiority beginning to form in her little mental sky, and see her beginning to distort her personality by developing an unconscious bitterness toward white people; when you have to concoct an answer for a five-year-old son who is asking, "Daddy, why do white people treat colored people so mean?"; when you take a cross-country drive and find it necessary to sleep night after night in the uncomfortable corners of your automobile because no motel will accept you; when you are humiliated day in and day out by nagging signs reading "white" and "colored"; when your first name becomes "nigger," your middle name becomes "boy" (however old you are) and your last name becomes "John," and your wife and mother are never given the respected title "Mrs."; when you are harried by day and haunted by night by the fact that you are a Negro, living constantly at tiptoe stance, never quite knowing what to expect next, and are plagued with inner fears and outer resentments; when you are forever fighting a degenerating sense of "nobodiness"—then you will understand why we find it difficult to wait. There comes a time when the cup of endurance runs over, and men are no longer willing to be plunged into the abyss of despair. I hope, sirs, you can understand our legitimate and unavoidable impatience.

You express a great deal of anxiety over our willingness to break laws. This is certainly a legitimate concern. Since we so diligently urge people to obey the Supreme Court's decision of 1954 [*Brown* v. *The Board of Education of Topeka*] outlawing segregation in the public schools, at first glance it may seem rather paradoxical for us consciously to break laws. One may well ask: "How can you advocate breaking some laws and obeying others?" The answer lies in the fact that there are two types of laws: just and unjust. . . .

Now, what is the difference between the two? How does one determine whether a law is just or unjust? A just law is a man-made code that squares with the moral law or the law of God. An unjust law is a code that is out of harmony with the moral law. To put it in the terms of St. Thomas Aquinas [Catholic theologian]: An unjust law is a human law that is not rooted in eternal law and natural law. Any law that uplifts human personality is just. Any law that degrades human personality is unjust. All segregation statutes are unjust because segregation distorts the soul and damages the personality. It gives the segregator a false sense of superiority and the segregated a false sense of inferiority. Segregation, to use the terminology of the Jewish philosopher Martin Buber, substitutes an "I-it" relationship for an "I-thou" relationship and ends up relegating persons to the status of things. Hence segregation is not only politically, economically and sociologically unsound, it is morally wrong and sinful. Paul Tillich [Protestant theologian] has said that sin is separation. Is not segregation an existential expression of man's tragic separation, his awful estrangement, his terrible sinfulness? Thus it is that I can urge men to obey the 1954 decision of the Supreme Court, for it is morally right; and I can urge them to disobey segregation ordinances, for they are morally wrong. . . .

I hope you are able to see the distinction I am trying to point out. In no sense do I advocate evading or defying the law, as would the rabid segregationist. That would lead to anarchy. One who breaks an unjust law must do so openly, lovingly, and with a willingness to accept the penalty. I submit that an individual who breaks a law that conscience tells him is unjust, and who willingly accepts the penalty of imprisonment in order to arouse the conscience of the community over its injustice, is in reality expressing the highest respect for the law. . . .

You speak of our activity in Birmingham as extreme. At first I was rather disappointed that fellow clergymen would see my nonviolent efforts as those of an extremist. I began thinking about the fact that I stand in the middle of two opposing forces in the Negro community. One is a force of complacency, made up in part of Negroes who, as a result of long years of oppression, are so drained of self-respect and a sense of "somebodiness" that they have adjusted to segregation; and in part of a few middle-class Negroes who, because of a degree of academic and economic security and because in some ways they profit by segregation, have become insensitive to the problems of the masses. The other force is one of bitterness and hatred, and it comes perilously close to advocating violence. It is expressed in the various black nationalist groups that are springing up across the nation, the largest and best-known being Elijah Muhammad's Muslim movement. Nourished by the Negro's frustration over the continued existence of racial discrimination, this movement is made up of people who have lost faith in America, who have absolutely repudiated Christianity, and who have concluded that the white man is an incorrigible "devil."

I have tried to stand between these two forces, saying that we need emulate neither the "do-nothingism" of the complacent nor the hatred and despair of the black nationalist. For there is the more excellent way of love and non-violent protest. I am grateful to God that, through the influence of the Negro church, the way of nonviolence became an integral part of our struggle. . . .

[T]hough I was initially disappointed at being categorized as an extremist, as I continued to think about the matter I gradually gained a measure of satisfaction from the label. Was not Jesus an extremist for love: "Love your enemies, bless them that curse you, do good to them that hate you, and pray for them which despitefully use you, and persecute you." Was not Amos an extremist for justice: "Let justice roll down like waters and righteousness like an ever-flowing stream." Was not Paul an extremist for the Christian gospel: "I bear in my body the marks of the Lord Jesus." Was not Martin Luther an extremist: "Here I stand: I cannot do otherwise, so help me God." And John Bunyan: "I will stay in jail to the end of my days before I make a butchery of my conscience." And Abraham Lincoln: "This nation cannot survive half slave and half free." And Thomas Jefferson: "We hold these truths to be self-evident, that all men are created equal . . ." So the question is not whether we will be extremists, but what kind of extremists we will be. Will we be extremists for hate or for love? Will we be extremists for the preservation of injustice or for the extension of justice? . . .

Before closing I feel impelled to mention one other point in your statement that has troubled me profoundly. You warmly commended the Birmingham police force for keeping "order" and "preventing violence." I doubt that you would have so warmly commended the police force if you had seen its dogs sinking their teeth into unarmed, nonviolent Negroes. I doubt that you would so quickly commend the policemen if you were to observe their ugly and inhumane treatment of Negroes here in the city jail; if you were to watch them push and curse old Negro women and young Negro girls; if you were to see them slap and kick old Negro men and young boys; if you were to observe them, as they did on two occasions, refuse to give us food because we wanted to sing our grace together. I cannot join you in your praise of the Birmingham police department. . . .

I wish you had commended the Negro sit-inners and demonstrators of Birmingham for their sublime courage, their willingness to suffer and their amazing discipline in the midst of great provocation. One day the South will recognize its real heroes. They will be the James Merediths,[1] with the noble sense of purpose that enables them to face jeering and hostile mobs, and with the agonizing loneliness that characterizes the life of the pioneer. They will be old, oppressed, battered Negro women, symbolized in a seventy-two-year-old woman in Montgomery, Alabama, who rose up with a sense of dignity and with her people decided not to ride segregated buses, and who responded with ungrammatical profundity to one who inquired about her weariness: "My feets is tired, but my soul is at rest." They will be the young high school and college students, the young ministers of the gospel and a host of their elders, courageously and nonviolently sitting in at lunch counters and willingly going to jail for conscience' sake. One day the South will know that when these disinherited children of God sat down at lunch counters, they were in reality standing up for what is best in the American dream and for the most sacred values in our Judaeo-Christian heritage, thereby bringing our nation back to those great wells

---

1. **James Meredith:** The first black student at the University of Mississippi. His efforts to enter the university in 1962 were met by white demonstrations and violence.—Eds.

of democracy which were dug deep by the founding fathers in their formulation of the Constitution and the Declaration of Independence.

Never before have I written so long a letter. I'm afraid it is much too
long to take your precious time. I can assure you that it would have been
much shorter if I had been writing from a comfortable desk, but what else
can one do when he is alone in a narrow jail cell, other than write long
letters, think long thoughts and pray long prayers?

41

✧

WOMEN'S LIBERATION

After its bright triumph of the early 1920s, interest in the movement for women's rights lagged, then gathered new steam in the 1950s. This resurgence resulted partly from a trend in the workforce: 27 percent of adult women worked outside the home in 1940, 33 percent in 1960, and 50 percent in 1980. With so many women in the workforce, they gradually made their concerns heard: equal pay for equal work; managerial positions in heretofore all-male administrations; elimination of sexual and physical harassment. Working wives, it turned out, often strained traditional male-dominant marriages, and both the divorce rate and the need for new child-care arrangements increased. Also, married or not, working women saw their lives focusing less exclusively on children and domesticity. They therefore looked increasingly to modern birth control devices and to abortion. (The Supreme Court declared abortion legal in 1973.) From 1960 to 1980, the birth rate decreased 50 percent.

But if these trends provided the underpinnings for the modern women's movement, true feminism—the struggle for women's liberation— came only with the addition of "consciousness raising" to these socioeconomic tendencies. Here, too, there was a crucial underlying trend: many more women were college-educated than ever before. In 1940 approximately 15 percent of American women had completed at least one year of college, and women earned about one-fourth of all bachelor's degrees given by U.S. colleges. By 1960, about 20 percent of all women had gone to college, and women earned one-third of all bachelor's degrees. By 1980, the percentage of women attending college had increased to 40 percent and women earned nearly half of all U.S. bachelor's degrees.

In part, Betty Friedan was addressing these millions of educated but underemployed women in her pathbreaking *The Feminine Mystique,* published in 1963 and excerpted below. Friedan attacked the mass media for brainwashing women into models of domesticity. The National Organization for Women (NOW), created in 1966 with Friedan's support, pressed for eliminating all discriminatory legal sexual distinctions. A half-century after the suffrage amendment, politics witnessed major gains for women. They became governors in numerous states, including Texas, one of the three largest. Women senators were elected from several states, including Florida, another of the three largest. Mayors in many of the nation's largest cities, including Chicago and Houston, were women. They held three cabinet positions under Jimmy Carter and one each under Reagan and Bush. Two women were appointed Supreme Court justices, and one ran as a Democratic party vice-presidential candidate. Women were commonplace in the American military force sent to the Persian Gulf in 1991, although not initially in official combat roles.

Betty Friedan was born in 1921 in Illinois and attended Smith College and the University of California at Berkeley. In the early 1960s Friedan was a wife and mother who, having lost her job as a newspaper reporter, was contributing to popular magazines. Noticing that editors frequently cut her references to women's careers in favor of more material on homemaking, she began to analyze the housewife fantasy and to interview housewives themselves. The result was *The Feminine Mystique* (1963), an instant best seller that catapulted its author to the forefront of the women's movement and earned her countless offers to lecture and teach. Friedan was the founding president of the National Organization for Women from 1966 to 1970 and also helped found the National Women's Political Caucus and the National Association to Repeal Abortion Laws. None of it was easy. "A lot of people," she recalled, "treated me like a leper."

Questions to Consider. Betty Friedan argued in *The Feminine Mystique* that American women suffered from a "problem that has no name." What was that problem? Was she the first to discover it? What were her methods of investigating and reporting it? Why did it have no name? Did Friedan name it? Would all American women have responded to Friedan's arguments? What kinds of women would have been most likely to respond? How revolutionary was her message? What social or political measures would be required to deal effectively with this problem?

————————◇————————

The Feminine Mystique (1963)

BETTY FRIEDAN

The suburban housewife—she was the dream image of the young American women and the envy, it was said, of women all over the world. The

Betty Friedan. Betty Friedan has been in the forefront of the women's movement since the publication of her best-selling book, *The Feminine Mystique* in 1963. She helped found the National Organization for Women (NOW) in 1966. (Jesse Nemerofsky/Photoreporters)

American housewife—freed by science and labor-saving appliances from the drudgery, the dangers of childbirth and the illnesses of her grandmother. She was healthy, beautiful, educated, concerned only about her husband, her children, her home. She had found true feminine fulfillment. As a housewife and mother, she was respected as a full and equal partner to man in his world. She was free to choose automobiles, clothes, appliances, supermarkets; she had everything that women ever dreamed of.

In the fifteen years after World War II, this mystique of feminine fulfillment became the cherished and self-perpetuating core of contemporary American culture. Millions of women lived their lives in the image of those pretty pictures of the American suburban housewife, kissing their husbands goodbye in front of the picture window, depositing their stationwagonsful of children at school, and smiling as they ran the new electric waxer over the spotless kitchen floor. They baked their own bread, sewed their own and their children's clothes, kept their new washing machines and dryers running all day. They changed the sheets on the beds twice a week instead of once, took the rug-hooking class in adult education, and pitied their poor frustrated mothers, who had dreamed of having a career. Their only dream was to be perfect wives and mothers; their highest ambition to have five children and a beautiful house, their only fight to get and keep their husbands. They had no thought for the unfeminine problems of the world outside the home; they wanted the men to make the major decisions. They gloried in their role as women, and wrote proudly on the census blank: "Occupation: housewife."

For over fifteen years, the words written for women, and the words women used when they talked to each other, while their husbands sat on the other side of the room and talked shop or politics or septic tanks, were about problems with their children, or how to keep their husbands happy, or improve their children's school, or cook chicken or make slipcovers. Nobody argued whether women were inferior or superior to men; they were simply different. Words like *emancipation* and *career* sounded strange and embarrassing; no one had used them for years. . . .

But on an April morning in 1959, I heard a mother of four, having coffee with four other mothers in a suburban development fifteen miles from New York, say in a tone of quiet desperation, "the problem." And the others knew, without words, that she was not talking about a problem with her husband, or her children, or her home. Suddenly they realized they all shared the same problem, the problem that has no name. They began, hesitantly, to talk about it. Later, after they had picked up their children at nursery school and taken them home to nap, two of the women cried, in sheer relief, just to know they were not alone. . . .

Just what was this problem that has no name? What were the words women used when they tried to express it? Sometimes a woman would say "I feel empty somehow . . . incomplete." Or she would say, "I feel as if I don't exist." Sometimes she blotted out the feeling with a tranquilizer. Sometimes she thought the problem was with her husband, or her children, or that what she really needed was to redecorate her house, or move to a better neighborhood, or have an affair, or another baby. Sometimes, she went to a doctor with symptoms she could hardly describe: "A tired feeling . . . I get so angry with the children it scares me . . . I feel like crying without any reason." (A Cleveland doctor called it "the housewife's syndrome.") A number of women told me about great bleeding blisters that break out on their hands and arms. "I call it the housewife's blight," said a family doctor in Pennsylvania. "I see it so often lately in these young women with four, five and six children who bury themselves in their dishpans. But it isn't caused by detergent and it isn't cured by cortisone." . . .

In 1960, the problem that has no name burst like a boil through the image of the happy American housewife. In the television commercials the pretty housewives still beamed over their foaming dishpans and *Time's* cover story on "The Suburban Wife, an American Phenomenon" protested: "Having too good a time . . . to believe that they should be unhappy." But the actual unhappiness of the American housewife was suddenly being reported—from the *New York Times* and *Newsweek* to *Good Housekeeping* and CBS Television ("The Trapped Housewife"), although almost everybody who talked about it found some superficial reason to dismiss it. . . .

Of the growing thousands of women currently getting private psychiatric help in the United States, the married ones were reported dissatisfied with their marriages, the unmarried ones suffering from anxiety and, finally, depression. Strangely, a number of psychiatrists stated that, in their experience, unmarried women patients were happier than married ones. So the door of all those pretty suburban houses opened a crack to permit a glimpse of uncounted thousands of American housewives who suffered alone from a problem that suddenly everyone was talking about, and beginning to take for granted, as one of those unreal problems in American life that can never be solved—like the hydrogen bomb. . . .

I do not accept the answer that there is no problem because American women have luxuries that women in other times and lands never dreamed of; part of the strange newness of the problem is that it cannot be understood in terms of the age-old material problems of man: poverty, sickness, hunger, cold. The women who suffer this problem have a hunger that food cannot fill. . . .

Are the women who finished college, the women who once had dreams beyond housewifery, the ones who suffer the most? According to the experts they are, but. . . . housewives of all educational levels suffer the same feeling of desperation.

The fact is that no one today is muttering angrily about "women's rights," even though more and more women have gone to college. In a recent study of all the classes that have graduated from Barnard College, a significant minority of earlier graduates blamed their education for making them want "rights," later classes blamed their education for giving them career dreams, but recent graduates blamed the college for making them feel it was not enough simply to be a housewife and mother; they did not want to feel guilty if they did not read books or take part in community activities. But if education is not the cause of the problem, the fact that education somehow festers in these women may be a clue.

If the secret of feminine fulfillment is having children, never have so many women, with the freedom to choose, had so many children, in so few years, so willingly. If the answer is love, never have women searched for love with such determination. And yet there is a growing suspicion that the problem may not be sexual, though it must somehow be related to sex. I have heard from many doctors evidence of new sexual problems between man and wife—sexual hunger in wives so great their husbands cannot satisfy it. . . .

Can the problem that has no name be somehow related to the domestic routine of the housewife? When a woman tries to put the problem into words, she often merely describes the daily life she leads. What is there in this recital of comfortable domestic detail that could possibly cause such a feeling of desperation? Is she trapped simply by the enormous demands of her role as modern housewife: wife, mistress, mother, nurse, consumer, cook, chauffeur; expert on interior decoration, child care, appliance repair, furniture refinishing, nutrition, and education? . . .

If I am right, the problem that has no name stirring in the minds of so many American women today is not a matter of loss of femininity or too much education, or the demands of domesticity. It is far more important than anyone recognizes. It is the key to these other new and old problems which have been torturing women and their husbands and children, and puzzling their doctors and educators for years. It may well be the key to our future as a nation and a culture. We can no longer ignore that voice within women that says: "I want something more than my husband and my children and my home."

42

✧

RIGHT TURN

The "Reagan Revolution" of the early 1980s was the culmination of two trends: the Republican campaign against "big government" and the new importance of the "Sun Belt" in national politics. Some historians argue that the "revolution" had actually begun much earlier—with Barry Goldwater, another staunchly conservative Republican.

Since the period of Reconstruction, white southerners had firmly opposed the Republican party. After all, it was Lincoln's party that emancipated the slave, fought against the Confederacy, and imposed military rule on the defeated South. Until 1960, when John F. Kennedy ran against Richard M. Nixon (and the issue for many white Southerners was Kennedy's Roman Catholic faith), the "Solid South" could be counted on to vote mostly Democratic. But by the 1960s many white Southerners had come to believe that the Democratic party, as a result of its alignment with urban minorities and organized labor, had become too liberal, and they felt alienated. Goldwater, though in many respects a conventional probusiness Republican, urged his party to "hunt where the ducks are," and Republicans seized the initiative, seeking to become the party of disaffected white Southerners as well as big business.

Goldwater received the Republican party's nomination for president in 1964, and his acceptance speech is reproduced below. It reflects the now classic Republican notion that true freedom demands that government "keep off people's backs," and that individuals need to be more self-reliant. When Goldwater argued that society must nurture "incentives and opportunities for the creative and the productive," he was in fact saying that he, like increasing numbers of Americans, was opposed to high taxes and welfare appropriations, a hallmark of the Democratic party from Franklin Roosevelt's day. He proposed to sell the Tennessee Valley Authority (TVA) and end agricultural subsidies, attacked the social security program, and advocated curbs on public ownership of utilities.

"In Your Heart You Know He's Right" was the slogan Republicans used in the 1964 presidential campaign. The Democrats twisted it around and campaigned, "In Your Heart You Know He Might," appealing to public apprehension over Goldwater's apparent willingness to use nuclear weapons. Lyndon Johnson won the 1964 election decisively. A new pattern was established, however. All six states that Goldwater carried were in the Deep South or Southwest, which would become the cornerstone of the coming Republican ascendancy.

Barry Goldwater was born in Phoenix, Arizona, in 1909. Having dropped out of the University of Arizona ("the worst mistake I ever made"), he entered the family's mercantile business, and when World War II broke out, volunteered for the Army Air Force. His career in politics began with election to the Phoenix City Council, and he went on to become a state senator and then a U.S. senator. After losing his bid for the presidency in 1964, he returned to Arizona; in 1968 he was again elected to the Senate. A staunch supporter of Nixon's policies in Vietnam, he attacked those who opposed the stepped-up bombing of Hanoi as "weak-kneed and jelly-backed." In 1972–1974, as the Nixon administration was sinking from the weight of the Watergate affair, Goldwater publicly pushed the president to "get rid of the smell" and disclose to the public the full extent of his involvement. In August 1974, acting as spokesman for party leaders, Goldwater informed Nixon that he would vote to convict him of abuse of power should he be tried in the Senate. The following day Nixon resigned. Goldwater served in the Senate from 1953 to 1965 and again from 1969 to 1986, when he retired to Arizona, an elder statesman of "New Right" Republicanism.

Questions to Consider. Do you think that Goldwater's program would have secured greater freedom for Americans? Goldwater believed that government-sponsored relief programs undermined individual liberty and institutionalized poverty. To what extent do you agree? Why did white Southerners respond so strongly to Goldwater's message?

Presidential Nomination Acceptance Speech (1964)

BARRY GOLDWATER

The good Lord raised up this mighty Republic to be a home for the brave and to flourish as the land of the free—*not* to stagnate in the swampland of collectivism—*not* to cringe before the bullying of Communism.

The tide has been running against freedom. Our people have followed false prophets. We must and we *shall* return to proven ways—*not* because they are old, but because they are *true.* We must and we shall set the tides running again in the cause of freedom.

This Party, with its every action, every word, every breath, and every heartbeat, has but a single resolve:

Freedom!

Freedom—made orderly for this nation by our Constitutional government.

Freedom—under a government limited by the laws of nature and of nature's God.

Freedom—balanced so that order, lacking liberty, will not become the slavery of the prison cell; balanced so that liberty, lacking order, will not become the license of the mob and the jungle.

We Americans understand freedom. We have earned it, lived for it, and died for it.

This nation and its people *are* freedom's model in a searching world. We *can be* freedom's missionaries in a doubting world. But first we *must renew* freedom's vision in our own hearts and in our own homes.

During four futile years, the Administration which we shall replace has distorted and lost that vision.

It has talked and talked and talked the *words* of freedom. But it has failed and failed and failed in the *works* of freedom.

Failures cement the wall of shame in Berlin. Failures blot the sands of shame at the Bay of Pigs. Failures mark the slow death of freedom in Laos. Failures infest the jungles of Vietnam. Failures haunt the houses of our once great alliances, and undermine the greatest bulwark ever erected by free nations—the NATO community.

Failures proclaim lost leadership, obscure purpose, weakening will, and the risk of inciting our sworn enemies to new aggressions and new excesses.

Because of this Administration, we are a world divided—we are a nation becalmed.

We have lost the brisk pace of diversity and the genius of individual creativity. We are plodding at a pace set by centralized planning, red tape, rules without responsibility, and regimentation without recourse.

Rather than useful jobs, our people have been offered bureaucratic make-work. Rather than moral leadership, they have been given bread and circuses, spectacle and even scandal.

There is violence in our streets, corruption in our highest offices, aimlessness among our youth, anxiety among our elders. There is virtual despair among the many who look beyond material success for the inner meaning of their lives. . . .

The growing menace to personal safety, to life, limb, and property, in homes, churches, playgrounds, and places of business, particularly in our great cities, is the mounting concern of every thoughtful citizen. Security from domestic violence, no less than from foreign aggression, is the most elementary and fundamental purpose of any government. A government that cannot fulfill this purpose is one that cannot long command the loyalty of its citizens. History demonstrates that nothing prepares the way for tyranny more than the failure of public officials to keep the streets safe from bullies and marauders.

We Republicans see all this as more, *much* more than the result of mere political differences, or mere political mistakes. We see this as the result of a fundamentally and absolutely wrong view of man, his nature, and his destiny.

Those who seek to live your lives for you, to take your liberties in return for relieving you of your responsibilities—those who elevate the state and downgrade the citizen—must see ultimately a world in which earthly power can be substituted for divine will. This nation was founded upon the rejection of that notion and upon the acceptance of God as the author of freedom.

Those who seek absolute power, even though they seek it to do what they regard as good, are simply demanding the right to enforce *their* version of heaven on earth. They are the very ones who always create the most hellish tyrannies.

Absolute power *does* corrupt. And those who seek it must be suspect and must be opposed.

Their mistaken course stems from false notions of equality.

Equality, rightly understood, as our Founding Fathers understood it, leads to liberty and to the emancipation of creative differences.

Wrongly understood, as it has been so tragically in our time, it leads first to conformity and then to despotism. . . .

The Republican cause demands that we brand Communism as the principal disturber of peace in the world today—indeed, the only significant disturber of the peace. We must make clear that until its goals of conquest are absolutely renounced, and its relations with all nations tempered, Communism and the governments it now controls are enemies of every man on earth who is or wants to be free.

We can keep the peace only if we remain vigilant and strong. Only if we keep our eyes open and keep our guard up can we prevent war.

I do not intend to let peace *or* freedom be torn from our grasp because of lack of strength or lack of will. *That* I promise you.

I believe that we must look beyond the defense of freedom today to its extension tomorrow. I believe that the Communism which boasts it will "bury us," will instead give way to the forces of freedom. . . .

During Republican years this again will be a nation of men and women, of families proud of their roles, jealous of their responsibilities, unlimited in their aspirations—a nation where all who *can, will* be self-reliant.

We Republicans see in our Constitutional form of government the great framework which assures the orderly but dynamic fulfillment of the whole man—and we see the whole man as the *great* reason for instituting orderly government in the first place.

We see, in private property and an economy based upon and fostering private property, the one way to make government a durable ally of the whole man, rather than his determined enemy. We see, in the sanctity of private property, the only durable foundation for Constitutional government in a free society.

And beyond that, we see and cherish diversity of ways, diversity of thoughts, of motives and accomplishments. We do not seek to live anyone's life for him—we seek only to secure his rights, guarantee him opportunity to strive, with government performing only those needed and Constitutionally-sanctioned tasks which cannot otherwise be performed.

We seek a government that attends to its inherent responsibilities of maintaining a stable monetary and fiscal climate—encouraging a free and competitive economy, and enforcing law and order.

Thus do we seek inventiveness, diversity, and creative difference within a stable order. For we Republicans define government's role, where needed, at *many* levels, preferably the one *closest* to the people involved.

Our towns and our cities, then our counties and states, then our regional compacts—and *only then* the national government! *That* is the ladder of liberty built by decentralized power. On it, also, we must have balance *between* branches of government at *every* level. . . .

And let our Republicanism, so focused and so dedicated, not be made fuzzy and futile by unthinking labels.

Extremism in the defense of liberty is no vice. Moderation in the pursuit of justice is no virtue. . . .

Our Republican cause is not to level out the world or make its people conform in computer-regimented sameness.

Our Republican cause is to free our people and light the way for liberty throughout the world.

43

✧

BACKLASH AND ANGER

The Supreme Court decision in *Brown* v. *The Board of Education of Topeka* in 1954 and the Montgomery bus boycott in 1955 marked the beginning of the modern civil rights movement, an enterprise that in the 1950s engaged the efforts of both blacks and whites. Within a few short years of these important victories, however, the character of the movement changed. Predominantly black civil rights organizations such as the National Association for the Advancement of Colored People (NAACP) and the Southern Christian Leadership Conference (SCLC) had initially welcomed the support and participation of whites, but in the early 1960s, when the primary objective of black civil rights activists was to secure voting rights, the savage white backlash that ensued fueled the anger of young African-Americans. Whites, they believed, should get out of their ranks.

Martin Luther King's "I have a dream" speech, made before the largest crowd ever assembled in the cause of civil rights, was a stunning moment of interracial harmony. But 1963's "March on Washington" marked the beginning of the end of peaceful multiracial protest. With massive and fiercely contested voter registration drives underway in the South and urban violence erupting in the North, the movement became fragmented. Perhaps the most militant of all African-Americans—"the angriest Negro in America"—was Malcolm X. That was how many whites, terrified of the rage his words could inspire in alienated blacks, described him. In the autobiography that appeared after his assassination he explained:

I *believe* in anger. The Bible says there is a *time* for anger [Whites called me] "a fomentor of violence." I would say point blank, "That is a lie. I'm not for wanton violence, I'm for justice. I feel that if white people were attacked by Negroes—if the forces of law prove unable, or inadequate, or reluctant to protect those whites from those Negroes—then those white people should protect and defend themselves from those Negroes using arms." . . .

Well, I believe it's a crime for anyone who is being brutalized to continue to accept that brutality without doing something to defend himself. . . .

In a celebrated interview conducted by Pierre Berton on Canadian television and reproduced in part below, Malcolm X made his position clear. He explained that since his conversion to Islam, he did not hate whites and that, contrary to what was being reported, he was not "pleased" at the assassination of President Kennedy. Rather, as a result of his experiences in the Middle East and his religious convictions, he believed "in recognizing every human being as a human being, neither white, black, brown, nor red." Nevertheless, he emphasized that blacks "are prepared to do *whatever* is necessary to see that our people, wherever they are, get the type of protection the federal government has refused to give them." One month after this statement, he was assassinated.

Malcolm Little was born in 1925 in Omaha; his family moved to Milwaukee and then to Lansing, Michigan. When he was two, his family's home was set afire; a few years later his father (according to rumor) was murdered by white supremacists. His mother suffered a nervous breakdown. After living in various foster homes in Michigan, Malcolm moved at age sixteen to Boston, where he lived with his sister, worked at odd jobs, and became involved with the city's underworld. "Big Red," as he was known then, made a quick reputation as a drug dealer, pimp, and numbers runner, but he was soon caught for breaking and entering and sentenced to prison. While in prison he immersed himself in a self-study program. Not long after his parole he heard the Black Muslim leader Elijah Muhammad speak, and received the "X" that signified his unknown African name. His appointment as the assistant minister at Detroit Temple No. 1 was the beginning of his career with the Muslims, and his travels in the Middle East and Africa as a representative of Muhammad affirmed his Islamic religious beliefs. Disillusioned by Muhammad's extramarital affairs, Malcolm broke with him and took steps to organize a black nationalist party (Organization of Afro-American Unity). It was while he was addressing an OAAU rally in New York in 1965 that he was gunned down. He was thirty-nine years old, married, and the father of six daughters.

Questions to Consider. Does the evidence suggest that Malcolm X was "the angriest Negro in America"? One year after the death of Malcolm X, Stokely Carmichael wrote a position paper for the Student Nonviolent Coordinating Committee (SNCC) in which he argued that it should be "black-staffed, black-controlled and black-financed. Whites can only subvert our true search and struggle for self-determination." Had Malcolm X lived, do you think he would have agreed? Do you agree with the argument that blacks should respond to white brutality with "whatever is necessary"? Would Malcolm have urged a similar response to male-against-female brutality, or to same-race brutality?

Interview with Malcolm X (1965)

PIERRE BERTON: At the time of President Kennedy's assassination, you made a speech that seemed to indicate that you were pleased that he had been assassinated. Certainly at that time, Elijah Muhammad indicated that you had been fired or suspended from the Black Muslim movement. How about that?

MALCOLM X: I had taken a subject as my topic that day, an approach that was designed to show that the seeds that America had sown—in enslavement, in many of the things that followed since then—all of these seeds were coming up today; it was harvest time. At the end of this particular lecture, during the question-and-answer period, somebody asked me what I thought of the assassination of President Kennedy. In line with the topic that I had just been discussing, I pointed out that it was a case of the chickens coming home to roost, by which I meant that this was the result of seeds that had been sown, that this was the harvest. This was taken out of context, and reported in one of the papers, and Elijah Muhammad, who had been waiting for me to make a move that would enable him to suspend me and get the support of the public in doing so, took advantage of that opportunity. He gave the impression that I was saying something against the president himself, because he felt that the public wouldn't go along with that.

BERTON: How did you feel, personally, about the president's assassination in that connection? Were you bothered about it? Were you angered by it? Or were you jubilant?

MALCOLM X: No. I was realistic, in that being at the forefront of this struggle of the black man in America—in his quest for respect as a human being—I had seen the many-faceted repercussions of this hate taking a grip on the American public. I think that many of the politicians took advantage of it and exploited it for their own personal benefit. So to me the whole thing was a case of politics, hate, and a combination of other things.

BERTON: There seems to me to have been a fair amount of hate in the Black Muslim movement itself.

MALCOLM X: Well, I won't deny that. But, at the same time, I don't think that the Black Muslim movement and its hate can be classified as the same degree or type of hate you find in the American society itself, because the

From David Gallen, *Malcolm X as They Knew Him* (New York: Carroll & Graf, 1992), 238–265.

Malcolm X talks to reporters in Washington in May, 1965. (Associated Press)

hate, so-called, that you see among black people is a reaction to the hate of the society which has rejected us. In that sense it is not hate.

BERTON: I'm not saying that the hate, or whatever it is, isn't understandable. I'm asking if it's effective to fight hate with hate?

MALCOLM X: In my opinion, I think that it is not fair to classify the reaction of people who are oppressed as hate. They are reacting to the hate of the society they have had put upon them or practiced against them. . . .

BERTON: . . . Let me ask you this about your God, Mr. X. Has he got any color? Is he black?

MALCOLM X: No.

BERTON: Is he white?

MALCOLM X: As a Black Muslim, who believed what Elijah Muhammad taught, I regarded God just as he taught, as a black man. Having since gone into the Muslim world and got a better understanding of the religion of Islam, I believe that God is the supreme being, and that color plays no part in his particular being.

BERTON: In fact, isn't the God of the Muslims and of the Jews and the Christians really the same God?

MALCOLM X: If they believe in the God who created the universe, then we all believe in the same God. I believe in the God who created the universe. Muslims call him Allah. Christians, perhaps, call him Christ, or by some other name. Jews call him Jehovah, and in referring to him they mean "the creative." We are all referring to the same God.

BERTON: Now, let me switch the subject briefly, and ask you what you mean when you say that the Black Muslims are not militant enough. Your new organization, I take it, will be more militant than the Black Muslims. In what way?

MALCOLM X: Well, the Black Muslim movement, number one, professes to be a religious movement. They profess the religion of Islam. But the Muslim world rejected the Black Muslim movement as a bona fide Islamic group, so it found itself maneuvered into a religious vacuum—or a sort of religious hybrid. At the same time, the government of the United States tried to maneuver the Black Muslim movement, with the press, into an image that was political instead of religious. So the Black Muslim movement came to be known as a political group. Yet, at the same time, it didn't vote; it didn't take part in any politics; it didn't involve itself actively in the civil rights struggle; so it became a political hybrid as well as a religious hybrid. Now, on the other hand, the Black Muslim movement attracted the most militant black American, the young, dissatisfied, uncompromising element that exists in this country—drawing them in yet, at the same time, giving them no part to play in the struggle other than moral reform. It created a lot of disillusion, dissatisfaction, dissension, and eventually division. Those who divided are the ones that I'm a part of. We set up the Muslim Mosque, which is based upon orthodox Islam, as a religious group so that we could get a better understanding of our religion; but being black Americans, though we are Muslims, who believe in brotherhood, we also realized that our people have a problem in America that goes beyond religion. We realized that many of our people aren't going to become Muslim; many of them aren't even interested in anything religious; so we set up the Organization of Afro-American Unity as a nonreligious organization which all black Americans could become a part of and play an active part in striking out at the political, economic, and social evils that all of us are confronted by.

BERTON: That "striking out," what form is it going to take? You talk of giving the Ku Klux Klan a taste of its own medicine. This is in direct opposition to the theory of nonviolence of Dr. Martin Luther King, who doesn't believe in striking back. What do you mean by "a taste of its own medicine"? Are you going to burn fiery crosses on their lawns? Are you going to blow up churches with the Ku Klux Klan kids in them? What are you going to do?

MALCOLM X: Well, I think that the only way that two different races can get along with each other is, first, they have to understand each other. That cannot be brought about other than through communication—dialogue— and you can't communicate with a person unless you speak his language. If the person speaks French, you can't speak English or German.

BERTON: We have that problem in our country, too.

MALCOLM X: In America, our people have so far not been able to speak the type of language that the racists understand. By not speaking that language, they fail to communicate, so that the racist element doesn't really believe that the black American is a human being—part of the human family. There is no communication. So I believe that the only way to communicate with that element is to be in a position to speak their language.

BERTON: And this language is violence?

MALCOLM X: I wouldn't call it violence. I think that they should be made to know that, any time they come into a black community and inflict violence upon members of that black community, they should realize in advance that the black community can speak the same language. Then they would be less likely to come in.

BERTON: Let's be specific here: suppose that a church is bombed. Will you bomb back?

MALCOLM X: I believe that any area of the United States, where the federal government has shown either its unwillingness or inability to protect the lives and the property of the black American, then it is time for the black Americans to band together and do whatever is necessary to see that we get the type of protection we need.

BERTON: "Whatever is necessary?"

MALCOLM X: I mean just that. *Whatever is necessary.* This does not mean that we should go out and initiate acts of aggression indiscriminately in the white community. But it does mean that, if we are going to be respected as human beings, we should reserve the right to defend ourselves by whatever means necessary. This is recognized and accepted in any civilized society. . . .

BERTON: There are some people going to go on trial in Mississippi for the murder of three civil rights workers. There are some witnesses who identify them as murderers, but the general feeling is they'll get off. Will you do anything about this if they get off?

MALCOLM X: I wouldn't say.

BERTON: You don't want to say?

MALCOLM X: Because, then, if something happened to them, they would blame me. But I will say that in a society where the law itself is incapable of bringing known murderers to justice, it's historically demonstrable that the well-meaning people of that society have always banded together in one form or another to see that their society was protected against repetitious acts by these same murderers.

BERTON: What you're talking about here is a vigilante movement.

MALCOLM X: There have been vigilante movements forming all over America in white communities, but the black community has yet to form a vigilante committee. This is why we aren't respected as human beings.

BERTON: Are you training men to use aggressive methods? Are you training men as the Black Muslim movement trained the elite core known as the Fruit of Islam? Have you got trainees operating now who know how to fight back?

MALCOLM X: Yes.

BERTON: Who know how to use knuckle-dusters and guns?

MALCOLM X: Yes, oh yes. The black man in America doesn't need that much training. Most of them have been in the army—have already been trained by the government itself. They haven't been trained to think for themselves and, therefore, they've never used this training to protect themselves.

BERTON: Have you got a specific cadre of such young, tough guys working for you or operating under your aegis?

MALCOLM X: We're not a cadre, nor do we want it to be felt that we want to be tough. We're trying to be human beings, and we want to be recognized and accepted as human beings. But we don't think humanity will recognize us or accept us as such until humanity knows that we will do everything to protect our human ranks, as others will do for theirs.

BERTON: Are you prepared to send flying squads into areas where the Negroes have been oppressed without any legal help?

MALCOLM X: We are prepared to do whatever is necessary to see that our people, wherever they are, get the type of protection that the federal government has refused to give them.

BERTON: Okay. Do you still believe that all whites are devils and all blacks saints, as I'm sure you did under the Black Muslim movement?

MALCOLM X: This is what Elijah Muhammad teaches. No, I don't believe that. I believe as the Koran teaches, that a man should not be judged by the color of his skin but rather by his conscious behavior, by his actions, by his attitude towards others and his actions towards others.

BERTON: Now, before you left Elijah Muhammad and went to Mecca and saw the original world of Islam, you believed in complete segregation of the whites and the Negroes. You were opposed both to integration and to intermarriage. Have you changed your views there?

MALCOLM X: I believe in recognizing every human being as a human being, neither white, black, brown nor red. When you are dealing with humanity as one family, there's no question of integration or intermarriage. It's just one human being marrying another human being, or one human being living around and with another human being. I may say, though, that I don't think the burden to defend any such position should ever be put upon the black man. Because it is the white man collectively who has shown that he is hostile towards integration and towards intermarriage and towards these other strides towards oneness. So, as a black man, and especially as a black American, I don't think that I would have to defend any stand that I formerly took. Because it's still a reaction of the society and it's a reaction that was produced by the white society. And I think that it is the society that produced this that should be attacked, not the reaction that develops among the people who are the victims of that negative society.

BERTON: But you no longer believe in a Black State?

MALCOLM X: No.

BERTON: In North America?

MALCOLM X: No. I believe in a society in which people can live like human beings on the basis of equality.

44

✧

WATERGATE

On June 17, 1972, five men were arrested for rifling the files and tapping the telephones of the Democratic National Committee in the Watergate office building in Washington, D.C. Thus was born the Watergate affair that transfixed the nation for the next two years. All five burglars, it turned out, were former agents of the Central Intelligence Agency (CIA). Two of the men, James McCord and G. Gordon Liddy, were currently working for the Committee to Re-elect the President (CRP, or, popularly, CREEP), an independent organization supporting President Richard Nixon's bid for reelection. McCord and Liddy had connections with another former CIA agent, E. Howard Hunt, who, like Liddy, now served as a White House aide. The other burglars were Cubans who had been associated with the Bay of Pigs operation in Cuba.

After the trial and conviction of the five burglars, McCord broke silence by indicating, first, that the head of CRP himself, none other than former Attorney General John N. Mitchell, had approved the break-in and, second, that White House agents had paid "hush money" to the burglars. Newspaper reporters, the Federal Bureau of Investigation, and a special Senate committee on campaign practices opened investigations and soon learned that CRP had used extortionist tactics to raise an illegal slush fund from corporations for the 1972 presidential campaign, and that CRP had used this fund to pay for burglaries, wiretaps, forgeries, phony demonstrations, and other "dirty tricks" to discredit and punish Nixon critics.

By the summer of 1973 it was clear that President Nixon's closest aides, including advisers H.R. Haldeman and John D. Ehrlichman and counsel John W. Dean, had tried to interfere with the Watergate investigations and were withholding valuable evidence, notably tapes of White House conversations during the period under question. When the Senate committee, wondering who (including President Nixon) knew what, requested access to the tapes, Nixon pleaded executive privilege and refused to release them; and when Archibald Cox, a special Watergate prosecutor whom Nixon had appointed, asked for the tapes, the president ordered Cox's dismissal, even though several Justice Department officials resigned in protest.

During the next few months more than thirty former Nixon advisers were indicted for federal crimes, including Dean, Ehrlichman, Haldeman, Mitchell, and former Secretary of Commerce and CRP finance chairman Maurice Stans. The House Judiciary Committee began preparing articles of impeachment against the president. On August 4, 1974, the Supreme Court ordered Nixon to release the tapes. Investigators, hoping to unearth the "smoking pistol" (direct evidence, if it existed, that the president himself had authorized the cover-up), were eager to examine them.

As suggested in the brief excerpts reprinted below, the tapes did indeed provide such evidence. According to the June 1972 conversations, Nixon knew of the Watergate break-in forty-eight hours after it happened; he also withheld evidence, authorized bribes, and used the FBI and the CIA to thwart congressional investigators. The September 1972 excerpt suggests Nixon's intent, in the aftermath of Watergate, to use the FBI and the Justice Department against the administration's enemies. In March 1973, the president elaborated on the nature of his enemies. A week later, in response to Dean's concern about washing money—"the sort of thing Mafia people can do"—for paying blackmail, Nixon replied that the money could be obtained. With such conversations made public and facing almost certain impeachment, Richard Nixon announced his resignation of the presidency on August 8, 1974. In the end, Nixon's bold diplomacy in foreign affairs seemed swallowed up by domestic sordidness. Nixon died in New York City in 1994.

Questions to Consider. The Watergate episode, as revealed in these tape transcriptions, illustrated the remarkable size and complexity of the White House staff and executive bureaucracy in the last third of this century; the constant, almost casual resort to the new technology of wiretapping and secret surveillance; and the phenomenal importance of money in high-level politics and the apparent ease of raising it. Might these features of the modern presidency have tended in themselves to promote the kind of domineering mentality that characterized the Nixon White House? Did the fact that Nixon felt assailed (not unlike Senator Joseph McCarthy) by "upper intellectual types" and a "dying" establishment affect his actions? How prominently did activist, Kennedy-style cold war attitudes and habits—the use of CIA operatives, references to the Bay of Pigs and national security—figure in the episode? Do future Watergate threats lie mainly in the nature of the modern presidency, or mainly in a special combination of anticommunism and status anxiety?

————————✧————————

White House Conversations (1972–1973)

June 23, 1972

HALDEMAN: Now, on the investigation, you know the Democratic breakin thing, we're back in the problem area because the FBI is not under control, because [Director Patrick] Gray doesn't exactly know how to control it and they have—their investigation is now leading into some productive areas. . . . They've been able to trace the money—not through the money itself—but through the bank sources—the banker. And it goes in some directions we don't want it to go. Ah, also there have been some [other] things—like an informant came in off the street to the FBI in Miami who was a photographer or has a friend who is a photographer who developed some films through this guy [Bernard] Barker and the films had pictures of Democratic National Committee letterhead documents and things. So it's things like that that are filtering in. . . . [John] Mitchell came up with yesterday, and John Dean analyzed very carefully last night and concludes, concurs now with Mitchell's recommendation that the only way to solve this . . . is for us to have [CIA Assistant Director Vernon] Walters call Pat Gray and just say, "Stay to hell out of this—this is ah, [our] business here. We don't want you to go any further on it." That's not an unusual development, and ah, that would take care of it.

PRESIDENT: What about Pat Gray—you mean Pat Gray doesn't want to?

HALDEMAN: Pat does want to. He doesn't know how to, and he doesn't have any basis for doing it. Given this, he will then have the basis. He'll call [FBI Assistant Director] Mark Felt in, and the two of them—and Mark Felt wants to cooperate because he's ambitious—

PRESIDENT: Yeah.

HALDEMAN: He'll call him in and say, "We've got the signal from across the river to put the hold on this." And that will fit rather well because the FBI agents who are working the case, at this point, feel that's what it is.

PRESIDENT: This is CIA? They've traced the money? Who'd they trace it to?

HALDEMAN: Well, they've traced it to a name, but they haven't gotten to the guy yet.

PRESIDENT: Would it be somebody here?

HALDEMAN: Ken Dahlberg.

PRESIDENT: Who the hell is Ken Dahlberg?

From Hearings Before the Committee on the Judiciary, House of Representatives, 93rd Congress, 2nd Session (Government Printing Office, Washington, D.C., 1974).

HALDEMAN: He gave $25,000 in Minnesota and, ah, the check went directly to this guy Barker.

PRESIDENT: It isn't from the Committee though, from [Maurice] Stans?

HALDEMAN: Yeah. It is. It's directly traceable and there's some more through some Texas people that went to the Mexican bank which can also be traced to the Mexican bank—they'll get their names today.

PRESIDENT: Well, I mean, there's no way—I'm just thinking if they don't cooperate, what do they say? That they were approached by the Cubans? That's what Dahlberg has to say, the Texans too.

HALDEMAN: Well, if they will. But then we're relying on more and more people all the time. That's the problem and they'll [the FBI] . . . stop if we could take this other route.

PRESIDENT: All right.

HALDEMAN: [Mitchell and Dean] say the only way to do that is from White House instructions. And it's got to be to [CIA Director Richard] Helms and to—ah, what's his name? . . . Walters.

PRESIDENT: Walters.

HALDEMAN: And the proposal would be that . . . [John] Ehrlichman and I call them in, and say, ah—

PRESIDENT: All right, fine. How do you call him in—I mean you just— well, we protected Helms from one hell of a lot of things.

HALDEMAN: That's what Ehrlichman says.

PRESIDENT: Of course; this [Howard] Hunt [business.] That will uncover a lot of things. You open that scab there's a hell of a lot of things and we just feel that it would be very detrimental to have this thing go any further. This involves these Cubans, Hunt, and a lot of hanky-panky that we have nothing to do with ourselves. Well, what the hell, did Mitchell know about this?

HALDEMAN: I think so. I don't think he knew the details, but I think he knew.

PRESIDENT: He didn't know how it was going to be handled though— with Dahlberg and the Texans and so forth? Well who was the asshole that did? Is it [G. Gordon] Liddy? Is that the fellow? He must be a little nuts!

HALDEMAN: He is.

PRESIDENT: I mean he just isn't well screwed on, is he? Is that the problem?

HALDEMAN: No, but he was under pressure, apparently, to get more information, and as he got more pressure, he pushed the people harder.

PRESIDENT: Pressure from Mitchell?

HALDEMAN: Apparently. . . .

PRESIDENT: All right, fine, I understand it all. We won't second-guess Mitchell and the rest. Thank God it wasn't [special White House counsel Charles] Colson.

HALDEMAN: The FBI interviewed Colson yesterday. They determined that would be a good thing to do. To have him take an interrogation, which he did, and the FBI guys working the case concluded that there were one or two possibilities—one, that this was a White House (they don't think that there is anything at the Election Committee) they think it was either a White House operation and they had some obscure reasons for it—nonpolitical, or it was a—Cuban [operation] and [involved] the CIA. And after their interrogation of Colson yesterday, they concluded it was not the White House, but are now convinced it is a CIA thing, so the CIA turnoff would—

PRESIDENT: Well, not sure of their analysis, I'm not going to get that involved. I'm (unintelligible).

HALDEMAN: No, sir, we don't want you to.

PRESIDENT: You call them in.

HALDEMAN: Good deal.

PRESIDENT: Play it tough. That's the way they play it and that's the way we are going to play it. . . .

* * * * *

PRESIDENT: O.K. . . . Just say (unintelligible) very bad to have this fellow Hunt, ah, he knows too damned much. . . . If it gets out that this is all involved, the Cuba thing, it would be a fiasco. It would make the CIA look bad, it's going to make Hunt look bad, and it is likely to blow the whole Bay of Pigs thing which we think would be very unfortunate—both for CIA, and for the country, at this time, and for American foreign policy. Just tell him to lay off. Don't you [think] so?

HALDEMAN: Yep. That's the basis to do it on. Just leave it at that. . . .

September 15, 1972

PRESIDENT: We are all in it together. This is a war. We take a few shots and it will be over. We will give them a few shots and it will be over. Don't worry. I wouldn't want to be on the other side right now. Would you?

DEAN: Along that line, one of the things I've tried to do, I have begun to keep notes on a lot of people who are emerging as less than our friends because this will be over some day and we shouldn't forget the way some of them have treated us.

PRESIDENT: I want the most comprehensive notes on all those who tried to do us in. They didn't have to do it. If we had had a very close election and they were playing the other side I would understand this. No—they were doing this quite deliberately and they are asking for it and they are going to get it. We have not used the power in this first four years, as you know. We have never used it. We have not used the Bureau, and we have not used the Justice Department, but things are going to change now. And they are either going to do it right or go.

DEAN: What an exciting prospect.

PRESIDENT: Thanks. It has to be done. We have been (adjective deleted) fools for us to come into this election campaign and not do anything with regard to the Democratic Senators who are running, et cetera. And who the hell are they after? They are after us. It is absolutely ridiculous. It is not going to be that way any more.

March 13, 1973

PRESIDENT: How much of a crisis? It will be—I am thinking in terms of—the point is, everything is a crisis. (expletive deleted) it is a terrible lousy thing—it will remain a crisis among the upper intellectual types, the soft heads, our own, too—Republicans—and the Democrats and the rest. Average people won't think it is much of a crisis unless it affects them. (unintelligible)

DEAN: I think it will pass. I think after the [Senator Sam] Ervin hearings, they are going to find so much—there will be some new revelations. I don't think that the thing will get out of hand. I have no reason to believe it will.

PRESIDENT: As a matter of fact, it is just a bunch of (characterization deleted). We don't object to such damn things anyway. On, and on and on. No. I tell you this it is the last gasp of our hardest opponents. They've just got to have something to squeal about it.

DEAN: It is the only thing they have to squeal—

PRESIDENT: (Unintelligible) They are going to lie around and squeal. They are having a hard time now. They got the hell kicked out of them in the election. There is not a Watergate around in this town, not so much our opponents, even the media, but the basic thing is the establishment. The establishment is dying, and so they've got to show that despite the successes we have had in foreign policy and in the election, they've got to show that it is just wrong, just because of this. They are trying to use this as the whole thing.

March 21, 1973

DEAN: So that is it. That is the extent of the knowledge. So where are the soft spots on this? Well, first of all, there is the problem of the continued blackmail which will not only go on now, but it will go on while these people are in prison, and it will compound the obstruction of justice situation. It will cost money. It is dangerous. People around here are not pros at this sort of thing. This is the sort of thing Mafia people can do: washing money, getting clean money, and things like that. We just don't know about those things, because we are not criminals and not used to dealing in that business.

PRESIDENT: That's right.

DEAN: It is a tough thing to know how to do.

PRESIDENT: Maybe it takes a gang to do that.

DEAN: That's right. There is a real problem as to whether we could even do it. Plus there is a real problem in raising money. Mitchell has been working on raising some money. He is one of the ones with the most to lose. But there is no denying the fact that the White House, in Ehrlichman, Haldeman and Dean, are involved in some of the early money decisions.

PRESIDENT: How much money do you need?

DEAN: I would say these people are going to cost over a million dollars over the next two years.

PRESIDENT: We could get that. On the money, if you need the money you could get that. You could get a million dollars. You could get it in cash. I know where it could be gotten. It is not easy, but it could be done. But the question is who the hell would handle it? Any ideas on that?

DEAN: That's right. Well, I think that is something that Mitchell ought to be charged with.

PRESIDENT: I would think so too.

45

✦

CHOICE AND LIFE

Except for a brief "baby boom" period after 1945, the number of children born to the average American woman has steadily decreased since the early nineteenth century. She had seven children on average in the early 1800s, four in the late 1800s, three in the early 1900s, two in the late 1900s. In the nineteenth century, the chief methods for limiting births were primitive contraception, abstinence, and, especially, abortion. In the early twentieth century, however, abortion became illegal in most states, and abstinence in marriage was less acceptable to husbands and wives. Improved contraception and delays in first marriages therefore became increasingly important birth-limiting measures. The falling birthrate since 1960 has come chiefly from a dramatic improvement in contraceptive techniques, especially contraceptive sterilization, the pill, the intrauterine device, and the vaginal sponge. Less important but still significant has been a rise in abortion rates, most notably in the five years that followed the historic 1973 Supreme Court decision in *Roe* v. *Wade,* which ruled restrictive state abortion laws unconstitutional.

Roe v. *Wade* reflected major changes in American society. These included advances in birth control technology, a desire to limit family size, and, especially, increased attention to the rights of women. One of these rights, according to modern feminists, is "reproductive free-dom," of which abortion on demand was a crucial part. *Roe* v. *Wade* also typified a notable long-term shift in how the Supreme Court has viewed Constitutional "rights"—or at least the question of which rights are the truly vital ones. In theory, all rights in the Constitution are of equal value, but over the years the Court, reflecting changes in social values, has always cherished some rights as more important than others. In the nation's early days, private property was given special consider-ation; later this came to include the rights of businesses and liberty of contract. Then, in the 1930s and 1940s, economic rights lost pride of place to the rights enumerated in the First Amendment. In recent years the right to vote and to attend racially integrated schools has been judged to be of fundamental importance. With the *Roe* v. *Wade* deci-sion, so has the right to privacy.[1]

---

1 In *Rust* v. *Sullivan* (May 23, 1991) the Supreme Court decided that medical personnel in family planning clinics receiving federal funds may not mention abortion or abortion facilities to clients.

Justice Harry Blackmun's decision, which invalidated the statutes of thirty states that forbade abortions except to save the mother's life, sparked bitter controversy. "Pro-life" forces, most affiliated with religious denominations and uncompromisingly opposed to abortion, denounced the ruling. They called for a Constitutional amendment defining human life as beginning at conception, picketed abortion clinics, and successfully urged Congress to curtail most Medicaid funds for abortions. Meanwhile, "pro-choice" advocates organized in support of the right of a woman (rather than the state) to choose whether or not to have an abortion. They also supported doctors' rights to perform abortions and poor women's rights to obtain them. By the 1980s, a political candidate's position on abortion could make or break a campaign, just as a Supreme Court nominee's position on *Roe* v. *Wade* could make or break a Court nomination.

Harry Blackmun, author of the *Roe* v. *Wade* decision, was born in Illinois in 1908. He grew up in the Minneapolis-St. Paul area and then headed east to attend Harvard College and Harvard Law School. Blackmun returned to Minneapolis to open a private practice before moving to Rochester, Minnesota, as legal counsel for the world-famous Mayo Clinic. A hard-working, serious-minded, moderate Republican, he was first appointed to the federal judiciary by President Dwight Eisenhower in 1959. Blackmun, a boyhood friend of Chief Justice Warren Burger, was promoted to the Supreme Court in 1970 after the Senate had rejected Richard Nixon's first two nominations to fill a recent vacancy. Although Blackmun was initially perceived as Burger's "Minnesota twin," the *Roe* v. *Wade* ruling (from which Justices Byron White and William Rehnquist dissented) marked the beginning of his drift away from the conservative Burger wing of the Court toward the more liberal wing associated with Justice William Brennan.

Questions to Consider. On what two Constitutional grounds did the appellant seek to overturn restrictive Texas abortion laws? Of the three reasons commonly given to justify restricting abortions since the nineteenth century, which did Blackmun consider most important? Where in the Constitution did he find grounds for the right to privacy claimed by the appellant? Did Blackmun consider a woman's right to privacy a guarantee of an absolute right to abortion? The State of Texas (the appellee) argued that states could restrict abortion because the state has a "compelling interest" in protecting the right of an unborn fetus under the provisions of the Fourteenth Amendment. How did Blackmun deal with this argument? Why did he call Texas's position "one theory of life"? Why did Blackmun discuss "trimesters" and "viability" at such length? If medical technology were to shift the point of viability from the third to the second trimester, would that undercut the force of *Roe* v. *Wade*?

———————✧———————

Roe v. *Wade* (1973)

HARRY BLACKMUN

The principal thrust of appellant's attack on the Texas statutes is that they improperly invade a right, said to be possessed by the pregnant woman, to choose to terminate her pregnancy. Appellant would discover this right in the concept of personal "liberty" embodied in the Fourteenth Amendment's Due Process Clause; or in personal, marital, familial, and sexual privacy said to be protected by the Bill of Rights.

It perhaps is not generally appreciated that the restrictive criminal abortion laws in effect in a majority of States today are of relatively recent vintage. Those laws, generally proscribing abortion or its attempt at any time during pregnancy except when necessary to preserve the pregnant woman's life, are not of ancient or even of common law origin. Instead, they derive from statutory changes effected, for the most part, in the latter half of the nineteenth century. . . .

Three reasons have been advanced to explain historically the enactment of criminal abortion laws in the nineteenth century and to justify their continued existence.

It has been argued occasionally that these laws were the product of a Victorian social concern to discourage illicit sexual conduct. Texas, however, does not advance this justification in the present case, and it appears that no court or commentator has taken the argument seriously. . . .

A second reason is concerned with abortion as a medical procedure. When most criminal abortion laws were first enacted, the procedure was a hazardous one for the woman. . . . Modern medical techniques have altered this situation. Appellants refer to medical data indicating that abortion in early pregnancy, that is, prior to the end of first trimester, although not without its risk, is now relatively safe. . . . The State retains a definite interest in protecting the woman's own health and safety when an abortion is proposed at a late stage of pregnancy.

The third reason is the State's interest—some phrase it in terms of duty—in protecting prenatal life. Some of the argument for this justification rests on the theory that a new human life is present from the moment of conception. The State's interest and general obligation to protect life then extends, it is argued, to prenatal life. Only when the life of the pregnant mother herself is at stake, balanced against the life she carries within her, should the interest of the embryo or fetus not prevail. Logically, of course, a legitimate State interest in this area need not stand or fall on acceptance

From *Roe* v. *Wade*, 410 U.S. 113 (1973).

of the belief that life begins at conception or at some other point prior to live birth. In assessing the State's interest, recognition may be given to the less rigid claim that as long as at least *potential* life is involved, the State may assert interests beyond the protection of the pregnant woman alone. . . .

The Constitution does not explicitly mention any right of privacy. In a line of decisions, however, going back perhaps as far as *Union Pacific R. Co.* v. *Botsford* (1891), the Court has recognized that a right of personal privacy, or a guarantee of certain areas or zones of privacy, does exist under the Constitution. . . . These decisions make it clear that only personal rights that can be deemed "fundamental" or "implicit in the concept of ordered liberty," are included in this guarantee of personal privacy. They also make it clear that the right has some extension to activities relating to marriage, procreation, contraception. . . .[1]

This right of privacy, whether it be founded in the Fourteenth Amendment's concept of personal liberty and restrictions upon state action, as we feel it is, or, as the District Court determined, in the Ninth Amendment's reservation of rights to the people, is broad enough to encompass a woman's decision whether or not to terminate her pregnancy. The detriment that the State would impose upon the pregnant woman by denying this choice altogether is apparent. Specific and direct harm medically diagnosable even in early pregnancy may be involved. Maternity, or additional offspring, may force upon the woman a distressful life and future. Psychological harm may be imminent. Mental and physical health may be taxed by child care. There is also the distress, for all concerned, associated with the unwanted child, and there is the problem of bringing a child into a family already unable, psychologically and otherwise, to care for it. In other cases, as in this one, the additional difficulties and continuing stigma of unwed motherhood may be involved. All these are factors the woman and her responsible physician necessarily will consider in consultation. . . .

On the basis of elements such as these, appellants argue that the woman's right is absolute and that she is entitled to terminate her pregnancy at whatever time, in whatever way, and for whatever reason she alone chooses. With this we do not agree. Appellant's arguments that Texas either has no valid interest at all in regulating the abortion decision, or no interest strong enough to support any limitation upon the woman's sole determination, is unpersuasive. The Court's decisions recognizing a right of privacy also acknowledge that some state regulation in areas protected by that right is appropriate. As noted above, a State may properly assert important interests in safeguarding health, in maintaining medical standards, and in protecting potential life. At some point in pregnancy, these respective interests become sufficiently compelling to sustain regulation of the factors that govern the abortion decision. The privacy right involved, therefore, cannot be said to

---

1. References to prior court decisions have been omitted.

be absolute. In fact, it is not clear to us that the claim . . . that one has an unlimited right to do with one's body as one pleases bears a close relationship to the right of privacy previously articulated in the Court's decisions. The Court has refused to recognize an unlimited right of this kind in the past.

We therefore conclude that the right of personal privacy includes the abortion decision, but that this right is not unqualified and must be considered against state interests in regulation. . . .

Appellee [the state of Texas] argues that the State's determination to recognize and protect prenatal life from and after conception constitutes a compelling state interest. We do not agree fully. . . .

The Constitution does not define "person" in so many words. Section 1 of the Fourteenth Amendment contains three references to "person." The first, in defining "citizens," speaks of "persons born or naturalized in the United States." The word also appears both in the Due Process Clause and in the Equal Protection Clause. "Person" is used in other places in the Constitution. . . . But in nearly all these instances, the use of the word is such that it has application only postnatally. None indicates, with any assurance, that it has any possible prenatal application. All this, together with our observation, that throughout the major portion of the nineteenth century prevailing legal abortion practices were far freer than they are today, persuades us that the word "person," as used in the Fourteenth Amendment, does not include the unborn. . . .

Texas urges that, apart from the Fourteenth Amendment, life begins at conception and is present throughout pregnancy, and that, therefore, the State has a compelling interest in protecting that life from and after conception. We need not resolve the difficult question of when life begins. When those trained in the respective disciplines of medicine, philosophy, and theology are unable to arrive at any consensus, the judiciary, at this point in the development of man's knowledge, is not in a position to speculate as to the answer.

In view of all this, we do not agree that, by adopting one theory of life, Texas may override the rights of the pregnant woman that are at stake. We repeat, however, that the State does have an important and legitimate interest in preserving and protecting the health of the pregnant woman, whether she be a resident of the State or a nonresident who seeks medical consultation and treatment there, and that it has still *another* important and legitimate interest in protecting the potentiality of human life. These interests are separate and distinct. Each grows in substantiality as the woman approaches term and, at a point during pregnancy, each becomes "compelling."

With respect to the State's important and legitimate interest in the health of the mother, the "compelling" point, in the light of present medical knowledge, is at approximately the end of the first trimester. This is so because of the now established medical fact, referred to above . . . that until the end of the first trimester mortality in abortion is less than mortality in normal childbirth. It follows that, from and after this point, a State may regulate the abortion procedure to the extent that the regulation reasonably relates to the preservation and protection of maternal health. Examples of permissible state regulation in this area are requirements as to the qualifications of the person who is to perform the abortion; as to the licensure of that person; as to the facility in which the procedure is to be performed, that is, whether it must be a hospital or may be a clinic or some other place of less-than-hospital status; as to the licensing of the facility; and the like.

This means, on the other hand, that, for the period of pregnancy prior to this "compelling" point, the attending physician, in consultation with his patient, is free to determine, without regulation by the State, that in his medical judgment the patient's pregnancy should be terminated. If that decision is reached, the judgment may be effectuated by an abortion free of interference by the State.

With respect to the State's important and legitimate interest in potential life, the "compelling" point is at viability. This is so because the fetus then presumably has the capability of meaningful life outside the mother's womb. State regulation protective of fetal life after viability thus has both logical and biological justifications. If the State is interested in protecting fetal life after viability, it may go so far as to proscribe abortion during that period except when it is necessary to preserve the life or health of the mother.

Measured against these standards, the Texas Penal Code, in restricting legal abortions to those "procured or attempted by medical advice for the purpose of saving the life of the mother," sweeps too broadly.

To summarize and to repeat:

A state criminal abortion statute of the current Texas type, that excepts from criminality only a *life saving* procedure on behalf of the mother, without regard to pregnancy stage and without recognition of the other interests involved, is violative of the Due Process Clause of the Fourteenth Amendment.

(a) For the stage prior to approximately the end of the first trimester, the abortion decision and its effectuation must be left to the medical judgment of the pregnant woman's attending physician.

(b) For the stage subsequent to approximately the end of the first trimester, the State, in promoting its interest in the health of the mother, may, if it chooses, regulate the abortion procedure in ways that are reasonably related to maternal health.

(c) For the stage subsequent to viability the State, in promoting its interest in the potentiality of human life, may, if it chooses, regulate, and even proscribe, abortion except where it is necessary, in appropriate medical judgment, for the preservation of the life or health of the mother.

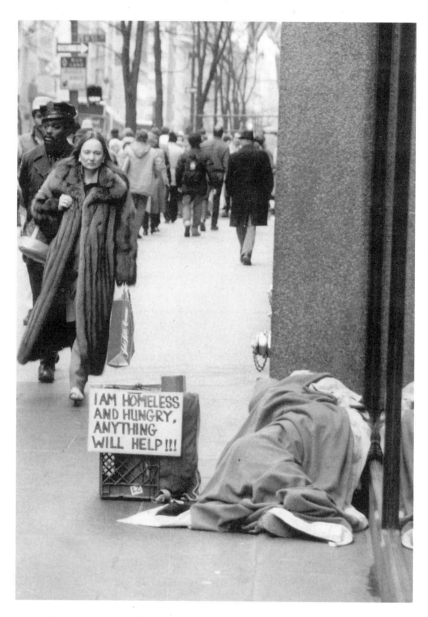

Cityscape. (AP/Wide World Photos)

CHAPTER EIGHT

◆

Modern Times

46

✧

ENTERPRISE UNLEASHED

Ronald Reagan first made his mark in politics with a televised appeal in 1964 on behalf of conservative Senator Barry Goldwater, the Republican presidential candidate. Reagan argued a position popular with the Sunbelt and the suburbs where Republicans were beginning to show strength—that federal government high taxes, social programs, and regulations were strangling individual freedom and threatening to drag the country "down to the ant heap of totalitarianism." He also showed himself to be a brilliant speaker—relaxed, confident, earnest, and poised, with a warm voice, a gift for turning a phrase, and a knack for seeming simultaneously friendly and determined. The speech failed to rescue Goldwater's foundering campaign, but it did launch Reagan's own political career, which led first to the California governor's mansion and then to the White House.

Reagan's major victory in the presidential election of 1980 can be traced to several sources. The Democratic candidate, incumbent Jimmy Carter, was widely perceived as a weak president, unable to lift the country from a lingering economic slump or to rescue American diplomatic hostages from the clutches of Moslem fundamentalists in Iran. But Reagan was himself a strong candidate, promising repeatedly (as he had on Goldwater's behalf sixteen years before) to cut taxes, deregulate business, balance the federal budget, and increase military spending—in brief, to restore unregulated capitalism and global supremacy, the twin pillars of the American system. That some of these promises appeared contradictory, mutually exclusive, or impossible was no problem, Reagan argued. According to "supply-side economics," which Reagan popularized, the country could accomplish these ends simply by cutting taxes enough to trigger massive investment and rapid growth, thus generating higher tax revenues despite lower tax rates. Reagan's Republican rival, George Bush, dismissed this notion as "voodoo economics." Nevertheless, Reagan's form of voodoo proved enormously popular with the American business community, which aggressively supported and financed his candidacy. President Reagan's inaugural address, excerpted below, signaled his determination to follow through on his campaign promises.

Born in 1914, Ronald Reagan won initial fame in Hollywood, where he worked in films and was president of the Screen Actors' Guild. During the 1950s he appeared on television and did publicity for General Electric Company. A two-term governor of California, he was by 1980 both a seasoned politician and a seasoned actor—photogenic, comfortable before the cameras, and possessing a mellifluous, compelling voice. No president since Franklin D. Roosevelt, with whom Reagan has often compared himself, used the electronic media so effectively or to such political advantage. His critics labeled him "the Teflon president" because he managed for years to escape unscathed from scandal or policy gaffes. But his friends called him "the Great Communicator," perhaps the finest of the century.

Questions to Consider. What was the nature of the "crisis" that Reagan saw in the United States in 1981? How did this crisis manifest itself at the government level? Why did Reagan say "government is the problem"? Did the president propose specific steps to deal with this? What steps did he propose for forcing government to live "within its means"? How, given these principles, was it possible for Reagan to oversee the biggest increase in the federal deficit in American history?

✧

First Inaugural Address (1981)

RONALD REAGAN

These United States are confronted with an economic affliction of great proportions. We suffer from the longest and one of the worst sustained inflations in our national history. It distorts our economic decisions, penalizes thrift, and crushes the struggling young and the fixed-income elderly alike. It threatens to shatter the lives of millions of our people.

Idle industries have cast workers into unemployment, causing human misery and personal indignity. Those who do work are denied a fair return for their labor by a tax system which penalizes successful achievement and keeps us from maintaining full productivity.

But great as our tax burden is, it has not kept pace with public spending. For decades, we have piled deficit upon deficit, mortgaging our future and our children's future for the temporary convenience of the present. To continue this long trend is to guarantee tremendous social, cultural, political, and economic upheavals.

From *The New York Times,* January 21, 1981.

The winning team. President-elect Ronald Reagan and Vice-President-elect George Bush at their first post-election news conference, November 7, 1980, after demolishing the Democratic ticket in the wake of the Iran hostage crisis. (© 1980 AP/Wide World Photos)

You and I as individuals can, by borrowing, live beyond our means, but only for a limited period of time. Why, then, should we think that collectively, as a nation, we are not bound by that same limitation? . . .

In this present crisis, government is not the solution to our problem. Government is the problem.

From time to time, we have been tempted to believe that society has become too complex to be managed by self-rule, that government by an elite group is superior to government for, by, and of the people. But if no one among us is capable of governing himself, then who among us has the capacity to govern someone else?

All of us together, in and out of government, must bear the burden. The solutions we seek must be equitable, with no one group singled out to pay a higher price.

We hear much of special interest groups. Our concern must be for a special interest group that has been too long neglected. It knows no sectional boundaries or ethnic and racial divisions, and it crosses political party lines. It is made up of men and women who raise our food, patrol our streets, man our mines and our factories, teach our children, keep our homes, and heal us when we are sick—professionals, industrialists, shop-keepers, clerks, cabbies, and truckdrivers. They are, in short, "We the people," this breed called Americans. . . .

So, as we begin, let us take inventory. We are a nation that has a government—not the other way around. And this makes us special among the nations of the earth. Our government has no power except that granted it by the people. It is time to check and reverse the growth of government, which shows signs of having grown beyond the consent of the governed.

It is my intention to curb the size and influence of the federal establishment and to demand recognition of the distinction between the powers granted to the federal government and those reserved to the states or to the people.

All of us need to be reminded that the federal government did not create the states; the states created the federal government.

So there will be no misunderstanding, it is not my intention to do away with government. It is, rather, to make it work—work with us, not over us; to stand by our sides, not ride on our backs. Government can and must provide opportunity, not smother it—foster productivity, not stifle it.

If we look to the answer as to why, for so many years, we achieved so much, prospered as no other people on earth, it was because here, in this land, we unleashed the energy and individual genius of man to a greater extent than has ever been done before. Freedom and the dignity of the individual have been more available and assured here than in any other place on earth. The price for this freedom has been high at times. But we have never been unwilling to pay that price.

It is no coincidence that our present troubles parallel and are proportionate to the intervention and intrusion in our lives that result from unnecessary and excessive growth of government. . . .

So with all the creative energy at our command, let us begin an era of national renewal. Let us renew our determination, our courage, and our strength. And let us renew our faith and our hope. We have every right to dream heroic dreams. . . .

In the days ahead, I will propose removing the roadblocks that have slowed our economy and reduced productivity. Steps will be taken aimed at restoring the balance between the various levels of government. Progress may be slow—measured in inches and feet, not miles—but we will progress. It is time to reawaken this industrial giant, to get government back within its means, and to lighten our punitive tax burden. And these will be our first priorities; on these principles there will be no compromise.

47

✧

SPIRIT AND CULTURE

Writing in 1884, an American archbishop who understood the importance of wholehearted Roman Catholic participation in the nation's social and political life wrote the following:

Republic of America, receive from me the tribute of my love and my loyalty. . . . *Esto perpetua.* Thou bearest in thy hands the hopes of the human race, thy mission from God is to show to nations that men are capable of [the] highest civil and political liberty. . . . Believe me, no hearts love thee more ardently than Catholic hearts, . . . and no hands will be lifted up stronger and more willing to defend, in war and peace, thy laws and thy institutions than Catholic hands. *Esto perpetua.*

In an address written nearly a century later and reproduced in part in the document below, Hispanic bishops echo these sentiments, affirming their love for the United States, "although the struggle has been difficult."

Similarly to nineteenth-century Irish Catholics who endured years of discrimination in America, Hispanic Catholics have been forced to cope with the effects of racism. Recognizing this, the Catholic church has addressed the particular difficulties that confront Hispanic Americans, and Hispanic religious have led efforts to end the suffering of the community.

In terms of the number of people who call themselves believers, and also as a percentage of the total population, the Christian church in America is larger than it has ever been—in spite of all its difficulties. The denominations showing the most growth are Southern Baptists and Roman Catholics, and to a great degree the astonishing increase in the latter is explained by the fact that Hispanics are the fastest-growing immigrant group. As the document suggests, the Catholic church has worked hard to establish a relationship with Hispanics, organizing itself to deal with the most urgent problems of the community and linking the foundations of the Christian gospel with the historical identity and traditions of the Hispanic people.

Questions to Consider. What is meant by *mestizaje?* According to the pastoral message, what is the relationship between the Hispanic family

and the Christian faith? What special problems of the Hispanic community do the pastors address? In their view, what elements in American
society endanger both the *mestiza* tradition and religious convictions?

Pastoral Message of the Hispanic Bishops (1982)

Four hundred fifty years after your apparition in our lands, we, your sons,
come as the shepherds of our Hispanic people in the United States of North
America. We come full of joy and hope, but we also come saddened and
preoccupied with the suffering of our people.

We are the shepherds of a people on the march. Walking with our people,
we come to you, Mother of God and our mother, so that we may receive
a renewed spirit. We want to be filled with enthusiasm to go out and
proclaim the wonders of God that have taken place in our history, that
are taking place at this time in our lives and that will take place in the
future. . . .

I. Our Pilgrimage Throughout History

A. THE BIRTH OF A NEW PEOPLE

At a unique moment in the history of this world, three radically different
and totally unknown worlds met: indigenous America, Africa and Europe.

The clash carried many of the indigenous people to slavery and death,
and made them strangers in their own land. The Africans were violently
wrenched from their lands and transplanted to far-off countries as slaves.
This initiated a shock whose reverberations are experienced even today.
There also began at that time a *mestizaje,* an intertwining of blood and
culture that in effect brought about the birth of a new people.

The roots of our Latin American reality are grounded in their threefold
inheritance. It is our identity, our suffering, our greatness and our
future. . . .

B. OUR FAITH

Our ancestors had a strong sense of religiosity. Their lives were centered
in their God. They were a people of spiritual values, of wisdom and hu-
manizing customs.

From *Origins Magazine* (August 12, 1982), 145–152.

The missionaries brought us the knowledge of a personal God who, through his Son, invites us to a new life. The Gospel purified and enriched the beliefs of our lands.

Because of this our faith is personal and cultural, because the word was made flesh on our land when his mother arrived on the hill of Tepeyac. Little by little the Gospel has penetrated every aspect of our life and culture. It is the alpha and omega, the center of our very being. Faith penetrates our music, art, poetry, language, customs, fiestas—every expression of our life.

Faithful to our tradition we hope that the Gospel continues to transform our life and our culture.

C. OUR MESTIZAJE

The Hispanic people of the United States of North America is a people of *mestizaje*, an interlacing of the blood and culture of the indigenous, African and European peoples. In the present reality of our people we find a new intertwining: that of the Latin American people and those of the United States. From this second *mestizaje*, the Hispanic American people begin to emerge.

We are thus a new people and within our very being we combine the cultural riches of our parents. The Virgin of Guadalupe, our *madrecita mestiza*, comes to fill with joy and blessings the painful and difficult process of our *mestizaje*. . . .

E. OUR FAMILIES

It is almost impossible to explain this great gift from God. Words do not tell the whole story. For us the meaning of family is extended and includes parents, children, grandparents, aunts and uncles, "distant" relatives, neighbors, godparents and *compadres*, or intimate friends. The family is the first school of love, tenderness, acceptance, discipline and respect. In our homes we have come to experience the bonds of friendship, mutual support, concern for one another and the presence of God.

We have received from our families the thoughts and values that are the foundation and primary orientation of our lives.

The new Juan Diego who carried the message from heaven to the church of the United States was also a humble messenger: our mothers and grand-mothers. They taught their sons and grandsons to pray while their fathers struggled to earn their daily bread.

Their voice has echoed insistingly: "Don't miss Mass," "Marry in the church," "May God go with you." They have marked our souls with the love of God and have caused your image of Guadalupe, full of tenderness, to blossom throughout the nation. . . .

II. Our Reality

Much has been gained but the suffering continues. We are conscious of the oppression and exploitation of our people. We have seen bodies disfigured by hunger and saddened by the fear of the law; we have heard the cries of abandoned children mistreated by their own parents. We sense the loneliness of the elderly ignored by their relatives and the depression of prisoners whose greatest crime has been the lack of money to pay someone to defend them in court. We have shared the pain and the heat of farm workers and domestic laborers, the invisible slaves of modern society. In the jails and the detention camps there are some who have come to our country in search of work and freedom, yet who have been considered criminals. We have seen our youth with empty eyes because they have nothing to look forward to in life. We have been with the countless victims of the violence that grows daily in our neighborhoods and even in our families. We will not rest until all injustice is eliminated from our life.

We have shared with our people the fear that comes from racism and discrimination. The knowledge that we might be rejected, ridiculed or insulted paralyzes us.

Just as Juan Diego accepted his challenge, we now accept ours: that of being artisans of a new people.

A. OUR IDENTITY

We are people twice *mestizado*. We are in the beginning stages of our life as Hispanic Americans.

Every birth is at one and the same time joy and sadness. Our birth as a people has been the same. Constant rejection has been a part of our daily life.

Nevertheless, our parents taught us to love the United States, although the struggle has been difficult. Our people have always struggled to improve themselves. We love the peace founded on truth, justice, love and freedom *(Pacem in Terris)*. We have not taken up arms against our country but instead have defended it. We have fought to eliminate the injustices that rule our lives. The road has been long and difficult, littered with many obstacles, but we have made progress and will continue ahead with firmness and determination. . . .

C. CHALLENGES

There are certain challenges in our society which we must meet.

Our betterment in social life does not mean that we forget our roots—our Latin American *mestiza* tradition. The more we value our past, the more strength will we have to launch ourselves toward the building of our future.

Development of a more human life does not mean that we allow ourselves to be enslaved and destroyed by materialism, consumerism, social climbing, the desire for continuous pleasure and immediate gratification. All of this come from the idolatry of gold. These values are the cancer of society.

The modernization of the family does not mean that we abandon the greatest treasure of our Hispanic culture. The family is in great danger today. Divorce is on the rise, the elderly are forgotten and even cheated, children are abandoned and young people make the street their home. The spirit of individualism is killing the spirit of community that is the core of the family.

Christian unity does not mean religious indifference. Ecumenism must not lead us to lose our identity as Catholics. Affirming ecumenism, we reject every type of active proselytizing which is anti-ecumenical and destructive to our people. The great diversity of fundamentalist groups and their anti-Catholic spirit divide our families and our peoples. Our response is not one of fighting against these groups nor one of speaking ill of them or their intentions, but rather we will take their activities as a challenge to us Catholics to live more authentically and apostolically the life of the Gospel.

III. Artisans of a New Humanity

* * * * *

B. A REBIRTH OF THE CHURCH

The word of the Gospel takes human form the more it penetrates, encompasses and ennobles our culture. It is expressed by means of images, symbols, music, art and wisdom. The church is born out of our response to the word of Jesus. Today we are living a true rebirth of the Hispanic American *mestizo* church.

C. THE LIFE OF THE CHURCH

Faith comes to us from the church and calls us to be church. In time and space this life of the church takes various forms depending on concrete needs and conditions. With great joy we see:

—The birth of new parish life where each member places his or her talents at the service of the community. The wide participation of parishioners in the mission of the church is the beginning of a new day and the source of great hope for the church of the future;

—In the renewed parishes the church is the natural center of the life of the community. The parish forms leaders and moves the people to work together for the good of all;

—The base communities *(comunidades eclesiales de base)* cause the individual to experience faith and to feel like church;

—New family movements and Bible study groups have brought new life to our communities;

—The resurgence of ministries has engendered a new ecclesial life that has incorporated many into the mission of the church. We are all called to actively take part in the apostolate;

—Permanent deacons, men prepared and ordained for service to the people of God, have renewed the presence of the church in many places with their dedication and apostolic zeal. . . .

I. A MORE AUTHENTIC FOLLOWING OF JESUS

Christ is our only model and like him we ought to be ready to commit ourselves and to be steadfast in the proclamation of truth, always filled with compassion and mercy.

Our following of him demands us to raise our voice when life is threatened, defending and respecting everyone as persons created by God. We are obligated to fight for peace and justice.

Just as he opened up new horizons for us, so too must we raise up the farm worker, the migrant and the laborer. We must aid in the self-improvement of all in search of a better place in society.

48

❖

TECHNOLOGY AND WORK

After population growth, cheap land, and bountiful resources, it was technological innovation—the work of creative individuals such as Eli Whitney, Isaac M. Singer, Andrew Carnegie, and Henry Ford—that was the driving force of American industrialization. After World War II, modern industries like petrochemicals, aerospace, and electronics helped power an unprecedented twenty-five years of almost uninterrupted growth in real national income. At every hand, it seemed, technology yielded products of prosperity: plastics and pharmaceuticals, satellites and jetliners, televisions and computers.

By the 1970s, however, doubt had appeared concerning the future and even the benefits of technology. These doubts stemmed in part from the "oil shocks" of 1973 and 1979, when exploding petroleum prices produced not only stagflation—a combination of high unemployment and rising prices—but also concern about whether science could discover usable substitutes for hydrocarbon fuels. Another source of doubt came from fear that technology was destructive as well as creative. Evidenced by a rapidly growing environmental movement, this fear centered chiefly on nuclear-powered electric plants with their radiation dangers and on the petrochemical industry, whose "unnatural" nonbiodegradable products and byproducts polluted the nation's air, water, and soil.

A final source of technological doubt concerned not whether we could find new energy supplies or avoid poisoning ourselves but whether, given continuing stagflation and the success of foreign competitors such as Germany and Japan, the United States was technologically competitive—that is, technological enough. The first selection reprinted below, by physicist Robert Jastrow, summarizes these concerns and provides an answer that was characteristic of the early 1980s, when many of the technologies Jastrow mentions were first becoming known to the general public.

In contrast to the technological optimism of Robert Jastrow, Robert B. Reich's is a gloomier view. According to Jastrow, the globalization of the marketplace and the accelerated development of "hi-tech" industries will mean tremendous economic growth for the United States.

But Reich believes that these developments will benefit only the new intelligentsia, that "fortunate fifth" of persons who will earn excellent incomes as (for example) researchers, writers, communications specialists, and design engineers. The majority of "globally vulnerable" workers will not fare well in the global economy, and in fact, Reich argues, will be left far behind, thereby increasing the gulf between rich and poor in ways that could very well threaten America's social fabric.

Robert Jastrow was founder of the Goddard Institute for Space Studies of the National Aeronautics and Space Administration and chair of the committee that set priorities for the early moon explorations. Once called "one of the rare scientists with the gift of making the unimaginable imaginable," Jastrow is currently professor of earth science at Dartmouth College. His books include *Red Giants and White Dwarfs* and *God and the Astronomers.*

Robert Reich, who is currently serving the Clinton administration as secretary of labor, was born in Scranton, Pennsylvania, in 1946. Educated at Dartmouth, Oxford, and Yale, he taught at the John F. Kennedy School of Government and Harvard University, has written several books *(The Next American Frontier, Tales of a New America, The Work of Nations),* and has been a member of the governing board of the "good government" group, Common Cause.

Questions to Consider. In reading "Science and the American Dream," consider four questions in particular. First, with whom does it appear that Jastrow was arguing in this essay? Second, can Jastrow be accurately placed within the tradition of probusiness writers such as Andrew Carnegie? Third, can Jastrow be accurately fitted into the conventional liberal or conservative categories of modern American politics? Finally, if Jastrow's argument is correct, would his argument reassure some people more than others?

To what extent is Robert Reich merely using a different vocabulary to describe the old dichotomy between "white collar" and "blue collar" workers? Why, according to Reich, will the relationship between "symbolic analysts" and less sophisticated workers change so dramatically? If events prove Reich to be correct and great disparities in wealth result, what does he recommend to "close the gap"? Is his reasoning persuasive?

———————✦———————

Science and the American Dream (1983)

ROBERT JASTROW

Industrial productivity depends on technical innovations, engineering and general knowhow—areas in which American prowess has been unchallenged. How is it possible that American productivity leveled off in the last ten years, while the productivity of Japan and Germany increased rapidly? What happened? The experts have given many answers. They all sound convincing, but when I began to look into the situation I found that none passes the test of a comparison with the facts. Here are some frequently heard opinions on the causes of our decline, and the data that test their validity.

American labor has priced itself out of the market. The Japanese have captured our market with cheap labor.

True once but no longer. Japanese wages were pennies an hour in 1950, but factory wages in Japan are now about $10 an hour, nearly the same as in America. Steel and automobile workers in America make more than their counterparts in Japan but that is not true for industry across the board for the two countries.

We spend too much on social welfare, on defense, on government as a whole; the tax burden is oppressive.

The United States spends a smaller fraction of its GNP on social welfare than do its leading industrial competitors, Japan and West Germany. This item is surely not the main brake on American productivity.

And although we spend considerably more on defense than Japan and somewhat more than Germany, during the 1970s defense costs averaged only 5.5 percent of the American GNP—significant, but not large enough to slow down the whole economy.

In general, the United States spends approximately the same fraction of its GNP on government as Japan does—about 30 percent—and a considerably smaller fraction of GNP than West Germany spends.

Federal deficits are excessive; the federal debt has zoomed to astronomical levels.

Deficits in the federal budgets of our main competitors, Japan and Germany, are far greater than ours—three to four times larger as a fraction of GNP in recent years.

The federal debt in the United States has increased only 20 percent since 1954, when corrected for inflation. The astronomical zoom reflects inflated dollars.

From Robert Jastrow, "Science and the American Dream," *Science Digest* (March 1983), 46–48. First appeared in *Science Digest,* © 1983 by The Hearst Corporation. Reprinted by permission of the author.

Antipollution laws have increased the cost of doing business in America.

True, but no more so than in Japan, and less in some cases. In the steel industry, for example, although Japanese steel manufacturers spent nearly twice as much as we did on pollution control in the 1970s—$3.6 billion versus $1.9 billion between 1971 and 1977—they still had lower prices, and took away much of our market. In the automobile industry, Japanese restrictions on the emission of pollutants in automobile exhausts are far more stringent than the limits set by our own government, yet Japanese auto manufacturing costs are far lower.

American industry is not spending enough on R&D.

U.S. expenditures on industrial R&D are considerably higher than in Japan, as a fraction of GNP. The fraction of scientists and engineers engaged in R&D in industry is also higher. Furthermore, U.S. spending on industrial R&D increased throughout most of the '70s, during the period in which our economic growth was slowing down. This factor cannot explain the poor performance of the U.S. economy in the past decade.

The United States is not training enough engineers.

True; in recent years the Japanese have been turning out twice as many engineers as America in proportion to population. That growing pool of bright young engineers is a time bomb for America. Still, at the moment we lead the world in the number of scientists and engineers engaged in R&D in proportion to the size of the labor force, and we have done so throughout the recent period of slow economic growth in the United States.

Investment in plant and equipment is inadequate.

Total capital investment as a fraction of GNP is low in the United States compared with other countries. However, in the manufacturing industries—such as steel, autos, machine tools—investment in machinery and equipment increased nearly 40 percent as a fraction of total production between 1960 and 1978, just when industrial productivity growth was declining. Many economists favor this explanation, but it cannot be a major factor.

Business gets more help from the government in Japan than in the United States.

Differences between Japan and America in this respect are not as great as generally believed. U.S. government purchases of semiconductors, computers and aircraft for the defense and space agencies in the 1950s and 1960s nurtured the great growth industries in computing, semiconductors and aircraft, when they were weak and struggling, by paying a large part of their R&D costs and buying up most of their products. Between 1955 and 1967 the government bought 57 percent of all computers made in the United States, 40 percent of all semiconductors, and more than half of all aircraft. In America, as in Japan, these hi-tech industries prospered because of government support. . . .

There is no villain. The trauma we are passing through now is not a depression, but a natural interlude between two great waves of economic growth. American industry is shedding its skin, casting off old technologies and developing new ones. But the new skin has not yet hardened. Industries based on the new technologies—mainly computers and microelectronics but also robots, fiberoptics, long-distance communications, biotechnology, and exotic new materials—are still young. They have not yet developed to the point where they can take up the slack in employment and industrial output created by the decline of the aging enterprises—the smokestack industries of steel, chemicals, autos, and so on.

The potential for growth in the new hi-tech industries is mind-boggling in terms of new jobs and new wealth. The computing industry alone is expected to grow from its current $50 billion to at least $100 billion and growing at the rate of 18 percent a year. Robots, another major new industry, pack a double wallop. Not only do they increase industrial productivity, but the construction of robots itself is showing phenomenal growth, from $200 million in 1980 to a projected $2 billion by 1985.

Fiberoptics is another rapidly growing technology. These light-pipes, made from glass fibers the thickness of a horsehair, can carry voices and data in a stream of tiny laser pulses at the rate of millions of pulses a second. AT&T plans to use a message-carrying light-pipe in a telephone cable between Boston and Richmond. The new cable would have taken 2 million pounds of copper with the old-fashioned wire technology.

There is little question that growth in the hi-tech industries will more than make up for the decline in the smokestack industries. Projected growth of $50 billion in the computing industry alone in the next four years is enough to offset the combined losses in the shrinking steel and auto industries. And new jobs go with the growth—easily sufficient to replace the jobs lost in the smokestack industries. Hewlett-Packard, one of the medium-size hi-tech companies, employs 57,000 people, Xerox more than 100,000. Two more Hewlett-Packards and a Xerox in the 1980s will make up for all the jobs lost in the auto industry.

Other countries will vie with us for a share in the wealth generated by the new technologies. Japan is the most formidable competitor. That nation graduated 87,000 engineers in 1980, compared with 63,000 in the United States, and is rapidly closing the gap in total numbers of scientists and engineers engaged in R&D in industry. The Japanese built their initial successes on technology borrowed from the United States, as we once borrowed our technology from Europe. Now, still following in our tracks, they are working very hard to acquire their own base of innovative research in semiconductors, computing, robotics, fiber optics, superplastics and biotechnology.

I would bet my money on America in this competition. The Japanese have the advantages of long-range planning and very productive management of people. But their industrial organization tends to stifle initiative, especially youthful initiative. "The nail that stands up gets hammered down," says a Japanese proverb. Conformity and respect for elders are highly valued traits in Japan.

We Americans have the advantages of an open society and an upward mobility that gives free rein to the innovativeness and entrepreneurial energy of human beings. This is what counts most of all—human capital, and a society in which it is utilized to its maximum potential.

The Work of Nations (1991)

ROBERT B. REICH

Regardless of the profitability or market share of a nation's corporations, the economic success of a nation (or, more accurately, the region of the global economy denominated by the nation's political borders) must be judged ultimately by how well its citizens are able to live and whether these standards of living can be sustained and improved upon in the future. . . .

Increasingly, one's capacity to command both tangible and intangible wealth is determined by the value that the global economy places on one's skills and insights. The ubiquitous and irrepressible law of supply and demand no longer respects national borders. In this new world economy, symbolic analysts hold a dominant position. American symbolic analysts are especially advantaged. The quality of the nation's universities is unsurpassed; its best primary and secondary schools are among the finest in the world; no other country provides the same quality of on-the-job training within entire regions specializing in one or another kind of symbolic analysis. In this Americans can take pride.

For the two other major categories of worker, however, the law of supply and demand does not bode well. Routine producers, confronted with an immense and rapidly growing pool of unskilled and semiskilled laborers worldwide, find their incomes slipping and their jobs disappearing. In-person servers, while largely sheltered from such direct competition, suffer the indirect effects and find themselves in an increasingly precarious position. A shrinking labor pool within America's borders may ease their plight somewhat in the future, but competition from workers who otherwise would have entered into routine production, from immigrants, and from labor-saving machinery may offset much of the gain. Primarily as a result of these trends, the earnings of Americans (as well as those of citizens of

Robert Reich. Robert Reich, soon to be named Secretary of Labor, with President-elect Bill Clinton and Vice President-elect Al Gore, December 1992. (Wide World Photos)

many other nations) have begun to diverge. Hence the challenge: to improve the living standards of the majority of Americans now occupying the two latter categories, who are losing ground in the global economy.

The problem is far from insoluble. In fact, the range of potential solutions is well understood. Finding the political will to implement them poses a considerably greater challenge.

One response is to offset the polarizing tendencies of the new global economy through a truly progressive income tax, coupled with the closure of gaping tax loopholes.

Today, the ideal of tax progressivity seems faintly quaint in the United States, although several other industrialized nations continue to regard it as a viable means for moderating income inequities. By 1990, America's income-tax rate on its wealthiest citizens was the lowest of any industrialized nation. A more progressive income tax is no panacea for widening income disparities rooted in the emerging worldwide division of labor, of course, but it would at least ameliorate the trend. The contrary strategy—featuring a low marginal tax on the highest incomes and a growing reliance on Social Security payroll taxes, sales taxes, user fees, property taxes, and lotteries—moves us in exactly the opposite direction.

A second response to the widening gap is to guard against class rigidities by ensuring that any reasonably talented American child can become a symbolic analyst—regardless of family income or race. Here we see the upside of the globalized economy. Unlike America's old hierarchical and somewhat isolated economy, whose white-collar jobs were necessarily limited in proportion to the number of blue-collar jobs beneath them, the global economy imposes no particular limit upon the number of Americans who can sell symbolic-analytic services worldwide. In principle, all of America's routine production workers could become symbolic analysts and let their old jobs drift overseas to developing nations. The worldwide demand for symbolic analysis is growing so briskly that even under these circumstances real wages would still move steadily upward. . . .

Even under these most optimistic circumstances it is doubtful that there would be radical growth in the number of Americans who became research scientists, design engineers, management consultants, advertising and marketing specialists, film producers, directors, editors and publishers, software engineers, writers, architects, or—even if the world really needed them—investment bankers and lawyers. So other responses are also needed. One is to increase the number of Americans who could apply symbolic analysis to production and in-person services. There is ample evidence, for example, that access to computerized information can enrich production jobs by enabling workers to alter the flow of materials and components in ways that generate new efficiencies. Production workers empowered by computers thus have broader responsibilities and more control over how production is organized. They cease to be "routine" workers—becoming, in effect, symbolic analysts at a level very close to the production process. . . .

This abbreviated catalogue of ways to improve the plight of America's globally vulnerable citizens is not intended as a definitive guide, but rather to suggest the realms of policy in which such solutions are apt to be found. I do not want to minimize the difficulty of designing and executing such remedies effectively, but only to show that they are neither mysterious nor beyond our grasp. The fundamental difficulty is not in imagining or implementing solutions. The greatest challenge comes in summoning the political determination to embark upon them. Good education, training, health care, and public infrastructure—available to all Americans—will be costly.

The reader may appropriately object that "more money" is no solution. Clearly it is not the whole solution. *Methods* of educating, training, providing health care, and building and maintaining infrastructure can surely be improved upon. But while money may not be sufficient, it is certainly a necessary prerequisite, and the facile assumption that money already has been dedicated generously to these ends is false, as I will show in more detail in the next chapter.

If there are to be additional expenditures, who is to pay? Most working Americans, already under a heavy tax load, cannot afford to shoulder the added financial burden of higher levels of public spending. It would have to be borne instead by the one group of Americans whose earnings have been increasing—our symbolic analysts. Of course, symbolic analysts would also bear the cost of any changes in the tax code designed to redistribute income and thus to reduce the polarizing domestic effects of a globalized economy.

Thus a central question concerns the extent to which America's fortunate citizens—especially symbolic analysts, who, with about half the nation's income, constitute the greatest part of the most fortunate fifth of the population—are willing to bear these burdens. But herein lies a paradox: As the economic fates of Americans diverge, the top may be losing the long-held sense of connectedness with the bottom fifth, or even the bottom four-fifths, that would motivate such generosity.

Ironically, as the rest of the nation grows more economically dependent than ever on the fortunate fifth, the fortunate fifth is becoming less and less dependent on them. The economic interdependence that Tocqueville observed in nineteenth-century America is slipping away. Increasingly, the fortunate fifth are selling their expertise on the global market and are able to maintain and enhance their standard of living and that of their children even as that of other Americans declines. No longer does their well-being depend exclusively or primarily on the productivity, purchasing power, or wage restraint exercised by the other four-fifths of the population. The American executive software engineer, linked to his worldwide web by computer, modem, and facsimile machine, is apt to be more dependent on design engineers in Kuala Lumpur, fabricators in Taiwan, bankers in Tokyo and Bonn, and sales and marketing specialists in Paris and Milan than on routine production workers in a factory on the other side of town.

Yet without the support of the fortunate fifth, it will be almost impossible to muster the resources, and the political will, necessary for change. . . .

The direction we are heading is reasonably clear. If the future could be predicted on the basis of trends already underway, laissez-faire cosmopolitanism would become America's dominant economic and social philosophy. Left to unfold on its own, the worldwide division of labor not only will create vast disparities of wealth within nations but may also reduce the willingness of global winners to do anything to reverse this trend toward inequality—either within the nation or without. Symbolic analysts, who hold most of the cards in this game, could be confident of "victory." But what of the losers?

We are presented with a rare historical moment in which the threat of worldwide conflict seems remote and the transformations of economies and technology are blurring the lines between nations. The modern nation-state, some two hundred years old, is no longer what it once was: Vanishing is a nationalism founded upon the practical necessities of economic interdependence within borders and security against foreigners outside. There is thus an opportunity for us, as for every society, to redefine who we are, why we have joined together, and what we owe each other and the other inhabitants of the world. The choice is ours to make. We are no more slaves to present trends than to vestiges of the past. We can, if we choose, assert that our mutual obligations as citizens extend beyond our economic usefulness to one another, and act accordingly.

49

✦

THE URBAN ORDEAL

The rise of Reagan conservatism moved serious discussion of the problems of poverty and urban blight to the edges of party politics. That there *were* such problems was apparent. It was difficult to travel in any American city without encountering unprecedented numbers of homeless people, so many that census takers barely counted them, lawyers barely represented them, doctors barely treated them, and public health officers barely coped with their existence. It was also difficult to follow the daily news without being assailed by instances of criminal violence. Large sections of cities became off-limits for many people; at night most sections became off-limits for nearly everyone. Drug dealers carried deadlier weapons than most police officers. School administrators frisked pupils for firearms.

The statistics told their own story: life expectancy among black urban males was falling; real income for urban workers was also falling. Rates of illegitimate birth were rising, as were rates of urban drug addiction and rates of domestic violence, rape, and murder. For a time, Detroit became the murder capital of the world, only to be displaced soon after by Houston—which in turn was overtaken by Washington, D.C. And there were the comparisons. Calcutta, the sprawling Indian city, has long been a byword for nightmarish squalor. In 1990 a group of foreign businessmen maintained that life in Calcutta, though desperate, might be preferable to the misery and viciousness of New York City. An American journalist agreed.

But serious as these problems were, they were largely problems of the poor at a time when the national mood and the national leadership were unsympathetic to reforms. Nevertheless, those who have a will to reform often find a way, usually by changing the terms of debate and organizing from outside. Faced with an unwillingness to debate poverty, reformers in the 1980s talked instead about the needs of children. Faced with an unwillingness to debate violence, they talked instead about the ravages of firearms. Thus arose one of the most visible and influential initiatives of the 1980s—the Children's Defense Fund—and the career of Marian Wright Edelman, the woman who led it.

Marian Wright Edelman was born in 1939 in South Carolina. She attended Spelman College and Yale Law School and, in 1963, became a staff attorney for the National Association for the Advancement of Colored People. She was congressional liaison for Martin Luther King's Poor People's Campaign in 1968 and director of the Harvard Center for Law and Education before founding the Children's Defense Fund in Washington, D.C. The purpose of the Fund was to monitor and propose improvements in government policies and programs in child-related areas: child and maternal health, education, child care, child welfare, adolescent pregnancy prevention, youth employment, and family support systems. Called "the 101st senator on children's issues" and "the nation's most effective lobbyist on behalf of children," Edelman, with the Children's Defense Fund, initiated a major long-term campaign in 1983 to prevent teenage pregnancy and provide positive life options for youth. The following excerpt is from her 1987 book, *Families in Peril,* which encapsulated many of the arguments and data that earned the Fund its high reputation for effective advocacy.

Questions to Consider. What single factor, in Marian Wright Edelman's view, best accounted for black family deterioration? Why did she stress the point that both white and black children were suffering from poverty? Do any of her statistics surprise you? Of the six reasons she gave for child poverty generally, which do you find most, and least, persuasive? What is the "highest ideal" that Edelman referred to in her final paragraph?

---------------◆---------------

Defending Children (1987)

MARIAN WRIGHT EDELMAN

A 1985 Children's Defense Fund (CDF) study, *Black and White Children in America: Key Facts,* found that black children have been sliding backward. Black children today are more likely to be born into poverty, lack early prenatal care, have a single mother or unemployed parent, be unemployed as teenagers, and not go to college after high school graduation than they were in 1980. . . .

We also found that:

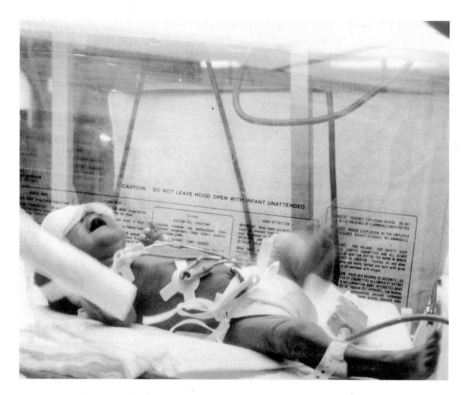

An innocent victim. A "crack baby," addicted to cocaine because the mother was an addict. Addictive illegal drugs were a plague throughout urban America. "Crack" cocaine, easily affordable and quickly addictive, was particularly deadly. (© 1990 John Chiasson/Gamma-Liaison, Inc.)

- Only four out of every ten black children, compared to eight out of every ten white children live in two-parent families.
- Births to unmarried teenagers occur five times more often among blacks than whites, although birth rates for black teens, married and unmarried, have been *declining*, while the birth rate among white unmarried teens has been *increasing* in recent years.
- In 1983, 58 percent of all births to black women were out of wedlock. Among black women under the age of twenty, the proportion was over 86 percent. For thirty years these out-of-wedlock ratios have increased inexorably. They have now reached levels that essentially guarantee the poverty of many black children for the unforeseeable future.

Since the main reason that black children live with only a mother is that most unmarried pregnant black women do not marry before giving birth, what has become of the fathers? They remain single. The pattern is quite clear. . . .

One crucial question is: When did the rate of marriage formation drop among young black males? In the 1970s it paralleled the decline of employment prospects of young black males, which resulted in only 29.8 percent of black teens and 61 percent of black twenty- to twenty-four-year-old men being employed by 1978. From 1978 to 1985 things got a bit worse for both black teens and males in their twenties.

Why did this economic disaster for black men occur? It is difficult to say precisely, but I think that the other factors which contributed included the softening of the labor market generally in the 1970s, poor education, continuing discrimination, and a reciprocal sense of defeatism among some inner-city and rural men. There is no question but that the number of Americans who wanted to work and could not find jobs was larger in 1980 than it had been in 1970. The economy absorbed unprecedented numbers of baby-boomers, women, and immigrants; in the process it left behind the same people who have always been at the end of the American line. . . .

The American family crisis is not just a black family crisis. Both public and private sector neglect and anti-family policy have contributed to a downward spiral for families and children, black and white. Those who suffer the most are of course the poor. Although the data on poverty, family dissolution, and teenage pregnancy are grimmer for blacks than for whites, the data for whites and for our society as a whole are themselves quite grim. In some respects (education, income of two-parent families, women's earnings, child nutrition, infant mortality) black rates have been improving and narrowing the gap between whites—or were doing so until the budget cuts and near-depression of the early 1980s. In certain other respects the gap has been narrowing because blacks have been standing still while whites are slipping backward. . . .

We must recognize that, if only by dint of their overwhelmingly majority status, whites make up most of the children and young adults about whom we should be concerned.

Nearly half of all black children in the United States are poor, an appalling figure. But a sixth of white children are poor, and that is also appalling. There are 8.1 million poor *white* children in the U.S., and 4.3 million poor black children—a two to one ratio. Together, more than one out of five American children are poor, including nearly one out of four children under the age of six.

Overall, children in America have become far poorer than other age groups. During the past fifteen years their poverty rates have soared, even as poverty among adults generally has stayed stable. . . .

Poverty is the greatest child killer in the affluent United States of the mid-1980s. More American children die each year from poverty than from traffic fatalities and suicide combined. Over a five-year period, more American children die from poverty than the total number of American battle deaths during the Vietnam War. . . .

Children are poor because our nation has lost its moral bearings. We must work to change the national climate and focus attention on families and children. Recent federal government policy has spawned a new set of beatitudes which measure success not by how many needy pregnant women can be provided cost-effective prenatal care to prevent infant deaths and birth defects, but by how many families can be denied Medicaid and turned away from public health clinics. . . .

Children are poor because their parents cannot find work. Today unemployment is at historically high levels, given the context of well over three years of economic recovery. . . .

Millions of children remain locked in poverty because hard-working parents cannot make enough income to provide for their basic needs. Recent governmental and private sector policies have resulted not only in high unemployment but in low wages for those who are working, increasing poverty and making the struggle of poor families harder. . . .

Poor families struggling to survive on meager wages have faced another burden: skyrocketing federal taxes. In 1979 a family of four with earnings at the poverty line paid less than 2 percent of its income in federal Social Security and income taxes. In 1986 that same family, if still earning (inflation-adjusted) poverty-line wages, has nearly 11 percent of its income taken by the federal government. Tax rates for single-parent families are even higher. . . .

Children are poor because of decreasing government support at a time of increasing need, which has resulted from economic recession, unemployment, low wages, and increased taxes on the poor. The America of the 1980s presents a cruel paradox: while the rich are getting richer and often getting more government help, the poor are getting poorer and receiving less help. The decline in federal assistance for children has made living in poverty a harsher existence for 13 million children, and it has crippled the efforts of their families to struggle back up out of poverty. . . .

Children are poor because of demographic changes and the growth of female-headed families. In 1970 one baby in nine was born to a single mother. In 1983 one baby in five was. If the trends continue, by 1990 one out of five white babies and three out of four black babies will be born into female-headed households. . . .

The United States today has the challenge and opportunity of showing the world a living justice by eradicating child poverty and putting a floor of decency under every American family. To do less is to betray our highest ideal. This task cannot be relegated just to government or to somebody else. Every individual has a responsibility to try to make a difference, to give imaginative flesh to the ideal of justice. We should aim high.

50

✧

BLOOD AND SAND

Since World War II, the Middle East, with its vast oil reserves, has been of strategic importance to both the United States and the Soviet Union. The presence there of Israel, a state with strong political and military ties to the United States virtually since Israel's founding in 1948, has made the area doubly important to American policy makers. As a consequence, every modern U.S. president has expended enormous financial and political resources to maintain American influence in the Middle East. There have been some successes from the standpoint of the American government. In 1953 President Dwight Eisenhower used the Central Intelligence Agency to replace an unfriendly government with a friendly one in oil-rich Iran; in 1958 he deployed the Sixth Fleet to maintain a friendly government in Lebanon. In 1978 Jimmy Carter helped bring about the so-called Camp David Accords between Israel and Egypt, the Arab world's most populous state.

But the United States has also experienced many failures in the region, not least in the very places where initial policies succeeded. In the late 1970s, for example, Islamic partisans seized control of Iran and its oil fields, taking fifty-two American hostages in the process. President Carter, unable to respond effectively, plummeted in public opinion polls and lost the 1980 election to Ronald Reagan partly because of his handling of the Iran crisis. President Reagan himself then came to grief when Israeli and Syrian invasions of Lebanon shattered that country's unity in 1982. Concerned about Syrian and Soviet influence, Reagan sent U.S. Marines to Beirut, the Lebanese capital, as part of a peacekeeping force, only to see more than two hundred of them killed in a terrorist attack. Just three months later, even though the president had called the American presence "essential," he ordered the force's withdrawal.

On August 2, 1990, Iraq, which had concluded a long and inconclusive war with Iran, invaded Kuwait, an oil-rich sheikdom abutting Iraq in the Persian Gulf not far from Kuwait's border with the desert kingdom of Saudi Arabia, the largest oil producer in the world. President George Bush immediately branded the Iraqi president, Saddam Hussein, a "bloody tyrant" and vowed that this brutal aggression "will not stand." During the following weeks the United States sent 250,000 troops to

312 Chapter 8 ❖ Modern Times

Saudi Arabia to protect it from Iraqi invasion and persuaded several European and Arab countries (including the dictator of Syria, a long-time U.S. foe) to send forces to join the Americans. The United States also obtained the backing of the United Nations Security Council for economic sanctions against Iraq, with a deadline of January 15, 1991, for Iraqi withdrawal from Kuwait. In November (after the congressional elections) another 200,000 American troops put still bigger teeth in the multinational force facing Iraqi soldiers across the borders of Kuwait.

In early January—after a historic debate that lasted several days and was broadcast live from gavel to gavel—the Senate and the House of Representatives voted to support President Bush's request for what everyone agreed was tantamount to a declaration of war: an endorsement of the U.N. resolution threatening military action if Iraq did not leave Kuwait by January 15. Saddam Hussein, however, made no move. On January 16, Bush ordered a full-scale air assault, including a dazzling array of electronic weaponry, against military targets in Kuwait and Iraq. That evening he delivered the following television address to explain and defend his decision.

Born in Massachusetts in 1924, George Bush was the son of Prescott Bush, a Wall Street banker and U.S. senator. He attended private schools and, after service with the navy in World War II, took a degree in economics at Yale, where he also played baseball. Bush then moved to Texas, where he made money in the oil business. He lost a race on the Republican ticket for the U.S. Senate before, in 1966, winning election to Congress from Houston. During the Nixon years, Bush served as U.N. ambassador and chairman of the Republican National Committee; under Gerald R. Ford he was chief of the Liaison Office in China and director of the Central Intelligence Agency. Defeated by Ronald Reagan for the 1980 Republican presidential nomination, Bush agreed to run as Reagan's vice-presidential nominee. This was the ticket that trounced Jimmy Carter in 1980 and mauled Walter Mondale in 1984. With a record of party loyalty and Reagan's popularity behind him, Bush easily won the nomination for president in 1988 and, with Dan Quayle on the bottom of the ticket, thrashed Democrat Michael Dukakis to keep the White House in Republican hands. Four years later, Bush himself lost the presidency to Democrat Bill Clinton.

Questions to Consider. President Bush gave several reasons for taking action against Iraq. Which of them seems to have been most important? What reasons did he give for taking military action rather than waiting for the economic sanctions possibly to produce results? Which reasons seem to have mattered most to him? What kind of war did the President seem to anticipate? What did he mean when he said this war would not be "another Vietnam"? What did he mean by "the new world order"?

———————— ✧ ————————

Address on the War with Iraq (1991)

GEORGE BUSH

Just two hours ago, allied air forces began an attack on military targets in Iraq and Kuwait. These attacks continue as I speak. Ground forces are not engaged.

This conflict started Aug. 2, when the dictator of Iraq invaded a small and helpless neighbor. Kuwait, a member of the Arab League and a member of the United Nations, was crushed, its people brutalized. Five months ago, Saddam Hussein started this cruel war against Kuwait; tonight, the battle has been joined.

This military action, taken in accord with United Nations resolutions and with the consent of the United States Congress, follows months of constant and virtually endless diplomatic activity on the part of the United Nations, the United States and many, many other countries.

Arab leaders sought what became known as an Arab solution, only to conclude that Saddam Hussein was unwilling to leave Kuwait. Others traveled to Baghdad in a variety of efforts to restore peace and justice. Our Secretary of State, James Baker, held an historic meeting in Geneva, only to be totally rebuffed.

This past weekend, in a last-ditch effort, the Secretary General of the United Nations went to the Middle East with peace in his heart—his second such mission. And he came back from Baghdad with no progress at all in getting Saddam Hussein to withdraw from Kuwait.

Now, the twenty-eight countries with forces in the gulf area have exhausted all reasonable efforts to reach a peaceful resolution, and have no choice but to drive Saddam from Kuwait by force. We will not fail.

As I report to you, air attacks are under way against military targets in Iraq. We are determined to knock out Saddam Hussein's nuclear bomb potential. We will also destroy his chemical weapons facilities. Much of Saddam's artillery and tanks will be destroyed. Our operations are designed to best protect the lives of all the coalition forces by targeting Saddam's vast military arsenal.

Initial reports from General [Norman] Schwartzkopf are that our operations are proceeding according to plan. Our objectives are clear: Saddam Hussein's forces will leave Kuwait. The legitimate government of Kuwait will be restored to its rightful place, and Kuwait will once again be free.

Iraq will eventually comply with all relevant United Nations resolutions, and then, when peace is restored, it is our hope that Iraq will live as a

From *The New York Times,* Jan. 17, 1991.

Aftermath of the war with Iraq. This tank was abandoned by Iraqis in their retreat. But to the cow who came looking for food it meant nothing. In the background an oil well burns out of control. (Magnum Photos)

peaceful and cooperative member of the family of nations, thus enhancing the security and stability of the Gulf.

Some may ask, why act now? Why not wait? The answer is clear. The world could wait no longer. Sanctions, though having some effect, showed no signs of accomplishing their objective. Sanctions were tried for well over five months, and we and our allies concluded that sanctions alone would not force Saddam from Kuwait.

While the world waited, Saddam Hussein systematically raped, pillaged and plundered a tiny nation no threat to his own. He subjected the people of Kuwait to unspeakable atrocities, and among those maimed and murdered, innocent children.

While the world waited, Saddam sought to add to the chemical weapons arsenal he now possesses, an infinitely more dangerous weapon of mass destruction—a nuclear weapon. And while the world waited, while the world talked peace and withdrawal, Saddam Hussein dug in and moved massive forces into Kuwait.

While the world waited, while Saddam stalled, more damage was being done to the fragile economies of the Third World, emerging democracies of Eastern Europe, to the entire world, including to our own economy.

The United States, together with the United Nations, exhausted every means at our disposal to bring this crisis to a peaceful end. However,

Saddam clearly felt that by stalling and threatening and defying the United Nations, he could weaken the forces arrayed against him.

While the world waited, Saddam Hussein met every overture of peace with open contempt. While the world prayed for peace, Saddam prepared for war.

I had hoped that when the United States Congress, in historic debate, took its resolute action, Saddam would realize he could not prevail, and would move out of Kuwait in accord with the United Nations resolutions. He did not do that. Instead, he remained intransigent, certain that time was on his side.

Saddam was warned over and over again to comply with the will of the United Nations, leave Kuwait or be driven out. Saddam has arrogantly rejected all warnings. Instead he tried to make this a dispute between Iraq and the United States of America.

Well he failed. Tonight twenty-eight nations—countries from five continents, Europe and Asia, Africa and the Arab League—have forces in the Gulf area standing shoulder to shoulder against Saddam Hussein. These countries had hoped the use of force could be avoided. Regrettably, we now believe that only force will make him leave.

Prior to ordering our forces into battle, I instructed our military commanders to take every necessary step to prevail as quickly as possible, and with the greatest degree of protection possible for American and Allied service men and women. I've told the American people before that this will not be another Vietnam, and I repeat this here tonight. Our troops will have the best possible support in the entire world, and they will not be asked to fight with one hand tied behind their back. I'm hopeful that this fighting will not go on for long and that casualties will be held to an absolute minimum.

This is an historic moment. We have in this past year made great progress in ending the long era of conflict and cold war. We have before us the opportunity to forge for ourselves and for future generations a new world order, a world where the rule of law, not the law of the jungle, governs the conduct of nations.

When we are successful, and we will be, we have a real chance at this new world order, an order in which a credible United Nations can use its peacekeeping role to fulfill the promise and vision of the U.N.'s founders. We have no argument with the people of Iraq. Indeed, for the innocents caught in this conflict, I pray for their safety.

Our goal is not the conquest of Iraq. It is the liberation of Kuwait. It is my hope that somehow the Iraqi people can, even now, convince their dictator that he must lay down his arms, leave Kuwait and let Iraq itself rejoin the family of peace-loving nations.

Thomas Paine wrote many years ago: "These are the times that try men's souls." Those well-known words are so very true today. But even as planes of the multinational forces attack Iraq, I prefer to think of peace, not war.

I am convinced not only that we will prevail, but that out of the horror of combat will come the recognition that no nation can stand against a world united. No nation will be permitted to brutally assault its neighbor. . . .

And let me say to everyone listening or watching tonight: When the troops we've sent in finish their work, I'm determined to bring them home as soon as possible. Tonight, as our forces fight, they and their families are in our prayers.

May God bless each and every one of them, and the coalition forces at our side in the Gulf, and may He continue to bless our nation, the United States of America.

51

CONTRACT

A striking feature of American politics since the election of Dwight Eisenhower in 1952 is that although the Republicans have won the presidency twice as often as the Democrats and thus have largely controlled both the executive and (through appointments) the judicial branches, they seemed unable to gain control of Congress. Even when they briefly controlled the Senate in the 1950s and 1980s, they remained the minority in the House of Representatives—a Democratic stronghold for over forty years.

The elections of 1994 abruptly changed all this. Midway through Democrat Bill Clinton's first term, the Republican party triumphed in congressional races throughout the country. When the dust settled, the Republicans had solid control of the Senate for the third time since 1952, a control strengthened in succeeding months when two Democrats switched parties. In the House the shift was even more dramatic; the Republicans gained over eighty seats, giving them, for the first time since World War II, a powerful majority. And although a Democrat still occupied the White House, many observers expected the presidency to revert to Republican domination in the near future.

The post-1994 Republicans were not only numerically strong. To a remarkable degree, they were also united. In the fall of 1994, some 367 Republican candidates for the House of Representatives publicly supported the "Contract with America," a bold set of procedural reforms and conservative policy initiatives devised mainly by Georgia Republican Newt Gingrich. Most of these candidates were elected. What was telling about the 1994 congressional elections, in fact, was that while Democratic incumbents were falling right and left, not one Republican incumbent lost. The Contract, reproduced below, thus became a major political document, and Gingrich became Speaker of the House, dedicated to passing as much of the Contract as he could as quickly as possible. For at least the first few months of their Washington reign, the Republicans enjoyed considerable success.

Voter analysis shows that Republicans won in 1994 because they enjoyed exceptional support among certain groups: young voters, especially young males; white Southerners, especially white male Southerners; and male voters everywhere, especially white males. The South thus completed a shift toward the Republican party that had begun with Barry Goldwater's campaign in 1964. Most of the new Republican congressional leaders were Southerners, and the national party leadership was Southern to an unprecedented degree. But the antiwelfare, anti–affirmative action, anti–illegal immigrant, antiunion, antiregulatory, anti–high tax, probusiness, and promilitary positions of the Republicans were clearly compelling to a great many American voters in addition to white male Southerners. Furthermore, two special interest groups appeared to have been influential: the National Rifle Association, which campaigned aggressively against Democrats who had supported a ban on assault rifles and a waiting period for buying handguns; and the loosely confederated antiabortion movement, which opposed prochoice, mostly Democratic candidates.

Republicans raised and spent lots of money. The average House candidate in 1994 spent $200,000; successful first-time Republican candidates spent $675,000. Fifteen of the top twenty fundraisers among successful first-year candidates were Republicans, who spent on average over $1 million per race. Many Republican newcomers to the House used their own funds for campaigning, sometimes to the tune of $250,000 or more. This pattern, and the fact that the "Contract with America" did not address key issues of campaign financing and special interest lobbying, helped fuel the skepticism of some observers, including Lewis Lapham, editor of *Harper's Magazine,* whose essay on the Contract and the Gingrich insurgency is excerpted below.

Born in 1943 in Pennsylvania, Newt Gingrich is the adopted son of an Army soldier. Gingrich attended Emory University, received graduate degrees in history from Tulane, and taught American history at West Georgia College before winning a House seat as a Republican in 1978. He cultivated a combative style, assailing Democrats in Washington for ethical lapses and big-spending liberalism. He also took advantage of television coverage of the House chamber to deliver partisan attacks from the floor, including verbal assaults on Democratic House Speakers Jim Wright and Tip O'Neill. Gingrich was elected Republican Whip in 1984 largely on the basis of his influence over younger Republicans and his reputation as a fire-breathing conservative who hated to compromise. He also raised major political money, attracting $2 million (including $410,000 from insurance, medical, securities, and legal interests) in 1993–1994 alone.

Lewis Lapham was born in 1935 to a San Francisco banking family and attended Hotchkiss School and Yale University. A newspaper reporter from 1957 to 1962 and a magazine writer during the 1960s, Lapham became managing editor of *Harper's* in 1971 and editor in 1975. The author of several books on class, status, and power in contemporary America, he is a member of the Council on Foreign Relations.

Questions to Consider. Of the eight recommendations of the "Contract with America" pertaining to the operations of the House of Representatives itself, which one strikes you as most important? Would implementation of the four recommendations on committee organization and work increase or decrease the internal power of the House leadership and of the committees themselves? Of the ten national policy recommendations in the Contract, which would be likely to have the greatest impact? Is there a common thread tying these recommendations together?

What does Lewis Lapham see as the main features of the Contract and of Gingrich Republicanism? What appears to bother Lapham most, corruption or hypocrisy? Is he persuasive in arguing that the militant conservatives of the 1990s actually resemble the countercultural activists of the 1960s? Is he right in saying that the conservatives already control most of America? Do you agree with Lapham that the Republicans offer everyone except the "propertied classes" mainly prisons and sermons?

———————◇———————

Contract with America (1994)

NEWT GINGRICH

As Republican Members of the House of Representatives and as citizens seeking to join that body we propose not just to change its policies, but even more important, to restore the bonds of trust between the people and their elected representatives. That is why, in this era of official evasion and posturing, we offer instead a detailed agenda for national renewal, a written commitment with no fine print.

This year's election offers the chance, after four decades of one-party control, to bring to the House a new majority that will transform the way Congress works. That historic change would be the end of government that is too big, too intrusive, and too easy with the public's money. It can be the beginning of a Congress that respects the values and shares the faith of the American family.

Newt Gingrich. Speaker of the House Newt Gingrich holds a copy of the Republican Party's "Contract with America." During the first one hundred days following the 1994 election, the Republican-controlled Congress passed many of its provisions. (Robert Trippett/SIPA Press)

Like Lincoln, our first Republican president, we intend to act "with firmness in the right, as God gives us to see the right." To restore accountability to Congress. To end its cycle of scandal and disgrace. To make us all proud again of the way free people govern themselves.

On the first day of the 104th Congress, the new Republican majority will immediately pass the following major reforms, aimed at restoring the faith and trust of the American people in their government:

First, require all laws that apply to the rest of the country also apply equally to the Congress;

Second, select a major independent auditing firm to conduct a comprehensive audit of Congress for waste, fraud, or abuse;

Third, cut the number of House committees, and cut committee staff by one-third;

Fourth, limit the terms of all committee chairs;

Fifth, ban the casting of proxy votes in committee;

Sixth, require committee meetings to be open to the public;

Seventh, require a three-fifths majority vote to pass a tax increase;

Eighth, guarantee an honest accounting of our federal budget by implementing zero baseline budgeting.

Thereafter, within the first hundred days of the 104th Congress, we shall bring to the House Floor the following bills, each to be given full and open debate, each to be given a clear and fair vote, and each to be immediately available this day for public inspection and scrutiny.

The Fiscal Responsibility Act

• A balanced budget/tax limitation amendment and a legislative line-item veto to restore fiscal responsibility to an out-of-control Congress, requiring them to live under the same budget constraints as families and businesses.

The Taking Back Our Streets Act

• An anti-crime package including stronger truth in sentencing, "good faith" exclusionary rule exemptions, effective death penalty provisions, and cuts in social spending from this summer's crime bill to fund prison construction and additional law enforcement to keep people secure in their neighborhoods and kids safe in their schools.

The Personal Responsibility Act

• Discourage illegitimacy and teen pregnancy by prohibiting welfare to minor mothers and denying increased AFDC for additional children while on welfare, cut spending for welfare programs, and enact a tough two-years-and-out provision with work requirements to promote individual responsibility.

The Family Reinforcement Act

• Child support enforcement, tax incentives for adoption, strengthening rights of parents in their children's education, stronger child pornography laws, and an elderly dependent care tax credit to reinforce the central role of families in American society.

The American Dream Restoration Act

• A $500-per-child tax credit, begin repeal of the marriage tax penalty, and creation of American Dream Savings Accounts to provide middle-class tax relief.

The National Security Restoration Act

• No U.S. troops under UN command and restoration of the essential parts of our national security funding to strengthen our national defense and maintain our credibility around the world.

The Senior Citizens Fairness Act

• Raise the Social Security earnings limit, which currently forces seniors out of the workforce, repeal the 1993 tax hikes on Social Security benefits, and provide tax incentives for private long-term care insurance to let older Americans keep more of what they have earned over the years.

The Job Creation and Wage Enhancement Act

• Small business incentives, capital gains cut and indexation, neutral cost recovery, risk assessment/cost-benefit analysis, strengthening of the Regulatory Flexibility Act and unfunded mandate reform to create jobs and raise worker wages.

The Common Sense Legal Reforms Act

• "Loser pays" laws, reasonable limits on punitive damages, and reform of product liability laws to stem the endless tide of litigation.

The Citizen Legislature Act

• A first-ever vote on term limits to replace career politicians with citizen legislators.

Further, we will instruct the House Budget Committee to report to the floor and we will work to enact additional budget savings, beyond the budget cuts specifically included in the legislation described above, to ensure that the federal budget deficit will be less than it would have been without the enactment of these bills.

Respecting the judgment of our fellow citizens as we seek their mandate for reform, we hereby pledge our names to this *Contract with America*.

Reactionary Chic (1995)

LEWIS H. LAPHAM

The 104th Congress assembled in Washington on January 4 amid a dark murmur of sworn oaths about rescuing the captive spirit of American success from the dungeons of big government, and as I listened to the right-wing radio broadcasters sending their furious signals from their newly installed transmitters in the basement of the Capitol, I was struck by the resemblance between this season's Republican revolution and the old countercultural rebellion of thirty years ago. Once again the partisans of a romantic anti-politics intended a guerrilla raid on the wicked cities of death and time. Although nobody described the mission in precisely those words, the exuberant cheers welcoming Newt Gingrich to the Speaker's chair in the House of Representatives (loud cries of "Newt!" "Newt!" "Newt!") swelled with high purpose and zealous intent, the applause rising to the pitch of enthusiasm appropriate to the arrival of a hero or a saint. Here at last was the purifying wind from the South, the politician who had been touring the country both before and after the November election preaching the gospel of revolt, sacker of shibboleths and government spending programs come to lead the American people out of the deserts of the welfare state.

Under the circumstances and given the fierce expectations gathered on the Republican side of the aisle, Gingrich's inaugural address as Speaker of the House was surprisingly and uncharacteristically mild. Pronouncing the occasion "historic," he put aside for the moment his familiar persona as arrogant bully and humbly introduced himself as an adopted child and a common man. . . .

Like so much else about the Republican risorgimento, the political passion was attached to a preferred image rather than a plain or ambiguous fact, not to the Gingrich who had just delivered a conciliatory speech but to the Gingrich renowned for being nasty and brutish and short—the militant Gingrich blessed with a boll weevil's appetite for destruction who had ordered a skull of *Tyrannosaurus rex* as an ornament for his new office in the Longworth building.

It was the scornful Gingrich who had come to stand during his sixteen years in Congress as the shared symbol of resentment binding together the several parties of the disaffected right—the Catholic conservatives with the Jewish neoconservatives, the libertarians with the authoritarians, Pat Robertson's Christian Coalition with the disciples of David Duke. Clearly a man for all grievances, Gingrich summed up (in his person as well as in his lectures on the decline and fall of American civilization) the whole of the conservative objection that since the dawn of the Reagan revolution in the early 1980s has comprised the course of required reading at the Heritage Foundation and the American Enterprise Institute. Over the last fifteen years I probably have read two or three thousand variations of the complaint—editorials in the *Wall Street Journal*, articles in *Commentary* and *The New Criterion*, the speeches of William Bennett and the columns of George Will, the soliloquies of Rush Limbaugh, the books in the line of frowning succession, from Allan Bloom's *The Closing of the American Mind* through George Gilder's *Wealth and Poverty*, Dinesh D'Souza's *Illiberal Education*, and Charles Murray's *Losing Ground*, etc.—but when I delete the repetitions and piece together what remains of a coherent narrative, the entire sum of the great suburban remonstrance fits within the span of a short fairy tale. As follows:

Once upon a time, before the awful misfortunes of the 1960s, America was a theme park constructed by nonunion labor along the lines of the Garden of Eden. But then something terrible happened, and a plague of guitarists descended upon the land. Spawned by the sexual confusions of the amoral news media, spores of Marxist ideology blew around in the wind, multiplied the powers of government, and impregnated the English departments at the Ivy League universities, which then gave birth to the monster of deconstruction that devoured the arts of learning. Pretty soon the trout began to die in Wyoming, and the next thing that anybody knew the nation's elementary schools had been debased, too many favors were being granted to women and blacks, federal bureaucrats were smothering capitalist entrepreneurs with the pillows of government regulation, prime-time television was broadcasting continuous footage from Sodom and Gomorrah, and the noble edifice of Western civilization had collapsed into the rubble of feminist prose.

The story somehow made more sense when set against the operatic backdrop of the Cold War, possibly because the familiar stage design recalled to mind the first act of *The Nutcracker Suite* when the toy soldier does battle with the army of horrific mice. The evil Soviet empire furnished the book and lyrics for the election campaigns of both Presidents Reagan and Bush, and for a few years it was possible to imagine that the fungus blighting the apple trees in the American orchard had something to do with the weather on the totalitarian steppe. The sudden tearing down of the Berlin Wall took everybody by surprise—the director of the CIA as well as the editors at *National Review*—and the tellers of the tale found themselves in pressing need of other antagonists to take the place of the grim but harmless ogre. The departure of the Russian trolls prompted a casting call for prospective bogeymen and likely villains. The Japanese couldn't play the part because they were lending the United States too much money; the Colombian drug lords were too few and too well connected in Miami; Manuel Noriega and Saddam Hussein failed the audition; the Arab oil cartel was broke; and the Chinese were busy making shirts for Ralph Lauren.

In the absence of enemies abroad, the protectors of the American dream began looking for inward signs of moral weakness rather than outward shows of military force; instead of examining the dossiers of foreign tyrants, they searched the local newspapers for flaws in the American character, and the surveillance satellites overhead Leipzig and Sevastopol were reassigned stations over metropolitan Detroit and the back lots of Hollywood studios. Within a matter of months the authorities rounded up as suspects a motley crowd of specific individuals and general categories of subversive behavior and opinion—black male adolescents as well as leftist English professors, multiculturalists of all descriptions, the liberal news media, the 1960s, the government in Washington, welfare mothers, homosexuals, drug criminals, performance artists, illegal immigrants. Some enemies of the state were easier to identify than others, but in all instances the tellers of the tale relied on images seen in dreams or on the network news rather than on the lessons of their own experience.

Believing themselves under assault from what they took to be the hostile forces of history, the heirs and servants of American oligarchy chose to cast themselves as rebels against "the system," as revolutionary idealists at odds with a world they never made. The pose was as lucicrous as it was familiar. Here were the people who owned most of what was worth owning in the country (the banks and business corporations as well as the television networks and most of the members of Congress) pretending that they were victims of a conspiracy raised against them by the institutions that they themselves controlled. What was even more extraordinary was the general likeness between their own revolutionary pretensions and the posturing of the 1960s counterculture that they so often and so loudly denounced. Although I had made occasional notes over a number of years about the similarities between the two camps of *soi-disant* revolutionaries, it wasn't until last October 19, during the course of a publisher's lunch at the Harvard Club in New York, that I fully appreciated the extent to which the reactionary chic of the 1990s mimics the set of 1960s attitudes memoralized by Tom Wolfe in the phrase "radical chic."

Sponsored by the Manhattan Institute (a think tank that funds rightist political theory) and meant to welcome the arrival of a new work of neoconservative doctrine (*Dictatorship of Virtue*, by Richard Bernstein), the lunch attracted a crowd of fifty individuals who for the most part were affiliated with publications and charitable foundations (among them *Forbes, Commentary,* and the John M. Olin Foundation) known for their allegiance to the miracle of finance capitalism. The intellectual tide last fall was running strongly in favor of more prisons and higher interest rates, and the mood in the dining room was smiling and complacent. The Democrats clearly were on their way to defeat in the November elections . . .

Listening to Bernstein talk about "the tyranny of the left" crushing the universities under the iron heel of "moralistic liberalism," I understood that I was revisiting a make-believe time and place not unlike the one that used to be known as the Age of Aquarius. . . . Thirty years ago it was "the conservative establishment" that was at fault, a conspiracy largely composed of university professors, government bureaucrats, and network television executives who couldn't play guitar and trembled at the sound of Dylan's harmonica. Now it is "the liberal establishment" that is at fault, a conspiracy largely composed of university professors, government bureaucrats, and network televison executives who can't quote freely from *The Federalist* and tremble before the wisdom of Alvin Toffler and Arianna Huffington. . . .

But to whom do they then direct their protests, and what names do they put on their placards and cast like stones into the teeth of time? How do they organize the sullen draft of their hastily recruited enemies into coherent legions and simple slogans?

As so often in moments of rhetorical crisis, it was the belligerent Gingrich who answered the questions with the phrase "discredited liberal establishment," which connoted both the absence of virtue and the presence of a monolith not unlike the old Soviet Union. Understood as a conspiracy of dunces, the "discredited liberal establishment" could be held responsible for all the mistakes that had been made with the planning of the American Eden. It was the "discredited liberal establishment" that opened the Pandora's box out of which sprang the three evil spirits that wrecked the economic and spiritual environment. As follows:

THE WELFARE STATE

To hear the story told on the fairways of the nation's better golf courses, the American welfare state is a foreign country that resembles Rwanda or Chiapas. Although administered as a protectorate by the U.S. government and supplied with an ungodly sum of money, the metaphysical terrain is so harsh, and the moral climate so poor, that we can never rescue the place, and we would all be better off if we just withdrew our army of Harvard sociologists and let the local rulers sign a treaty with the Baptist Church. If the line of argument is familiar, it is because it so closely parallels the argument advanced by the radical Sixties left in opposition to the Vietnam War. Why continue to underwrite an expensive and futile expedition doomed to certain failure?

The blurring of the distinctions between crime and race and moral behavior plays to the prejudice of an audience eager to believe the worst that can be said of people whom they would rather not know, and to the extent that the word "poor" can be made to serve as a synonym for "black," the big-city slums become alien nations on the wrong side of the cultural and economic frontiers. Gingrich is especially skillful at conveying his point in the unspoken subtext, and during last year's election campaign he often summarized the nation's troubles in a single sentence made to the measure of the six o'clock news: "It is impossible to maintain civilization with twelve-year-olds having babies, fifteen-year-olds killing each other, seventeen-year-olds dying of AIDS, and eighteen-year-olds receiving diplomas they cannot read."

What he had in mind (and what his audiences knew he had in mind) was the desolation of Harlem or East Los Angeles. . . .

Murray and Hernstein's book *The Bell Curve* argues that the excessive number of crimes committed by black people, as well as their poverty and lack of employment, can be attributed, more or less directly, to their low I.Q. ratings. The pseudoscientific speculaton adds a few more brush strokes to the standard portrait of black people as synonyms for catastrophe. The image deletes the greater part of the black presence in the country—the rise of the black middle class over the last thirty years, the successes achieved under the rules of affirmative action, the real ratios between impoverished white and black people (two white to one black), the dramatis personae appearing in television situation comedies, the complexion of the United States Army—but it is an image that serves the plotlines of a bedtime story about the wages of sin.[1] As conditions in the slums deteriorate, which they inevitably must as a consequence of their designation as enemy countries, the slums come to look just the way they are supposed to look in the suburban imagination. The burned-out buildings and the number of dead in the streets support the notion that crimes allied with poverty can be classified as individual moral problems rather than a common political problem. At long last and with a clear conscience, the governing and possessing classes can comfort themselves with the thought that poor people deserve what they get, that their misery is nobody's fault but their own. The bleak prospect confirms the Republican faith in prisons and serves as an excuse for imposing de facto martial law on a citizenry construed as a dangerous rabble. Even the sunniest neoconservative optimisms carry the threat of stern punishment, and the tone of the intolerant scold that appears in the speeches of Gingrich and Bennett (as well as in those of Irving Kristol, Charles Krauthammer, and Michael Novak) has been most succinctly expressed by *Washington Times* columnist Cal Thomas: "If we will not be constrained from within by the power of God, we must be constrained from without by the power of the State, acting as God's agent."

THE LIBERAL NEWS MEDIA

Among the partisans of the populist and suburban right, no article of faith is more devoutly held than the one about the feral cynicism of the metropolitan news media. Although nobody at the mall ever can remember seeing a journalist who didn't look like the boy or girl next door, the crowd sitting around the tables in the food court likes to think that the news comes to them from sallow-faced leftists who cut up the wholesome American moral fabric into patches of socialist propaganda and strips of pornographic film.

The supposition bears comparison to Jane Fonda's belief in the innocence of Ho Chi Minh. The manufacture and sale of the nation's news is the

---

1. In the proposal submitted to prospective publishers of *The Bell Curve,* Murray didn't mince words about the bigotry that he meant to confirm and sustain. "[There are] a huge number of well-meaning whites who fear that they are closet racists, and this book tells them they are not. It's going to make them feel better about things they already think but do not know how to say." *[Lapham's footnote]*

work of very large, very rich, and very timid corporations—the Washington Post Co., Fox Broadcasting, and Turner Network Television. The managers of the commercial television networks, like the publishers of large and prosperous newspapers, define news as anything that turns a profit, no matter how indecent the photograph or how inane the speeches, and they seldom take chances with any line of thought that fails to agree with what their audiences wish to see and hear.

The *Wall Street Journal*, probably the most widely read newspaper in the country, heavily favors the conservative side on any and all questions of public policy, and both the *Washington Post* and the *New York Times* fortify their op-ed pages with columnists who strongly defend the established order—William Safire and A. M. Rosenthal in the *Times*, Charles Krauthammer, George Will, and Richard Harwood in the *Post*. The vast bulk of the nation's talk-radio shows (commanding roughly 80 percent of the audience) reflect a conservative bias, and so do all but one or two of the television talk shows that deal with political topics on PBS, CNN, and CNBC. . . .

As proof of the absurdity implicit in the complaint about the liberal news media, I can think of no better demonstration than the one offered by Rush Limbaugh to the C-Span cameras in mid-December of last year at the Radisson Hotel in Baltimore. Ripe with self-congratulation and glistening under the lights like a Las Vegas lounge comic, Limbaugh appeared as the principal banquet speaker before an audience of newly elected Republican congressmen attending a three-day conference organized by the Heritage Foundation and meant to acquaint them with their tasks as saviors of the Republic. Eager and young and as freshly scrubbed as a cohort of college fraternity pledges, they laughed on cue at Limbaugh's sniggering jokes about President Clinton, condoms, and mushy-headed liberals. Limbaugh told them that in Washington they would find themselves surrounded on all sides by enemies, by newspaper columists and anchorpersons as treacherous as Cokie Roberts, who would cajole them with flattery and then betray them for the price of a cheap headline. "You are going to be hated," Limbaugh said. "Remember that you are targets. Remain hostile."

After twelve years of the administrations of Presidents Reagan and Bush, and two years of the neo-Republican presidency of Bill Clinton, the notion of Washington as a city somehow hostile to political conservatives of any kind was as preposterous as Limbaugh's posing as a victim of liberal tyranny and persecution. . . .

THE MARBLE RUIN OF AMERICAN CIVILIZATION

The last of the dearly beloved tales told around the campfires of the reactionary right is the one about the once sacred temples of American art and political philosophy turned into pornographic movie theaters by the same crew of guitarists and literary critics that poisoned the pure streams of

Republican economic thought. The story has so many variants and inflections that it is hard to fix the precise tone of indignation (sometimes choleric, sometimes wistful or smug), but it invariably entails the assigning of subversive motives to the universities, the Hollywood movie companies, the popular-music business, the publishing industry, the Broadway stage, and the aforesaid liberal news media. Although the bad news sometimes takes grandiose forms—Irving Kristol informing the guests at conservative banquets that rock and roll music presents a greater threat to Western civilization than world Communism—for the most part it comes down to a complaint about a cheapened sense of aesthetics and school curricula debased by trendy (i.e., leftist) political alloys. Instead of reading Chaucer, students read the works of minor African poets; instead of going to see Shakespeare's plays, they gape at the sins of the flesh paraded through the courtyard of *Melrose Place.*

Again, as with so many of the other excited announcements emanating from the press offices of the right, the facts of the matter have been suborned by the preferred image. The mournful defenders of classical learning and Renaissance humanism ignore the point that the United States makes business its culture and its culture a business. Art is what sells, and education is what draws a paying crowd. . . . Children learn by example as well as by precept, and they have only to look at Times Square and Disneyland, or consider the triumphs of Roseanne or Ronald Perlman, to know that society bestows its rewards on the talent for figuring a market, not on a knowledge of Thucydides.

Nor is the popular culture by any means as immoral as it is dreamed of in the philosophy of the academic deans on the neoconservative and Christian right. As measured by its lists of best-selling books and long-running Broadway plays, as well as by its successful television comedies, sporting events, and popular songs, the American cultural enterprise (in 1995 as in 1895) is as irremediably conservative as it is relentlessly sentimental. During any Sunday's playing of the Top 40, the rap songs and heavy-metal rhythms show up at the bottom of the list, but as the countdown proceeds upward toward a kindly and forgiving providence, the music turns increasingly sweet and melodic. The lyrics almost always affirm the wisdom of a Rod McKuen poem or a speech by Peggy Noonan—love will last forever; our love will never die; you are the only one; my love for you is like a thousand points of light. . . .

The joke about the marble ruin is that American civilization never was much of a match for Periclean Greece. When the tellers of the sad Republican tale agree to take questions on the subject (reluctantly and usually in a hurry to leave the lecture hall), it turns out that the lost culture for which they grieve is the culture best expressed by the sensibility of the 1950s, the musical comedies of Rodgers and Hammerstein, the history of the world as told by Disney and Time Life, the list of great books that everybody owns but nobody has read.

Hoisted up by the cranes of populist bombast to the platforms of great expectation, the newly enskied 104th Congress confronts an ancient problem in socioeconomics—how does a wealthy and increasingly nervous plutocracy preserve its privileges while at the same time maintaining its reputation as an oppressed minority and a noble cause? . . .

What they have in hand is a dissenting rhetoric best suited to cries from the wilderness, a feeling for nostalgia, a faith in the claptrap futurism of Alvin and Heidi Toffler, the dubious economic theory inherited from the early days of the Reagan revolution, and an instinct for repression. Although convenient to pop quizzes and the nightly television news, the syllabus of glib answers bears comparison to the secrets of the universe packaged for sale in the supermarket press, and it isn't likely to prepare the class for the midterm examination. The electorate last fall was saying something about its fear and uneasiness, about jobs being sent overseas and the future (their own and that of their children) beginning to look like the receding objects seen through the wrong end of a telescope. For the last ten or fifteen years, the parties of the right have managed to convert the emotions rooted in economic anxiety into the politics of cultural anxiety, substituting the questions of moral conduct and deportment (the marble ruin, the heathen poor) for the more intractable ones about the division of the national spoils.

But the act is getting harder to perform, and the audience in the first ten rows has begun to figure out the trick with the coins and the scarves. Let the interest rate continue to rise, and who will applaud the futurist cant ("Parallel Transformations!" "Paradigms!" "Quality Management!") so dear to the heart of Speaker Gingrich? Let the chimera of a balanced budget drift off into the haze of what Washington calls "the out years," and people might begin to notice the difference between the big print and the small print in the Contract With America.

The paragraphs in large print postulate a return to an imaginary time and place in which the work of government could be performed by a volunteer fire department—a few hardy fellows cleaning up the village green after a winter storm, a benign judge adjudicating the occasional land dispute or divorce proceeding, a friendly county official awarding the rights of way for five hundred miles of railroad track in Kansas. The provisions in small print grant the propertied classes the freedom to acquire more property—a freedom expressed, among other ways, in the form of capital-gains tax breaks in the amount of $25 billion a year—and for everybody else, more police and more sermons.